Ventura Troubleshooting Guide

John Abraham

Wordware Publishing, Inc.
Plano, Texas

Library of Congress Cataloging-in-Publication Data

Abraham, John (John Thomas)
      Ventura troubleshooting guide / by John Abraham.
            p.   cm.
      Includes index.
      ISBN 1-55622-121-5
      1. Desktop publishing.   2. Ventura publisher (Computer program).
I. Title.   II. Title: Ventrua trouble shooting guide.
Z286.D47A27   1989
686.2'2544536— dc20   89-70437
                                                                 CIP

ISBN 1-55622-121-5

10 9 8 7 6 5 4 3 2 1
9001

All inquiries for volume purchases of this book should be addressed to Wordware Publishing, Inc.,
at the above address. Telephone inquiries may be made by calling:

(214) 423-0090

Contents

Contents

About This Book

Ventura Troubleshooting Guide was written to help the Ventura Publisher user who may have problems using the software. This book covers all versions of Ventura Publisher, including 1.0, 1.1, 1.1 Patch 1, 1.1 Patch 2, and 2.0. With this book the average user should be able to solve most Ventura Publisher problems.

So you can quickly find the solutions to your problems without reading the entire book, each chapter has an introduction and a Topic Guide. The Topic Guide categorizes common problems and known software bugs and directs you to the appropriate parts of the extensive Question and Answer section which makes up the bulk of each chapter.

The first nine chapters discuss and answer questions about each menu. Following chapters identify what hardware and software is compatible with Ventura Publisher, how to choose the most efficient computer products to work with Ventura Publisher, how to respond to the menu error screens, and how to design page layouts, from planning to the finished product.

The purpose of this book is to offer helpful advice to those using Ventura Publisher. Reading this book will save you time and possibly prevent your losing files. The book assumes you are familiar with using a keyboard; it does not assume you know the difference between saving a chapter file and saving a text file. This book not only tells you the difference, it explains how Ventura Publisher saves files, because the best way to troubleshoot a problem is to understand how Ventura Publisher works. The Ventura Troubleshooting Guide is designed like an auto repair manual.

You may have a bit of retraining ahead of you because of Ventura Publisher's use of a mouse. We have left the typewriter era when a carriage return or manual push was needed to advance from one line to another. With the advent of word processors, it will take practice to stop hitting the Return key at the end of every line.

Now, with desktop publishers entering the PC world, word processors will be used simply as text editors. It will be the desktop publisher that will create the final document. With this change in direction, users must also change the way they prepare documents.

Improper file preparation in the text processing stage can doom a project. This book makes it clear what should be considered for proper document setup in Ventura Publisher.

I would like to thank all the Ventura Publisher user groups around the country, especially the West Coast area, for sending me some of the questions included in this book. I also received considerable help attending the various desktop publishing conferences around the country.

Ventura Publisher Overview

Ventura Publisher is the leading desktop publishing product on the market. It operates under GEM, a graphic software package developed by Digital Research, which looks and operates like Microsoft Windows without color. It has drop-down menus from which you make selections with the mouse. You will find it easy to search for any option you need. Ventura Publisher is a very powerful desktop publisher. It gives you two or more ways to accomplish most page layouts. Consequently, Ventura Publisher uses a lot of memory. The total memory needed is the most important factor to consider when using Ventura. Ventura documentation states that the software will operate with 512K of memory, but you will find that this is not adequate for Version 1.1 and above. At least 640K bytes of memory is recommended.

There are plenty of things that can go wrong with Ventura Publisher if your system is not installed or configured correctly. The number one rule to remember is to keep the system configuration as simple as possible. Keep close to this rule when choosing printers, monitors, and scanners. If you don't, Ventura Publisher will give you a number of error windows to get around or will completely lock up the computer. Expanded or extended memory will not help when using Versions 1.0, 1.1, 1.2. and 2.0 Base, due to the GEM interface software and its 640K bytes limit. OS/2 DOS breaks this barrier and opens the door to a new era for Ventura Publisher.

Now lets look at the possible trouble areas that should be avoided. First, there are the computer's internal devices such as hard disk drives. Ventura Publisher needs plenty of disk space, but purchasing a 100Mb or greater disk drive may be a mistake. The problem is the size of the driver needed to run the hard disk drive. The driver's size must be considered whenever adding an extra or larger hard drive to your computer. It is possible that the driver could use too much memory to run Ventura Publisher properly. If you have an extra or large hard disk drive, you must develop batch files or boot diskettes to get Ventura Publisher to run correctly.

The other areas of concern are the external devices such as monitors, scanners, printers, and digitizers, etc. These devices also need memory-resident drivers to operate, so be careful which device you choose.

Monitors come in all shapes and sizes, from nine-inch to nineteen-inch, two-full-page displays. Many of the new monitors on the market today have a monitor board and a driver that use memory. Monitors are discussed in Chapter 11.

Scanners have the fewest problems. Either the scanner outputs in a format compatible with Ventura Publisher or it doesn't. Ventura Publisher translates some scanner file formats into a GEM format and others it leaves alone. The important thing is that the scanner and software must be able to output in the proper format.

Welcome to the world of Ventura Desktop Publishing!

CHAPTER 1
Fundamentals

This chapter answers questions on the basic fundamentals of using Ventura Publisher including installing, reinstalling, and loading the software. This chapter also includes questions on hardware and software considerations and Ventura Publisher's capabilities and features.

Having Ventura Desktop Publisher installed incorrectly is one of the most common problems. It is important you follow the install program provided on Ventura Publisher Disk #1. This program, called VPPREP, is a completely self-contained, menu-driven installation program. To use it, insert Disk #1 in drive A, type VPPREP at the A: prompt, and press Enter. Then, just answer the questions correctly and let Ventura Publisher do the rest. If you have problems, locate your problem in the Topic Guide which will direct you to the solution.

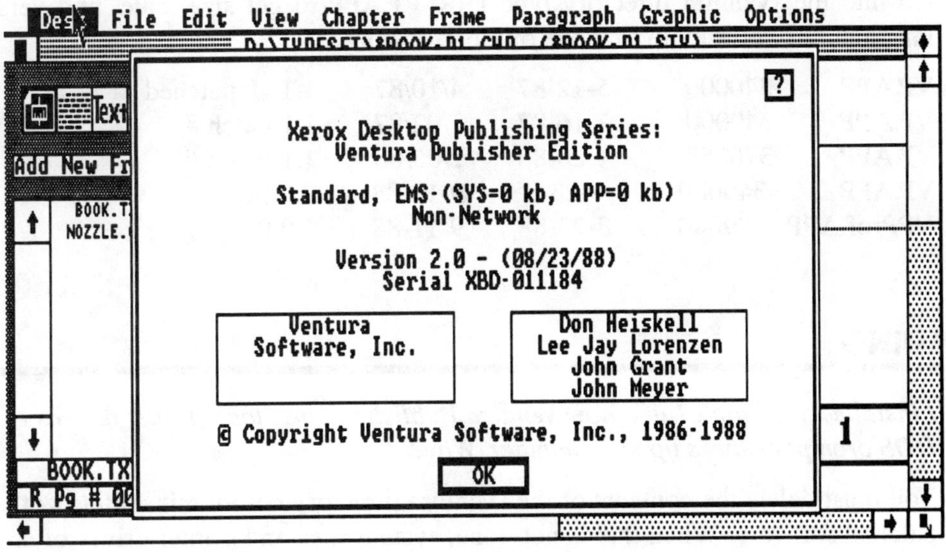

Topic Guide

INSTALLING

1. *I have just installed Ventura Publisher and now, when I type VP.BAT, all I get is the cursor in the upper left corner of the screen.*

   This is what happens when Ventura Publisher is installed with the wrong monitor driver. Reinstall with the correct monitor choice.

2. *How can I tell what version of Ventura Publisher I have?*

   Go into the \Ventura directory type DIR VP.APP to get size, date, and version information. You should find one of the following:

VP.APP	340000	5-12-87	4/10/87	1.1 Unpatched
VP.APP	340000	7-16-87	7/02/87	1.1 Patch #1
VP.APP	376368	4-20-88	2/05/88	1.1 Patch #2
VP.APP	340000	8-23-88	9-11-88	2.0 Base
VPProf.APP	499040	8-23-88	9-11-88	2.0 P.E.

LOADING

3. *I installed 1.1 Patch 1 and now Ventura Publisher won't load. It just returns to the DOS prompt or locks up my computer. Why?*

   You must delete the contents of the \Ventura directory before reinstalling with the patched software. When this is not done, system files and printer drives often are not overwritten correctly. If this problem is suspected, the date of files in the VENTURA directory can be compared with those on the patch disk. In this case VP.APP showed a date of 5/12/87 (unpatched version) instead of 7/16/87 (patched version).

4. *I'm in DOS attempting to load Ventura Publisher, but Ventura is telling me that the chapter is not in the proper format. What is wrong, is my program gone?*

   No, the problem is a corrupted chapter file that Ventura Publisher is attempting to load. There is no way to correct this problem short of rebuilding the chapter.

5. *When Ventura Publisher begins loading, it sends me back to the DOS prompt. Why?*

   The computer does not have enough memory or the style sheet is corrupted. To check to see if the style sheet is the cause, in the VENTURA directory, delete the .INF files. Then try loading Ventura Publisher. If Ventura Publisher loads the default style with no problem, then try to load the style sheet that Ventura Publisher was attempting to load before you deleted the INF files. If the computer locks up or returns you to DOS when you attempt to load a style sheet by name, then it is the style sheet that is the problem.

6. *Can I abort loading a chapter once it has begun?*

   No. Once Ventura Publisher has started loading a chapter, you must let it finish before executing any other instructions.

7. *Ventura Publisher is locking up every time I try to load. Why?*

   Check to see if you have enough disk space. Ventura Publisher makes temporary files when you are processing documents. When the document is saved, Ventura Publisher must store the temporary files into memory so that it can rewrite the text files. These files appear as lost clusters when you do a DOS CHKDSK command.

8. *When I tried to bring up Ventura Publisher, the system tried to load something from the A drive. I tried all the installation diskettes, and finally, when I inserted disk #11 into the system, Ventura Publisher loaded. Why do I have to have a diskette in the A drive to bring up Ventura Publisher?*

   A properly installed Ventura Publisher system does not require a diskette in drive A. Ventura Publisher holds information in the INF files that tells Ventura Publisher what disk drive you were working on when you quit the last time. Ventura Publisher will then attempt to load the style sheet off that drive. Also this problem can occur if you modified your AUTOEXEC.BAT file and inserted an incorrect path statement. If your path was set up to look first at the A drive, this could cause the problem.

9. *I can't seem to get Ventura Publisher to load files on my R drive. Why?*

The R drive is the clue. You are working on a network with a non-network version of Ventura Publisher.

10. *Why is Ventura Publisher taking longer to load now than it did previously?*

Merging a lot of font files into the width file will cause Ventura Publisher to load the width file slower than usual. To avoid this, do not merge the new files with the OUTPUT.WID file when you add fonts to your system. Then when you load Ventura Publisher, delete your INF files. This will cause Ventura Publisher to load the old, smaller OUTPUT. WID file instead of the larger new font width table. That's because Ventura Publisher's INF files remember the last width table loaded.

HARDWARE AND SOFTWARE CONSIDERATIONS

11. *What page description languages does Ventura Publisher support?*

Version 1.0 supports PostScript only. Version 1.1 and all patches support PostScript and Interpress page description languages. PostScript is currently available on the Apple LaserWriter and several other laser printers, as well as Linotronic typesetters. Interpress is supported only in context with a PC-on-the-net type Ethernet setup. Ventura Publisher creates an Ethernet master print file, then you send the print file to the Interpress printer operating on the network.

12. *Why doesn't Ventura Publisher see the other drives on my computer?*

Ventura Publisher was developed to show the normal disk drive configuration A B C. To get it to show the other drives, you are required to edit the VP.BAT file; find the following line:

```
DRVRMRGR VP %1 /S=SD_CGA_5.CGA/M=nn
```

The /M=nn is for the type of mouse installed (nn=32 for the MicroSoft Bus Mouse); at the end of the line, type /X=D:, /X=F:, etc. for the disk drives available. For example the following line will access D and F drives:

```
DRVRMRGR VP %1 /S=SD CGA 5.CGA/M=nn/X=D/X=F
```

13. *Can Ventura Publisher run on an IBM 3270 PC?*

Not in version 1.0. The 3270 PC is supported in version 1.1 and 2.0.

14. *I did a disk optimize and now Ventura Publisher has slowed down to a snail's pace. What happened?*

    Increase your buffers slightly to help Ventura Publisher find files.

15. *Is Ventura Publisher compatible with the new IBM PS/2 Computer Series?*

    Yes, all but the PS/2 Model 25 which seems to give Ventura Publisher trouble due to the graphic board installed.

16. *Does Ventura Publisher support the Datacopy scanner?*

    Ventura Publisher supports two image formats, GEM and PC Paintbrush. If the scanner can output to one of these formats, it does not make any difference to Ventura Publisher which brand it is.

17. *Do I need to purchase printer drivers, fonts, or other software to run Ventura Publisher?*

    No. Ventura Publisher comes complete with drivers and basic fonts for all printers and graphic displays listed.

Memory

18. *When a document exceeds the RAM available and has to be paged out to the hard drive, what sits in that area on the hard drive? Are they text or image files?*

    Primarily text data, although some overhead data used to describe and format the pages is also stored. Line art and image data are stored in the graphics buffer and are refreshed directly from their source.

19. *How much memory and hard disk space does Ventura Publisher use?*

    For version 1.0 Ventura Publisher uses about 470K bytes. Version 1.1 uses about 540K bytes, but this amount can be reduced to the 470K bytes mark by altering the VP.BAT file to include the /A switch. This will degrade your graphics buffer and printer buffer memory. Version 2.0 requires 580K bytes with the /A switch. The amount of hard disk space depends on what printer is installed and how many printer fonts are loaded. The range is from about 1Mb for PostScript to about 3Mb for the HP LaserJet and Xerox 4045.

20. *Can you give me a Ventura Publisher memory map or information on how Ventura Publisher uses memory?*

    The external memory is the amount available for loading files. The mouse and display drivers reduce the amount of external memory. The screen graphics and printer use a 64K buffer for screen drawing and to load the printer driver at print time. The /A switch reallocates memory from the graphics/printer buffer and increases the external memory. The graphics/printer buffer is a first-in, first-out memory area. When drawing the screen, it will format as much of the screen as it can in the buffer, then dump it onto the screen and start on the next part of the screen. If the screen is complex or if the buffer is made smaller by the /A switch, more formatting and dumping of the screen is required to draw the screen. This is what causes the delay you see in screen formatting.

At print time, the printer driver has to be loaded into the same graphics printer buffer where screen formatting information has been sitting. Therefore, the screen information is dumped and the printer driver is loaded. That is why the screen information has to be reloaded when the print job ends. The /A switch has an effect on printing. If the /A switch is set to any value larger than 16, rastorizors such as JLaser and dot matrix will not work. On a 512K system, the only printers that will work are HP and PostScript. Epson, JLaser, and similar printers will not work because they require more memory.

RAM Disk

21. *I have a 4Mb RAM disk. Can I operate Ventura Publisher from the RAM disk?*

    Yes. From the DOS prompt, set up a temporary substitute drive with the same designator that the RAM drive will eventually have (be sure the RAM disk is not active).

    a. Type C:SUBST E:=VPRAM at the DOS prompt. Create directory on hard disk first.

    b. Install Ventura Publisher to drive E. (Typeset and Ventura directories will become subdirectories of VPRAM directory.)

    c. Reboot and set up RAM disk as E.

    d. Copy VP.BAT from VPRAM directory to root directory and use an ASCII editor to insert E: as the first line in the file.

    e. Set up Autoexec.Bat to create a Ventura directory on the RAM drive E: and then input this line in Autoexec.Bat:

       copy c:\vpram\ventura*.* E:\ventura <cr>.

    f. Type vp <cr>. This should allow you to run Ventura Publisher from the RAM drive. Make sure that you keep all your files on the hard disk so when you quit Ventura Publisher, you don't have to copy the entire E drive back to the substitute drive.

22. *Can a RAM disk or expanded memory allow me to manipulate larger documents than with a 640K bytes machine?*

Only in Ventura Publisher 2.0 Professional Extension. Ventura Publisher 1.1 currently addresses 640K bytes of memory. Additional memory will not enable you to access larger documents at this time.

VENTURA PUBLISHER CAPABILITIES AND FEATURES

23. *Can you change the size of the crop marks that Ventura puts on the page?*

The crops marks are hard coded in the internal code and cannot be adjusted.

24. *Is kerning in 1.1 universal or for selected letter pairs?*

The kerning in 1.1 is for selected letter pairs according to industry standards. Kerning was devised to correct spacing for certain character combinations and has little or no value for others.

25. *Is there any way to have Ventura strip away all the tags in a text file?*

Yes. Simply tag all paragraphs as body text.

26. *Does Ventura automatically reformat pages when changes are made, and how long does this take?*

Yes. This is an important feature of Ventura Publisher. Any change made to the size of a picture or any addition or deletion of text will automatically reformat the current page. If another page is accessed, it will also be reformatted. A typical four-column page on a Xerox 6065 or Compaq Deskpro takes under one second to reformat.

27. *Is there any limit to the number of pages I can have in one document?*

Ventura 1.0 formats chapters. Each chapter can be up to 150K bytes of text in a 640K bytes system. This translates to approximately 70 to 100 pages of single-spaced typewritten text. Up to 64 chapters can then be combined together, effectively creating a document of over 5,000 pages.

Ventura 1.1 and 2.0 develop chapters differently. The 1.1 limit is that no text file can consist of more then 500K bytes. In the 2.0 Professional Extension, the file has no limit if you're using expanded memory. Text files can now be developed as large as 1Mb or more. The only actual limit to the number of pages per chapter is the page counter which goes to 9,999.

28. *Does Ventura Publisher work on a network?*

Not until the 2.0 network version. It is possible to use Ventura Publisher 1.1 on a PC that is connected to a network, but the Ventura Publisher software and all related files must reside on the PC's own local hard disk. Ventura Publisher 2.0 Base and Professional Extension cannot allow a network running in background due to their extensive use of available memory.

29. *Does Ventura Publisher have full integration of graphics and text?*

Yes. What you see on the screen is what you will print. Pictures are moved around the screen by simply dragging them from one place to another. The text flows around the new picture location.

30. *Is Ventura Publisher a true "What you see is what you get" (WYSIWYG) program? For example, If you are using 72 point size will it show up as 72 point on the display?*

Yes. This is completely true if you are using a PostScript printer as your output device and you are using a PostScript font. If you are printing on any other printer, you must have a screen font on the disk to see the font displayed in its true size. What Ventura Publisher will do for the users of other printers is leave space around the closest font it can find that is smaller to make up for the room the true font occupies.

31. *What sort of hyphenation is provided in Ventura Publisher?*

Ventura Publisher uses a hyphenation algorithm combined with two dictionaries. The system dictionary contains a list of words that the algorithm would hyphenate incorrectly. The user dictionary lets the user add words to be hyphenated differently than the algorithm allows. The user dictionary overrides the system dictionary and the system dictionary overrides the algorithm. The result is accurate, fast hyphenation.

32. *I have an 80Mb hard disk which is in eight partitions 10Mb each. I installed Ventura Publisher onto the E drive, but when I use the backup button to search other directories, it only gives me a choice between A, B, or E. Why can't I access the other drives?*

Unfortunately, the inability to list other drives by using the backup button is a restriction imposed by the GEM environment. You can, however, access data on these drives by going to the directory line and inserting the appropriate drive letter and file filter (i.e., C:*.TXT) for the text or pictures you want to retrieve. Another way is also available in version 1.1 (but not in version 1.0). In the VP.BAT file, at the end of the line which begins with DRVRMRGR, add X=/N: where N is replaced by the drive designator. Do this for each drive you want to add. For example, to add drives D and E, the line would end with ../X=D:/x=E:.

33. *How fast is Ventura Publisher?*

Ventura Publisher is very fast compared to many other MS-DOS packages. Text formatting speed is in excess of 20,000 characters per second on an AT, and text screen drawing speed, with multiple fonts and columns, takes approximately 1 to 1.5 seconds on an XT and is virtually instantaneous on an AT.

34. *What scientific capabilities (e.g., equations) does Ventura Publisher have?*

Ventura Publisher includes a complete symbol font. This symbol font includes both greek and math characters in several sizes. This works well for simple equations. However, Ventura Publisher 1.0 and 1.1 are not particularly well suited to complex mathematical formulas like triple integral, large summation (sigma) signs, or chemical equations. Version 2.0 has full scientific and mathematical functions.

GEM

35. *I have been using GEM and recently added Ventura Publisher. Now when I retrieve some of my GEM files, they don't look right. What is the problem?*

There is a known software bug in GEM that is not evident when operating it as a stand-alone product. However, when Ventura Publisher is loaded, it modifies certain GEM files causing this bug to appear. The makers of GEM are aware of the problem and may be working on a patch. Meanwhile, Ventura Publisher has supplied a workaround for users with DOS 3.0 and higher. Users with DOS versions below 3.0 can request GEM Version 1.01.

36. *Does Ventura Publisher provide clip art?*

No. Ventura Publisher can, however, accept clip art provided with GEM Draw. You can also design your own library of symbols, and those can be used repeatedly in multiple documents.

37. *Since GEM Draw prints to plotters and Ventura Publisher is GEM based, can Ventura Publisher print to plotters?*

No. Ventura Publisher provides a completely different set of drivers which are designed for publishing. These drivers include downloadable fonts. Plotters are very inefficient for drawing large numbers of characters at small sizes.

38. *I understand there are some problems using GEM Desktop with Ventura Publisher. Is there any workaround that will allow them to coexist without affecting each other?*

This was a problem with Ventura Publisher 1.0 when it existed in a subdirectory called GEM. Since version 1.1, the program files are loaded in a directory named VENTURA and the data files in TYPESET. If you are still using Ventura Publisher 1.0 and you have DOS 3.0 or higher, you can install Ventura Publisher and GEM separately in a way that they will not affect each other. This is done by using the DOS SUBST utility to trick the computer into thinking it has another drive. This drive can then hold the GEM directory and not allow the two programs to mix.

39. *Does Ventura Publisher use GEM?*

GEM stands for Graphics Environment Manager. GEM is a graphic system software developed by Digital Research. It was used by them to develop GEM Draw, GEM Graph, and other applications. Ventura Publisher includes a GEM Runtime software and uses it as an interface.

Foreign Languages

40. *Does Ventura Publisher support the Russian language?*

No. Ventura Publisher does not support Russian or any other Cyrillic language.

41. *What sort of foreign characters are provided in Ventura Publisher?*

Ventura Publisher provides a full international character set in one to three typefaces, depending on the printer. The typefaces are Helvetica, Times Roman, and Courier. Ventura Publisher also provides Symbol (greek and mathematics) characters for selected printers.

42. *Can Ventura Publisher generate foreign language documents?*

Yes. Ventura Publisher contains a full international character set which is used to create any of the Romance languages. Characters are generated by using the MS-DOS keyboard utility to activate the international character set before loading Ventura Publisher. Once it is loaded, you can input text and Ventura Publisher will display the appropriate characters. Ventura Publisher does not provide hyphenation for foreign languages and cannot translate words from English to a foreign language.

Color

43. *Do I need to display in color in order to print in color?*

No. Color information is stored even if your screen can't display it. You can create color documents on a monochrome monitor.

44. *Can Ventura Publisher handle color?*

Yes. Ventura Publisher supports up to eight colors and can print to the Xerox 4020 Color Ink Jet printer. Using an enhanced graphics board and color monitor, text can be displayed in color.

45. *Does Ventura support color PostScript printing?*

Yes, in Version 2.0 Ventura Publisher has upgraded their PostScript interpreter to support PostScript versions 52 and higher which supports color codes required by the new printers. This can make for very impressive forms, overheads, book covers, need I say more.

46. *Does Ventura Publisher support color separation?*

Yes. Ventura Publisher version 2.0 supports color separation for text and Ventura Publisher internal graphics only, such as ruling lines and graphics boxes, etc.

Word Processor

47. *Does Ventura Publisher have its own word processor?*

Ventura Publisher does have a text editor. This text editor lets you edit text within multiple columns, with full proportional spacing, automatic hyphenation, and multiple fonts. The screen shows, at all times, what will print. Ventura Publisher does not have a full-function word processor.

48. *When I key text into a document using Ventura Publisher's text editor, why won't the screen scroll when full?*

Ventura Publisher's text editor was not designed to be a full-function word processing system. It provides basic text editing capabilities under the assumption that a word processor will be used to generate large blocks of text.

VENTURA PUBLISHER UTILITIES

49. *I tried to convert a DXF file using Ventura Publisher's DXFTOGEM utility. The system locks up every time; can you tell me why?*

This may not be a lockup at all. The original Ventura Publisher 1.0. was released with a bugged conversion utility that slows the conversion process. The 1.0 DXF to GEM conversion takes a long time to complete (10 to 15 minutes), and it may appear as if the system has locked up. Watch the disk write light; there should be some disk activity (disk write light flashing) during the conversion process. If there is no indication that disk activity is taking place and the screen does not change after 15 to 20 minutes, the problem may be related to the software bug. This was fixed in the 1.1 version.

TXTTOPCX

50. *What is this TXTTOPCX utility that is on the #11 disk?*

The TXTTOPCX utility can convert 25 lines of text to create a screen reproduction. It can capture the display screen from any program, such as Sidekick or other background utilities that capture screen displays to a file. At the DOS prompt, type the command TXTTOPCX filename % and press Enter. Replace filename with the name of the file to convert, and % with the type of display in use:

> EGA with enhanced monitor, use: C

> EGA with monochrome monitor, use: M

> Color card with color monitor, use: O

> AT&T 6300 or Xerox 6065, use: A

> This utility creates a file of the same name with a PCX extension. This utility does not convert boldface or reverse video.

51. *The Ventura Publisher Guide says: "Any text file of up to 25 lines or less can be converted to a graphic PC Paintbrush file." The words "text file" mean an ASCII file. When TXTTOPCX is used to convert a 25-line ASCII file, it sometimes does not seem to perform as advertised. Sometimes the converted file is double-spaced, and only half of it shows up. When a 25-line text file is converted, only 24 lines result with one line lost. Why?*

Here are the following limitations of TXTTOPCX:

> (25 lines x 80 characters per line = 2000 characters. However, the absolute maximum conversion possible is 3 characters less than this—i.e., 1997. This is necessary to allow for a carriage return (CR) and end-of-file marker at the end.

> This ideal maximum conversion is possible only with an ASCII file which has no <CRs> before the one at the very end.)

> * Maximum printable characters per line: 79.

CHAPTER 2
File Menu

The File menu is the "Input\Output" utility of Ventura Publisher. It is one of two menus that allow you to access the disk drives and printer for output purposes (the other is the Options menu). The File menu also allows you to delete files from disk and develop and remove directories.

CAUTION

Beware of warnings in the DOS File Ops option. When you elect this menu option, the default could destroy your entire root directory. On the File Spec line it defaults to C:*.*. This bomb can be exploded if you are not alert to the messages on the screen, and you select Delete Matching File(s) and Done. Ventura Publisher begins deleting every file in your root directory.

Other than the preceding caution, the File menu has a lot of good things to offer. In version 2.0 the only change is the help box in the upper right corner.

Take a look at the File menu. Notice the ellipsis (...) after certain choices. This lets you know that a dialog box or boxes will appear when you click on those choices. In most cases the dialog box is an item selector. The Load Text/Picture... option has a dialog box requiring you to select the format of the file to import before offering an item selector. Due to the complexity of loading graphics, the Load Picture option is covered in more detail in Chapter 10, Load Picture Option and Graphic Packages. The Abandon... option has a dialog box that is more like a warning box than a dialog box. The three that don't have the ellipse are direct activation choices. Click on one of them, and Ventura Publisher executes the command directly.

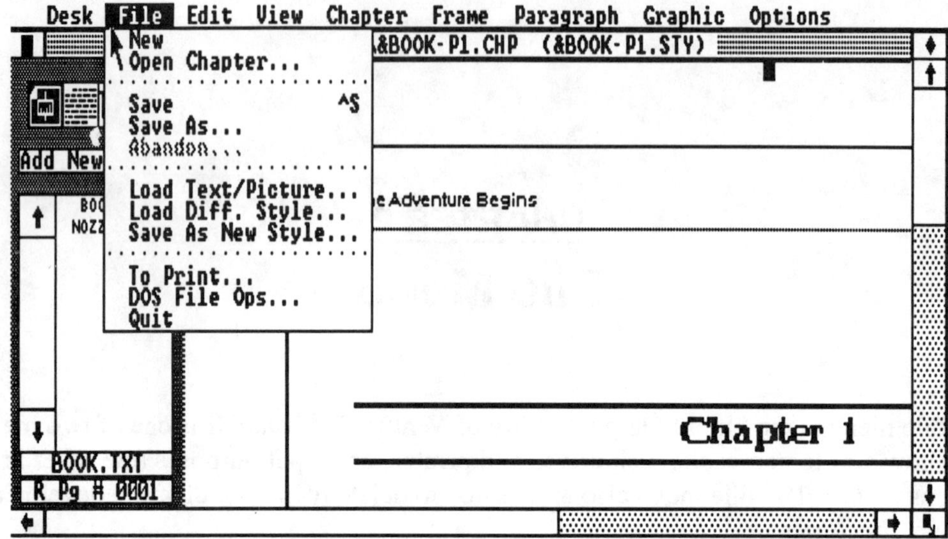

Topic Guide

Topic	Questions	Page
Open Chapter	1 - 13	15
Save	14 - 21	19
Load Text	22 - 38	21
WordPerfect	39	25
WordStar	40	25
Displaywrite	41 - 42	25
PFS Word	43	25
Smart Word	44	26
dBASE	45	26
Macintosh	46	26
ASCII	47 - 53	26
Hex	54	27
To Print	55 - 66	28
Dos File Ops	67	31

OPEN CHAPTER

1. *I would like to get information about the data contained in the chapter file, what it means and how I can modify it.*

   The data in the chapter file is used by Ventura Publisher to link all parts of a chapter together (text, style sheet, pictures, caption files, etc.). How Ventura Publisher uses this data is proprietary information and cannot be released. Any attempt to modify the data contained in the chapter file could seriously alter the document when loaded. This will produce less than satisfactory results or will fail to load altogether. It is never recommended that you attempt to edit the chapter file.

2. *Ventura Publisher is telling me to break the files I have in half. How do I do that so that Ventura Publisher understands?*

   One way to do this is to break the file inside the word processor and then change the name of the second file. After loading the chapter again you load the second file into a frame or add it to an inserted page.

3. *I have a text file which is too large to bring into Ventura Publisher in one chapter file. I have divided the file into two text files and created two chapter files within Ventura Publisher. How can I get the two chapters to print as though they were one chapter? Chapter 1 finishes with about ten lines of text on the last page. How do I get chapter 2 to start on the same page chapter 1 ended on?*

   The easiest solution is to move those ten lines of text from chapter 1 to chapter 2, so chapter 1 ends at the bottom of a page. Then chapter 2 will continue the document beginning at the top of the next page. Use the page counter to start page numbering in chapter 2 to follow the last page number from chapter 1.

4. *Ventura Publisher is locking up when it begins to load my file. It shows the first line of text in a bad font type, then shows me one more line and locks up. Why?*

   Try deleting the INF files in the VENTURA directory.

5. *I just loaded a chapter file and it does not look like it did when I last saved it. Why does it look different?*

   Remember that the format of each document (page layout, margins, fonts, width tables, etc.) is controlled by the style sheet associated with the document. If you modify a style sheet for a particular document, all other documents which use that style sheet will also be affected. Care should be taken before saving changes to a style sheet. If the style sheet is used by several other documents, it is best to create a new style sheet by using the Save As New Style option in the File menu. Also, remember that after a chapter is saved, the style sheet used for that chapter is retained on the screen and in memory. If you exit Ventura Publisher, the last style sheet used will be in memory when you next execute Ventura Publisher. Check that it is the correct style sheet for your next project before loading new text files and changing tag attributes or page layouts.

6. *I can't load chapter files that were developed in Ventura Publisher version 1.1 Patch 1. Why?*

   After installation of a patch, Ventura Publisher reloads all the dialog boxes to defaults. Check the Directory line to see if it is pointed to the proper directory.

7. *I've tried to load a chapter on one computer and it caused a lockup. I've loaded the same chapter on another computer and it loaded fine.*

   The problem is in the CONFIG.SYS file. Set the buffer size and the number of files to 15. Then reboot the computer and the chapter should load fine.

8. *I can load a chapter from an IBM PS/2 system with no problem. But when I attempt to load it to any other computer system, I can't seem to get it to load. Why?*

   This is a problem with the way each computer system is configured. Go to the CONFIG.SYS file and make sure it is the same on both systems. This makes the two computers compatible as far as Ventura Publisher is concerned. Also look at the AUTOEXEC.BAT to make sure that it's not putting any files in resident memory. Finally do a CHKDSK on the C drive. The last set of numbers is the amount of RAM available. This number should be above 570K bytes; if not, make room by deleting items from either CONFIG.SYS or AUTOEXEC.BAT.

9. *I copied my chapters to a new hard drive I purchased for Ventura Publisher, but now I cannot get my chapters to load anymore. What did I do?*

   You moved files via the DOS command instead of the Multi-chapter feature on the Options menu. This technique does not rewrite the chapter pointers which is the way Ventura Publisher knows where to find the files.

10. *How do I load a chapter?*

    Go to the File menu and click on Open Chapter. The item selector appears. If your chapter is in the TYPESET directory and the directory reads "C:\TYPESET*.CHP," your file should be present on the list. If your file exists on a disk or different directory, press the backup button with your mouse (see following screen).

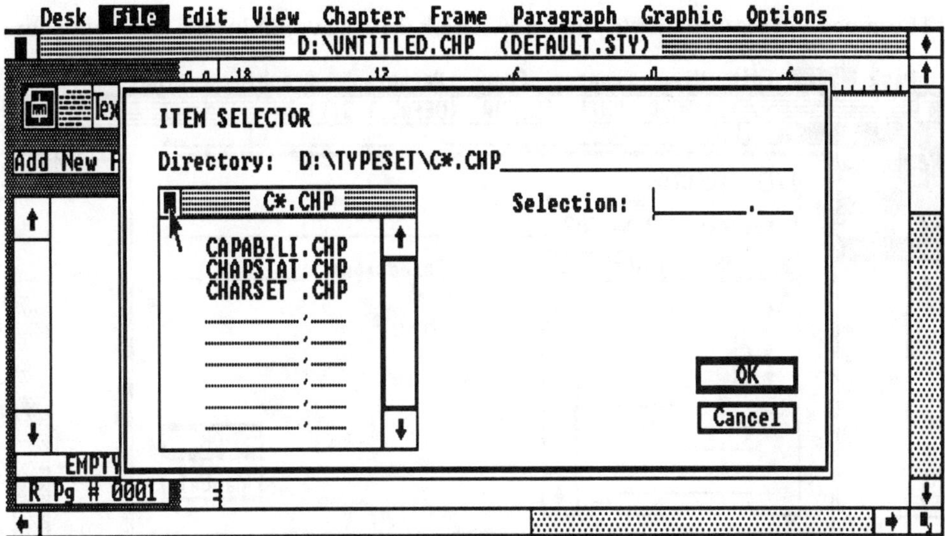

The first press will display all the directories on the active drive with black diamonds
to the left (see screen below).

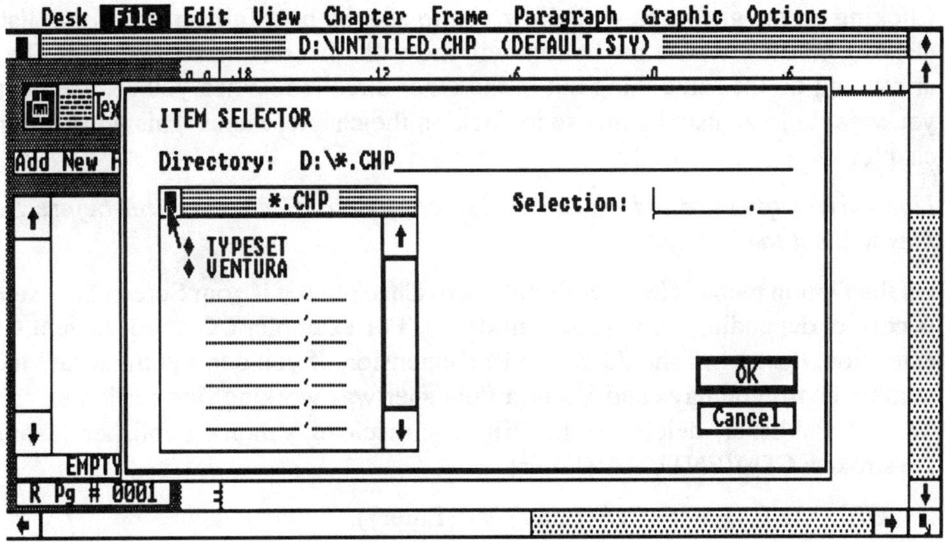

The second press will display all known disk drives available (see following screen).

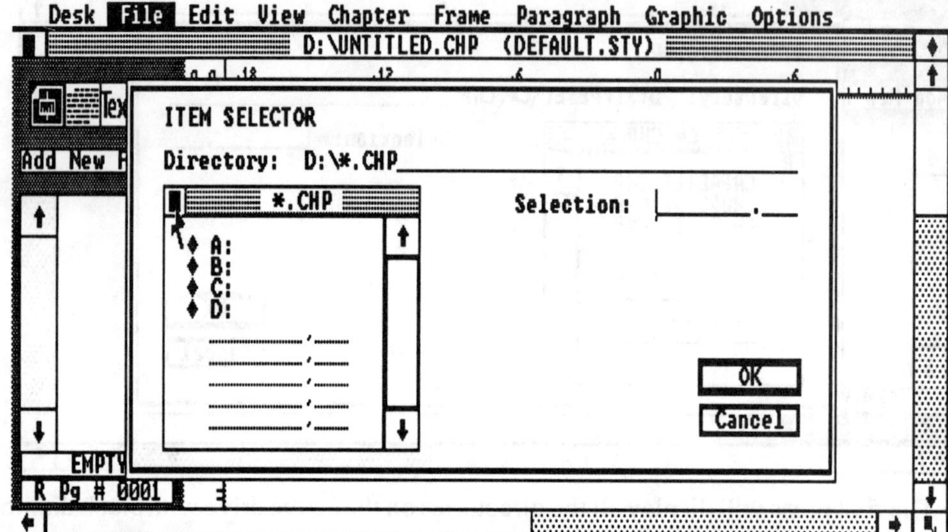

If you can't see it in the file list, notice the gray area on the right side of the list. Clicking on the gray area will allow you to see the next full screen of that list, or clicking on the arrow at the bottom will move the list one name at a time. The top arrow will do the same thing but in the other direction. When you see the chapter you want to load, use the mouse to click on the chapter name. This will load your chapter file.

11. *I loaded a chapter file and I got a weird screen font that I've never seen before. Some files will not load. Why?*

On the Option menu select Set Printer Info. Check to see if your Screen Font setting is correct depending on your screen driver. For example, CGA will have a CGA extension; PostScript should have a PSF extension. If you don't know what kind of graphic board you have and Ventura Publisher was working fine earlier, exit from Ventura Publisher, delete the INF files, and reload Ventura Publisher (example keystrokes: CD\VENTURA {Enter}

　　　DEL *.INF {Enter} CD\{Enter} VP{Enter}).

This should let Ventura Publisher renew the program by not reading the INF files when loading.

12. *I had graphics in frames that were fine, then later I opened the chapter file and all the graphics and frames were offset, not in the same location. What would make this happen?*

This is a classic example of a corrupted chapter file. Since a chapter file is a proprietary file, Ventura Publisher does not release its true format. This file is the key file for all Ventura Publisher chapter operations. Ventura Publisher loads the chapter file differently each time it is called upon. This is, done so that no one can monitor the opening of the files or duplicate the programs algorithm. To tell you how the file is corrupted is impossible. But chapter files can be easily corrupted by a system lockup during a save, or the file being opened and saved by an editor. If you open a chapter file, it looks like a regular ASCII file that can be read with no outward appearance of machine program codes, which leaves the user with the assumption that this file can be edited easily. This assumption would be a fatal one. Unfortunately, once a chapter file has been edited/corrupted there is no way to restore that chapter short of recreation of the chapter file.

13. *I created a document, typing all the text directly into Ventura Publisher. I saved the text file but when I recall the chapter, it can't find my file. Why?*

If the text file was saved to a directory that did not exist, it is lost. Ventura Publisher does not verify directories before it attempts to write files to disk. If you misspell the directory, Ventura Publisher will dump the file and your data is lost. Always make sure to verify the directory name before saving files in Ventura Publisher.

SAVE

14. *After I save a document, the Alt 197 code turns into a 97 on the screen. This only happens after the save. If I fix it, it's great until I save. Why?*

It's not in the saving process; it's a MultiMate/Ventura Publisher compatibility bug. This problem has been fixed in Patch 2 of version 1.1 of the software.

15. *When a MultiMate file is pulled into Ventura Publisher and then saved, tag names often appear in the document, chopped, with trailing dots. The tag names also appear in the assignment list as being chopped. What is wrong?*

Save the document to ASCII under MultiMate, or pull it into Ventura Publisher and select the File Type/Rename option in the Edit menu. Now select the Save option in the File menu. This will save the chapter file with your text file in an ASCII format. The drawback is that you now have a document which cannot be edited in MultiMate. This problem has been fixed in Patch 2. The best solution is to be registered and receive Patch 2 which will enable MultiMate to load properly.

16. *I created a chapter file and saved it, and now I can't find it. What happened to it?*

Make sure when you save a file that you are saving it to the correct directory and that you have spelled the filename correctly. Most errors of this type are the result of using the wrong directory or making a typo when keying the name of the file to be saved.

17. *I tried to save a chapter but the system locked during the save, causing Ventura Publisher to write a 0 byte file. How do I get this file back?*

Your odds of retrieving this information are not good. Since the file was not erased, the possibility that it is sitting in a lost cluster is your only hope. To see if there are any lost clusters, go to DOS and type CHKDSK/F. The /F will repair any cluster that is lost due to lockups. Any recovered files will be on the root directory with the name FILEnnnn.CHK (nnnn = numbers). You can look at these files by using the TYPE command. You can rename and/or delete the files as you see fit.

18. *A chapter file was created and saved. Ventura Publisher was reinstalled and the chapter file was lost. What happened?*

Reinstalling Ventura Publisher should not affect existing chapter files. The installation procedure will only overwrite existing Ventura Publisher software files. Make sure files are saved correctly using the Save command on the File menu. Use a filename different from the sample files created by Ventura Publisher.

19. *How do I find out what directory my files are going to when I save my chapter?*

Go to the Options menu and click on the Add Chapter option. You will be able to click on a file, then select Open File. This will show you what is in the files and the path for the files.

20. *During a save, my chapter file locked up and when I opened the file, the caption file was lost. How do I get it back?*

There is a possibility that the file is still present if Ventura Publisher saved a file with a .$AP extension. If it is available, then rename it to a .CAP file, using the following DOS command: REN filename.$AP to filename.CAP. If the file is not available, there's no other way to reinstate a lost caption file.

21. *Why is my system locking up everytime I try to save a document?*

There are two reasons this could happen, lack of disk space or lack of memory. Run CHKDSK on the hard disk in the drive where Ventura Publisher is installed. BYTES AVAILABLE ON DISK must be no less then 2Mb. The total memory should be no less then 575K bytes for version 2.0, and no less then 560K bytes with the use of expanded memory and the Professional Extension. For the Network version, you need 500K bytes plus 500K bytes expanded memory per node.

LOAD TEXT

22. *Are you supposed to use two spaces between sentences?*

Ventura Publisher is a true typesetting program and in a typeset document, the single space is standard. If you require a double space you may continue to press spacebar twice between sentences.

23. *How do I bring a Wang word processor file into Ventura Publisher?*

Wang is not supported by Ventura Publisher. The only way to load this file is to translate it into ASCII format. This format will load into Ventura Publisher with no problem.

24. *I've tried to load a text file which is well below the published limitations concerning file size. I still get an error which states there is not enough memory to load this file. Why won't it load into Ventura Publisher?*

Although the manual references file sizes which should load into Ventura Publisher, there are certain variables which could affect file loading. The one area that causes the most confusion is the format of the text file to be loaded. Text files that contain a paragraph end (carriage return) at the end of each line are formatted differently than those that contain large paragraphs of text with only a few paragraph ends per Ventura Publisher page. Tabs and paragraph ends are memory-intensive. In high concentrations they cause Ventura Publisher to display memory loading error messages even though the size of the text file would not appear larger than Ventura Publisher could load.

25. *How do you load a text file into Box Text?*

That is a function that Ventura Publisher does not support.

26. *I have attempted to load a text file. A message indicated the file loaded but I don't see it in the frame. How do you load the text?*

This is a common problem. Go to the File menu and select Load Text / Picture. Select Text from the Type of File option. Select your word processing software package or ASCII in the Text Format option. Select One or Several in the # of Files option. Click on OK. Ventura Publisher will display a list of files in the directory you have selected. From the list, an item selector will appear and you can select the proper filename.

You are now ready to load your file into a frame. The frame needs to be active for Ventura Publisher to load into a frame. When the frame is not active, Ventura Publisher will load the file into the assignment list. To load your file into the frame, activate the frame by clicking inside the frame area and click on the file in the assignment list. This should load the file.

27. *I put a paragraph marker in a paragraph without any text. But when I saved it and then reloaded the file later, the paragraph tag was not there. Why?*

This indicates the @parafiltr option is turned on. With no text before the paragraph marker, the paragraph filter deletes the paragraph marker.

28. *Ventura Publisher is giving an error message that this frame is too complex to format. I understand that when this error message appears I have used the maximum amount of line elements allotted to that frame. Can you tell me how to calculate the number of line elements in a frame?*

The term line element includes the unit called text element. The following examples illustrate the number of elements used to create a line with one tab and a line with a tab using dot leaders. TE stands for text element; each line always uses at least one line element.

"A - Z" uses a total of 4 elements: TE TE TE and 1 line element.

"A" is one text element, the hyphen character "-" is another, and "Z" is the third, Add 1 line element for a total of 4 line elements for this line.

"A .... Z" uses a total of 6 elements: TE TE TE TE TE and 1 line element. "A" is the first text element, a space placed before the dot leaders is the second element, the dot leaders themselves are the third element, a space placed after the dot leaders is the fourth element, and "Z" is the fifth element. Add 1 line element for a total of six line elements for this line.

29. *I have Ventura Publisher installed on C and files on D that I want to access. When I use the backup button to select a drive, D is not there. Is there a way to add D to the dialog box?*

Ventura Publisher does not search the system to find out what drives you have available. There is a way to add the drive to the dialog box. For example, if you were using the Load Text/Picture option, the procedure would be as follows:

a. Select the File menu Load Text/Picture option. Choose file format and OK. This will obtain an initial item selector dialog box. Do not use the backup switch yet.

b. Place the cursor on the directory line and press Esc to erase its contents. Then, type in the specification needed to reach the files on the desired new drive, D in this case.

c. Select OK and the item selector should show the list of files on the D drive.

d. Load one of the files. The step of loading is what tells Ventura Publisher which pointers to assign to this file during loading of the document. In this case it makes Ventura reference the D drive.

e. Go to the File menu and select Quit. This causes the information about availability of the new drive (D in this case) to be written to an .INF file.

f. From then on, when Ventura Publisher is started, the .INF file will tell Ventura Publisher that the new drive is available. It will be available by using the backup switch.

NOTE

If the file to be loaded already exists on the new target drive, it is only necessary to load it and quit. You don't need to save it, and you can even select Abandon to answer the prompt as Ventura Publisher quits. If the target drive does not contain suitable files to be loaded, then access a file on the installed drive and use Save As to put it on the target drive. When you quit Ventura Publisher, the necessary .INF information will be recorded.

30. *I cannot see all my files on my directory even though I know that they are there. Can you help me?*

This is a shortcoming of the software package. Ventura Publisher can only see about 100 files in a single directory, although the documentation states it can see 120.

31. *Will my formatting or codes be lost when I transfer a file from my regular word processor into Ventura Publisher?*

No. Ventura Publisher accepts text directly from word processors and stores text and formatting information back to the word processor. All text attributes (such as boldface and underline) and paragraph format information (called tags) are passed freely back and forth. However, since Ventura Publisher is a typesetting-like product, the word processor concepts of centering, double spacing, headers, footers, footnotes, and auto-numbering (to name a few) are totally different. Therefore, this information is ignored.

32. *How do I load more than one text file on the same page?*

Put multiple frames on the page and load the other files inside separate frames.

33. *Can Ventura Publisher load Interleaf or Documenter files?*

ASCII text can be from any source, assuming a physical mechanism exists for transferring the files to Ventura Publisher. Graphics are stored in different formats and are therefore incompatible.

34. *When I read my word processing files into Ventura Publisher, the text does not align the way it did in my word processor. Why not, and how do I fix it?*

Some word processors do not insert true tab characters when tabs are used, they only insert spaces. These spaces do not translate correctly in Ventura Publisher and cause the columns to be misaligned. Make sure you are setting the tabs correctly in your word processor. If all else fails, delete the spaces within Ventura Publisher and use the tabbing feature provided in the Paragraph menu.

35. *I am trying to use an @@ symbol by entering it through my word processor. After I saved my document and recalled it, the @@ symbol was missing. Why?*

The @@ symbol is a command-type character to Ventura Publisher. In order to get the symbol to work, enter it twice in succession, that is, @@@@.

36. *What are the compatible word processors for Ventura Publisher?*

The following word processors are compatible with Ventura Publisher: Xerox Writer, WordStar, MultiMate, Microsoft Word, WordPerfect 4.2 & 5.0, Displaywrite III and IV, in DCA format. Ventura Publisher is capable of accepting files from any program that can export a standard ASCII file.

37. *I can't get Ventura Publisher to show me anything in the TYPESET directory. Why?*

This is a common problem. It may mean the INF files are corrupted. Delete them and let Ventura Publisher rewrite the program loading files.

38. *When I load Ventura Publisher, I cannot find my word processing file. It is showing some files, but not the ones that I need. Is there anything that I'm not doing?*

Use the Load Text/Picture selection on the File menu. Make sure you are in the right subdirectory for your word processing file. A newly installed system defaults to the TYPESET directory. Use the mouse to point to the backup button in the item selector dialog box. Pressing the mouse once will display all subdirectories. Point to your word processing directory and press the mouse button once. Now select the file you want to load.

WordPerfect

39. *I used the Outline feature in WordPerfect. Now in Ventura Publisher it doesn't line up. Does Ventura Publisher understand this attribute?*

Break the numbers with paragraph returns. Then use the Breaks and Indent First Line options in the Paragraph menu to make them appear the way you like.

WordStar

40. *Does Ventura Publisher support the WordStar 2000 format?*

Not as yet. WordStar 2000 can be formatted to DCA.

Displaywrite

41. *Does Ventura Publisher support DCA/Displaywrite III?*

DCA is supported in Revisable format in version 1.1. DCA files of this type have the extension RFT.

42. *How do I change a Displaywrite III file into a DCA format to bring into Ventura Publisher?*

That is a four-step process, as follows:

    a. With Displaywrite loaded, at the Main menu press 6 [Utilities].

    b. Inside Utilities, press 6 again [Document Conversions].

    c. Type in the document's name and press Enter.

    d. Type in the name you want to name the DCA formatted file (Displaywrite III will place the RFT extension).

PFS Word

43. *Can I load files created by PFS Word?*

PFS Word is not one of the word processors currently supported by Ventura Publisher. Ventura Publisher can, however, read files generated by virtually any word processor if they are saved in a straight ASCII format.

Smart Word

44. *I'm trying to import files from Smart Word Processor but I can't seem to get them in when I save them in ASCII format.*

Ventura Publisher does not put carriage returns at the end of each line. This will let Ventura Publisher load the file without paragraph returns. Ventura Publisher can only load paragraphs under 8,000 characters. The Smart Word Processor did not have any carriage returns at the end of each paragraph, and so the file was too large (over 8,000 characters before reaching a carriage return).

dBASE

45. *I tried to load a dBASE III file which was output from dBASE as an ASCII file and it didn't load. Why?*

Try deleting and retyping the first few lines using the ASCII mode of your word processor to make sure there are not any hidden control characters in the file. Then try importing it as a WordStar file.

Macintosh

46. *Can any of the Macintosh word processing files be transferred into Ventura Publisher?*

The word processing files can be transferred using a MAC bridge or communications program. These files should be transmitted as standard ASCII files.

ASCII

47. *My ASCII files are not loading the tab code into Ventura Publisher correctly. When Ventura Publisher displays the file, the tabs are not spaced correctly. Why?*

You must implant the Ventura Publisher code for tab inside your ASCII files using your word processor or text editor.

48. *When I load an ASCII text file, all the text runs together with no resemblance to the original file. What am I doing wrong?*

Try loading the text as a WordStar file. The WordStar filter will recognize line endings that the ASCII filter might ignore.

49. *Why are columns in ASCII files brought into Ventura Publisher not aligning properly even when I use the Courier fixed-space font?*

It is due to the space width used as a default by Ventura Publisher. Change the Ems spacing in Alignment on the Paragraph menu to equal .6 Ems. You can do this by changing the Normal and Minimum Space Width to a measurement less than one. On the Xerox 4045 the measure is .83 for space width; other printers will vary.

50. *I loaded an ASCII file and now my lines are too far apart. How do I close up the distance?*

    There are probably returns at the end of each line, which makes Ventura Publisher see them (and space them) as paragraphs. Replace the hard returns with <9> (this is a tab) in the file and Ventura Publisher will read it in as a line break and not individual paragraphs. You can also do the same thing inside Ventura Publisher in Text mode, but some word processors that can read various text formats may be quicker.

51. *I have a 15K bytes ASCII file which will not load into a chapter. Can you tell me why?*

    Ventura Publisher cannot handle single paragraphs larger than 7K bytes. Make sure that the file has hard line breaks by breaking the file into two or more paragraphs.

52. *I cannot read in characters above ASCII 128 created in my WordStar document. Why?*

    The US version of WordStar will strip characters above 128. Try the UK WordStar filter.

53. *I am downloading ASCII files from a mainframe but Ventura Publisher is just locking up instead of loading. What's wrong?*

    This problem results when there are no hard returns in the text file. Load through the WordStar filter instead of the ASCII filter. This will allow the file to load so you can edit inside Ventura Publisher.

Hex

54. *Can Ventura Publisher load hex characters over 80h?*

    This capability was not available until Ventura Publisher version 1.1 Patch 2. In that patch the hex is extended.

TO PRINT

55. *I have a high-speed computer and I just can't print successfully from Ventura Publisher. Instead I get assorted garbage or the system locks up altogether when trying to print. I checked my installation and I have done everything correctly, my CONFIG.SYS and AUTOEXEC.BAT files are fine, and CHKDSK shows adequate free memory and disk space. My hardware also checks out fine. What's happening?*

If all else fails, reinstallation may be necessary. Here are two questions to explore before you reinstall.

1. If you have a high-speed computer, can it be slowed down? In a number of cases users have been unable to print successfully after installing Ventura Publisher with processors running at top speed. Before reinstalling, slow your computer down to low speed and reinstall that way. After completing the installation, you will probably be able to speed up again and operate successfully.

2. Is your floppy A drive a high-density drive? If so, installation of Ventura Publisher is being done from double-density disks via a high-density drive. Theoretically, this is fine. In practice, manufacturing tolerances for high-density disks occasionally cause slight read errors which cause slight errors to occur during the installation. These errors can occur without triggering any error messages, yet they do affect Ventura Publisher's behavior after installation. The only way to eliminate this source of possible trouble is to do a disk-for-disk copy of the Ventura Publisher software disks onto high-density disks. Then use the high-density disks to reinstall.

56. *My graphics print OK but the text does not.*

Verify the correct print driver and width table. The quality statement at the bottom of the Set Printer Info in 1.1 and at the top in Patch 2 and Version 2.0 menu should indicate Ultimate.

- Exit Ventura Publisher to DOS, Change to Ventura subdirectory, type DIR *.SFP to list your PORTRAIT fonts, then DIR *.SFL to list your LANDSCAPE fonts.

- Verify a minimum of 24 fonts; also verify that none of the fonts are zero (0) bytes.

- Make sure you're not pre-downloading fonts or other drivers for word processing, database, or other software packages prior to going into Ventura Publisher.

- Test Print &Book-P1 Page 1 with and without graphics. If you still have problems, reinstall Ventura Publisher after erasing the VENTURA directory.

57. *I have a document that printed in 10 minutes with version 1.0 but now takes 16 minutes in version 1.1. Why?*

Ventura Publisher is managing the fonts differently in version 1.1 and that could account for the difference in speed. Another factor is the choice of printer port. The TurboLaser card takes over a printer port, and the speed of printing varies with the port chosen. If a different port is selected when installing 1.1 that was not selected in 1.0, the print speed could be altered. According to the AST people, the COM2 port gives the fastest printing.

58. *I have created a page that will print in four colors. How can I print each color separately so that a printer can create four separate color plates to print my job?*

In version 1.1 you will have to create four new style sheets from the one you used to compose the document (make sure to leave the original style sheet unchanged). Use the Save As New Style selection from the File menu. On the first new style sheet, decide which color you would like to print first. Next, change the text tags for all the other colors, the ones you do not want to print, by modifying the Font selection in the Paragraph menu to change the color of the other text to White. Repeat this procedure for the other three style sheets and colors. The final result will be four style sheets that will produce only the text represented by a single color. To print, use the Load Different Style selection from the File menu to load each style sheet and then print the page for that color. To see the original document, load the style sheet that was originally used to create the document and all text will reappear. In 2.0 there is a setting for color separation built into the software.

59. *I attempted to block or hide an area of a picture with a white box so it wouldn't print. It looked great on the screen but it does not cover the graphic when it prints. Why?*

This is caused by the printer and/or driver in Ventura Publisher. Some printers can't print in the manner required to lay out the page with white boxes blocking out black boxes. The printer lays out the full black graphic instead of part of the graphic frame meant to show around the white box.

60. *My multiple-page document prints only the first few pages. Why?*

The problem here is usually handshaking between the printer and the computer serial port. When the printer buffer fills and causes DTR pin 20 to go low, the computer is supposed to halt transmission. The buffer on PostScript printers can contain from 1 to 6 pages before overflow. Power down the printer first to clear the previous print job. From Disk 11 of Ventura Publisher in the POSTSCPT subdirectory, copy ERHNDLR.PS to the printer, using the following command:

COPY A:/POSTSCPT/ERHNDLR.PS COM(n):<cr>.

The "n" stands for the number of the communications port (COM), for example COM1 or COM2. Repeat the printing of your multi-page document. When failure reoccurs there will be an error message on the last successful page. That error message will usually indicate the area where the problem is occurring. Only the first printed error message is reliable. This is usually caused by a bad cable.

61. *When I'm printing graphics, a portion of my image shifts.*

You have an accelerator board in your computer. Take out the accelerator board and it will work.

62. *I have created a multi-color drawing in PC Paintbrush and wonder why it does not display in color in Ventura Publisher. When I try to print the chapter to my 4020 color printer, the PC Paintbrush image comes out in red. Can you tell me why?*

Ventura Publisher reads only one bit plane when importing PC Paintbrush files, so it cannot reproduce your file in multi-colors. The Xerox 4020 drive written by GEM and used by Ventura Publisher treats the file as a mono-image, which is seen as the color red.

63. *How do I get the style sheet out of a C00 file?*

There is no style sheet inside a C00 file, just printer codes.

64. *Can I use communications packages to transmit a print file created by Ventura Publisher?*

Yes. This is one way to share a high quality printer among a number of computer systems. Print files created by Ventura Publisher can also be copied from one processor to another on a network. This allows access to different types of printers.

65. *I can't get Ventura Publisher to print all of my lines. It worked before; what happened?*

Delete your INF files. Check to see if anything has changed on your computer since the last time you worked on it. You may have a problem with disk space or not enough memory.

66. *My document printed yesterday, but now when it prints, the first line is missing. My top margin is set to .30. When I attempt to edit the text on the first line, it turns black and will not let me edit that line. Why?*

This problem was caused by having the frame background set to white 1. Change it to white hollow and your black line will go away and the first line should print.

DOS FILE OPS

67. *I'm trying to delete a chapter. How do I do this?*

Ventura Publisher allows you to delete files with the DOS_File Ops selection on the File menu. After you select this option, change the directory line to the name of the chapter file you want to delete, using .* for the extension. Then, click on Delete Matching Files. This deletes the chapter file and its associated files. For example, DIRECTORY LINE: [CHAPTER NAME.*].

CHAPTER 3
Edit Menu

The Edit menu is a short menu, but don't let the size fool you. When you become an advanced user, this menu will allow you to use some hidden power in Ventura Publisher. The Cut, Copy, and Paste features are very powerful. They allow you to copy or paste framed text, framed graphics, and Ventura Publisher text or graphics, from one page to another and from one chapter to another. This is extremely useful when you have already sized and scaled a graphic inside a frame, since it may have been a problem getting the graphic in the frame perfectly. The cut and paste process will load the frame with the same settings that exist in the other frame. You could even develop a library of framed text or graphics by saving each individual piece of text or graphics into small chapter files that could be reloaded to save time.

Remove Text/File allows you to delete files from the frames or the chapter pointers. This stops the chapter from attempting to load the deleted file.

File Type/Rename is a translate utility that is really undersold. It will translate any text file that Ventura Publisher can import into any other format Ventura Publisher imports. So if someone sends you a Microsoft Word file to edit at your station and you only have WordPerfect, you can load the file in Microsoft Word format, then use the File Type/Rename function to translate it to WordPerfect format. After saving the chapter file, you can load the text file into WordPerfect for editing.

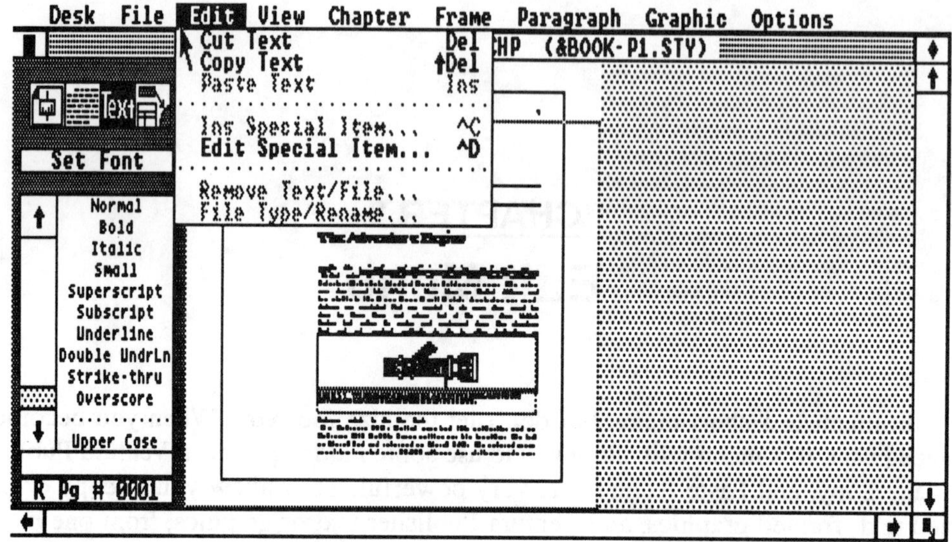

Topic Index

CUT AND COPY

1. *How do I cut and copy text?*

   In the Text mode, you place your mouse in the position that you want to start the copy and hold down the mouse button. Drag the cursor down the page to copy a block of text, or across the particular words that you wish to copy or cut. Once the desired text is highlighted, go to the Edit menu and select the Cut (Del) or Copy (Shift Del) option. The text will then be placed on the clipboard. There are three independent clipboards; Frame, Text, and Graphics. They can be pasted into any frame, chapter, or any multiple chapter/frames. The clipboards will keep the copy until something else is copied to the clipboard or the program is exited.

   Go to the chapter where you want the text to appear and click the mouse; this plants the text cursor. Go to the Edit menu and select the Paste (Ins) option. This will place the text in its new position. This text will also be rewritten to the text file when saved.

FLOW TO OTHER FRAMES

2. *I want to place my text from the third column on my page to a frame at the bottom of my page. For some reason the text will not go into the other frames that I have made to take the overflow. The rest is not showing up in the second frame that I drew. What's wrong?*

When using the Cut and Paste option in the Edit menu, Ventura Publisher cannot flow text into other frames like it does with regular loaded text files from the File menu. The cut text is kept in temporary memory in what Ventura Publisher calls the clipboard. This information comes and goes in blocks and Ventura Publisher cannot spool them into different frames. Instead of using the cut feature, break the text in your word processor in half and load your text files where you want them displayed.

View Menu

The View menu is a menu that an advanced user will not need to look at very often because most of the choices can be executed with keyboard shortcuts. Keyboard shortcuts are represented in the menus as a ^ (Ctrl) then a letter. For example, to execute Reduced view option, the keyboard shortcut is ^R, meaning you press and hold the Ctrl key and type R. Only the Facing Pages view cannot be accessed with keyboard shortcuts. The View menu is also another way to change from one operating mode to another. This method is important if you have the sidebar turned off to allow margin-to-margin viewing. This menu is self- contained; none of the options have ellipses leading to dialog boxes. Each time you click on an option, Ventura Publisher executes the command.

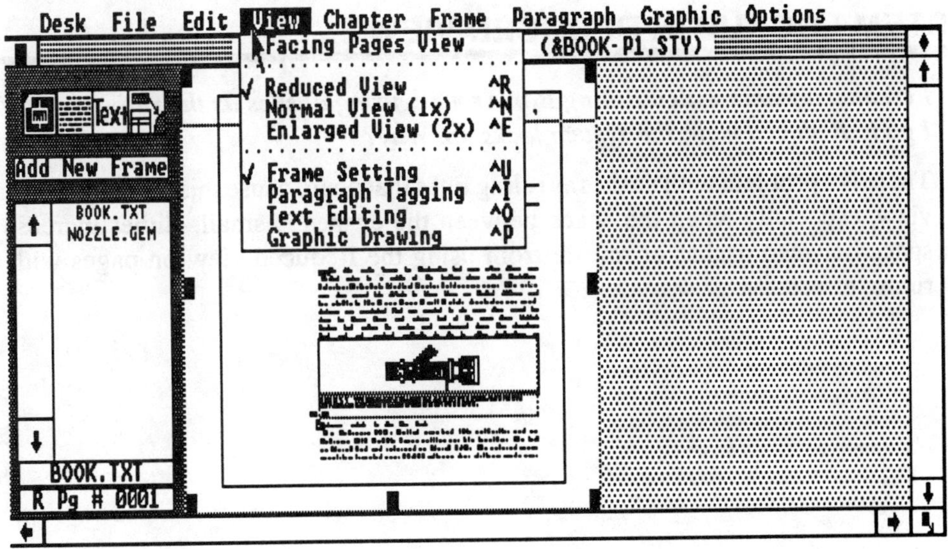

Topic Index

EDIT IN ALL VIEWS

1. *Can I edit text in all views?*

   Yes. All functions work in all views.

TWO-PAGE VIEW

2. *How do I see two pages of a document at once?*

   Under the View menu select Facing Pages view. Make sure Double Sides was selected in the Page Layout option of the Page menu for this feature to work.

SYSTEM LOCKUP IN REDUCED VIEW

3. *I created a frame with a Ruling Box Around, using dashes as the ruling line. When I go to Reduced view, the system locks up. Why?*

   There is a problem with dashes as ruling lines that could cause this lockup in Reduced view, especially when the space between the dashes is small. Either increase the space between dashes or refrain from using the Reduced view on pages with this ruling effect.

CHAPTER 5
Page / Chapter Menu

In version 2.0 the Page menu was renamed the Chapter menu. By either name, this menu controls the page settings for the entire chapter. It contains the header and footer controls for the chapter and individual pages, as well as settings for footnotes. Also, it lets you move throughout the document using the Go to Page option. As for differences in the two versions, Page Layout in 1.1 has changed to Page Size & Layout in 2.0; Widows and Orphans in 1.1 has changed to Chapter Typography in 2.0; and Chapter Counter in 1.1 has changed to Update Counters in 2.0. The Column Balance option has been moved into the Chapter Typography dialog box from the Frame menu in 1.1, thereby making this a more comprehensive menu.

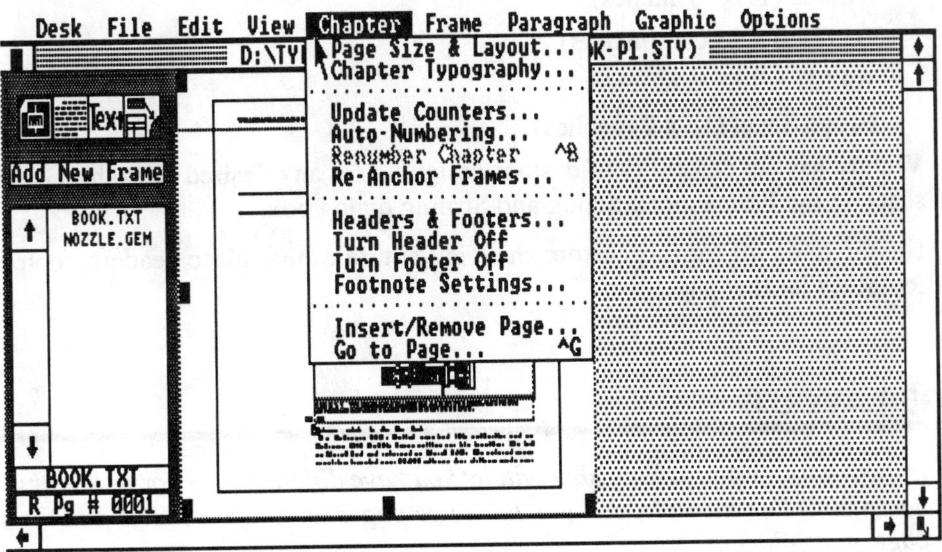

Topic Index

PAGE DIMENSIONS

1. *Can I produce an 11.5 x 15" page?*

Yes and no. Yes, Ventura Publisher is capable of producing portrait and landscape page sizes of:

Half (81/2 x 51/2 inches)

Letter (81/2 x 11 inches)

Legal (81/2 x 14 inches)

Double (11 x 17 inches)

B5 (17.6 x 25 centimeters)

A4 (21 x 29.7 centimeters)

Broad Sheet (18 x 24 inches).

Ventura has the capability of custom designing for any desired size, short of broad sheet, in the Frame menu Sizing and Scaling dialog box.

No, the trade off for this custom sheet is Ventura cannot place headers, footers, or footnotes for that page.

PAGE LAYOUT

2. *Is there a way Ventura Publisher will let you have different page formats within one document? For example, can you have five pages with two columns and the sixth page, one column.*

Simply draw a frame for the page that you want as one column and make the frame an entire column in width. Or, add a new page using the Add/Remove Page feature.

This will become an independent underlying page and can have different margins and column settings.

VERTICAL RULE SKIPS A PAGE

3. *I created a vertical rule between two columns. It shows up on the first page of my document, skips the second, and reappears on the third. Why?*

You probably have your Page Layout option set to Double Sided. You have set the Vertical Rule parameter for the right side of the page but have not turned it on for the left side. You can turn the left side on by changing the Setting For button from Right Page to Left Page. Whenever you have a condition that skips pages, check to see that you have set up the left and right pages for the same attributes. Or, simply click on the Copy To Facing Page button and this will automatically give your left and right pages a mirror effect.

AUTO-NUMBERING

4. *The Auto-Numbering in my document is showing all levels, for example: 1.,1.a.,1.b. I want to suppress the first number, for example: 1., a., b.*

There is a suppression feature in the Auto-Numbering dialog box that allows you to suppress the previous level. In your example, place the cursor at the left of the level 2 line and click on Suppress Level. Level 1 numbering will be suppressed for level 2 headings.

5. *Using Auto-Numbering, I can't get Ventura Publisher to start a section with the right letter, the letter "E." Can you help me?*

When using Auto-Numbering, you must understand that the starting point must always be stated as a number. To get Auto-Numbering to behave as intended, realize that E is letter number 5 of the alphabet and enter:

[*Chapter,A,5]

6. *I am trying to restart Auto-Numbering in my chapters using version 1.1. As I change the number sequence in one chapter, it changes the values in the other chapters as well. Why?*

The values for Auto-Numbering are stored in the style sheet. Style sheets that are used for multiple chapters carry the values from one chapter to another. The workaround is to make a separate copy of the style sheet for each chapter. Each style sheet would contain the Auto-Numbering values for its own chapter.

7. *My Auto-Numbering is not staying in sequence from one page to another. My first page ends on 4.a and my second page starts at 3.a; what's up?*

The second page was probably added on by the Add Page After Current Page option. In this case, Ventura Publisher detects an end-of-file marker which confuses the numbering scheme. These files need to be combined so that Ventura Publisher does not see the end-of-file marker.

8. *Sometimes I make a change to or activate Auto-Numbers, then save the chapter. When I reload the file, the Auto-Numbering changes that were made are not there. Why?*

If the only change made to a style sheet is within Auto-Numbers, those changes are not saved when the chapter is saved. This problem exists in version 1.1 unpatched and Patch 1, but is corrected in Patch 2. As a workaround, after you make Auto-Numbering changes, go into the Paragraph menu, select Font, and click on OK in that dialog box. This will cause a save of the style sheet and ensure that the Auto-Number changes are stored when the chapter is saved.

HEADERS & FOOTERS

9. *I want my left and right headers and footers to mirror each other. I don't see that happening when I set the page layout to show double pages. Why?*

You must go into the Frame mode and click on the footer frame. Go to the Page menu Headers and Footers option and choose the setting for Copy to Facing Page. This will make the two pages mirror each other. Another way to make this work is to click on Copy to Facing Page when you first make the header or footer.

10. *My footers are not printing. They display on the screen but they are not there, or only half the line prints when I print the chapter. Can you tell me why?*

There could be several reasons. First, check to see if your printer is capable of printing to the bottom of the screen. This may sound strange, but many laser printers have an effective print area that is less than a standard 8 1/2-by-11 page. Print the CAPABILI.CHP file to see how far your printer reaches toward each edge of the page. If this appears to be the problem, raise the bottom margin of your underlying page to raise the footer high enough to be printed. Another possibility is that the top margin in the frame which contains the footer is too large. Try reducing the top margin to raise the footer higher on the page.

11. *I cannot access the footer frame on one page. Why not?*

    Check to make sure that your Page or Chapter menu says Turn Footer Off, indicating that the footer is on. If it says Turn Footer On, click on this option to turn on the footer for this page.

12. *I cannot get the text inside the footer frame.*

    Check the margins of the footer frame and make sure they are not pushing the text below the visible area of the frame, making the frame appear to be empty.

13. *I have changed the Chapter Counter but it doesn't seem to be changing the header number. Why?*

    This is a problem that has been found in version 1.1. It doesn't seem to see a change in some of the dialog boxes if nothing else is changed but that dialog box. To fix this, go to the Paragraph menu, choose any option, click OK without changing anything, save the file, and exit Ventura Publisher. Then reload this chapter file and it should return with the header number changed.

14. *I would like to change the fonts on a running header so that the chapter title is a different typeface than the chapter number. How can I do this?*

    You use the paragraph tagging mode to change the whole generated header. The following procedure assumes that the chapter title will appear on the left of the page header, and the chapter number will appear on the right.

    a. Set the font for the generated header so that it provides the typeface you want for the chapter numbers.
    b. At the first page of the chapter, add a new page before the current page.
    c. On the new page, type the chapter title and press Enter. Ventura Publisher will ask you for a text filename for this new text, so you will have to assign it a name. Tag this new paragraph with a unique tag name, such as Chapter.
    d. Using the text editor, highlight the text and use the Set Font option to change to the desired typeface.
    e. Use the Page Down key to return to the first actual page of the chapter and select Headers & Footers from the Chapter menu.
    f. If you are using Double Pages (Left and Right), make the following changes for both the Left and Right Header (make sure both are turned on). You

should see a cursor at the beginning of the first line (Left). Erase whatever appears on that line.

g. Move the mouse cursor down to the selection box for 1st Match and select this box. You will see [*Tag Name] appear on line one.

h. Use the arrow key to move the cursor inside the right bracket and use the Backspace key to erase Tag Name.

i. Type in the name of the new tag you created on the previous page (Chapter was suggested). Your first line should now appear [<Chapter].

j. Move down to the fifth line labelled Right and erase that line if it is not blank.

k. Move the mouse cursor to the selection box Chapter # and select this box. This should complete the formatting of your header.

l. Select OK and you should now see the chapter title and the chapter number in different typefaces.

In version 1.1 it is possible to set an attribute with the Headers and Footers dialog box which will change the point size and weight of a word or words within the header or footer.

15. *I want to create one chapter file which will actually contain four small chapters of information. How can I set up Headers to allow me to show the chapter number and page number (e.g., 2 - 5) of each page? Doesn't page numbering run through the whole chapter file?*

You can create the appearance of multiple chapters within one chapter file.

a. Assuming each Chapter contains a line which says "Chapter 1, Chapter 2," etc., you can create a separate tag (i.e., Chapter Num) for that information. If you want Chapter 1, tag the word chapter and the number. If you want only the number to appear, tag only the number.

b. Go to the Page menu under Headers and Footers and turn on the headers for the left and right pages.

c. Decide which side of the page you want the chapter number to appear and move the cursor to that line.

d. Select 1st Match from the boxes at the lower portion of the dialog box. You will see [*Tag Name] appear on the line with the cursor.

e. Use the arrow keys to move the cursor inside the right bracket and then the Backspace key to erase tag name leaving [].

f. Enter the tag name you assigned to the Chapter number (e.g., Chapter Num). The line should now look like this [<Chapter Num].

g. Move the cursor outside the right bracket and add whatever separator you like to see between the chapter designator and the page number (space, dash, slash, etc.).

h. Select [P#] from the boxes at the lower portion of the dialog box. This will place either Chapter 1 or 1 in the header, followed by the separator and the page number.

Now that you have established your header, page through the document to determine where each chapter starts. Initially, you will find that the first page of each chapter will have the correct chapter number.

16. *How do you produce the typesetter's open quote and close quote in a header? The keystrokes that are in the manual don't work in the header dialog box.*

Put the code <169> to open the quote. Place the code <170> to close the quotes.

FIRST / LAST MATCH

17. *I am using the 1st Match/Last Match feature in the Headers and Footers dialog box. I need to have a different point size on the Last Match. How is this done?*

Use <Pnnn> in front of the Last Match code on the format line provided, where P = Point size and nnn = 1/72-inch per point. For example, <P072> = one inch.

18. *My headers and footers are not showing, but my header and footer frame is turned on using First and Last Match. What's happening?*

The First/Last Match option is matching with an empty paragraph return. The first tag must have text with it for the header/footer to display that first/last matched text.

19. *I am using First Match in my header, but on some pages the header is not maintaining the tag name. It is looking forward and picking up the next tag name on the next page. Why?*

This problem occurs when Page Break is set to Before/Until Left. Some users use this feature to insure that the chapters start on a left page. There is a workaround if you are creating blank right pages with this tag. You can use Insert Page Before Current Page. This replaces the page created by the tag with an inserted blank page and finds the correct First Match.

FOOTNOTE SETTINGS

20. *I have four footnotes on a page. As I began entering text to define the footnote references, I lost some text from footnote four as I expanded footnote three. Can you tell me what happened?*

Ventura Publisher supports one-half page of footnotes. In this particular instance the text added to footnote number three brought the effective area of the footnote to more than half a page, and the last few lines of footnote number four were dropped in order to accommodate the text above. There is not much that can be done about this problem. Ventura Publisher has always had a problem with footnotes and where they put things on the page.

21. *The footnote separator line width does not show up as the width that I entered. Why?*

The separator line begins over the asterisk (*) which Ventura Publisher uses as the footnote reference. This problem is because Ventura Publisher draws the separator line between two points, an origin point and a destination point. The origin point is taken at the left margin of the underlying page, in this case 1" from the left edge of the paper. The destination point should be 2" to the right of the margin, but a mistake was made in the software, and it is set at 2" to the right of the edge of the paper. This is a Ventura Publisher software limitation. As a workaround to get a given separator line width, simply enter that amount PLUS the left margin width in the Footnote Settings dialog box. For example, with a left margin of 1.00" and the desired separator line width of 2.00", enter Separator Line Width = 3.00". The Footnote Settings dialog box does not provide a way to start the separator line anywhere except at the left margin.

22. *My footnote separator line is being outdented outside my frame. Why?*

The footnote frame is larger than the margin of the underlying page so you must reduce the size of the footnote frame. This is done by clicking on Margins and Columns in the Frame menu. Set the Left and Right Margins to the same settings as the underlying page.

23. *I would like to move the separator line above the footnotes away from the text.*

The separator line is placed on the top of the footnote frame. The way to set it apart from your text is to set a tag on the footnote as a paragraph. In the Paragraph menu under the Spacing option, place some space in the Above area and this will push the information down away from the separator line.

24. *I have a footnote but it has a big fat line between it and the text. How do I get rid of it?*

In the Footnote Settings dialog box, check the Separator Line Width and Height of Line settings and make sure they are not showing some large settings like one inch.

25. *I can't get my footnotes to print. Why?*

Footnotes are under the same constraints as footers. They will not print on some printers because of the location on the page. Check to see where the footnote is located on the page. Then print the CAPABILI.CHP file located on your TYPESET directory. The outer white edge of this page is where the printer cannot print. Compare this page to the non-printing footer page. If the footnote is within the white area, it will not print. Change the page's bottom margin to allow the footnote space.

26. *I have a multi-page document in which there are many footnotes. On several pages there is a large block of white space under the last footnote entry and I cannot get the text to reformat to eliminate this space. I have tried to change margins and resize the footnote frame but nothing works. Why?*

What you have discovered is a Catch-22-type situation within Ventura Publisher. If you have 7 or 8 footnotes on a page, entering the text for the footnotes will expand the footnote frame upward to accommodate the text (up to one half page). As the footnote frame moves upward, text flows off the current page to the following page to make room for the frame. Let's say that you are entering text for footnote number 5 and as you do, the frame moves up and pushes the text containing the footnote reference for footnotes 5, 6, 7, and 8 onto the next page. As the footnote reference is moved to the next page, so also is the text for that footnote. The area of the footnote frame it formerly occupied is now left blank. If you were to shrink the footnote frame to flow text back from the next page, the footnote reference for footnote 5 would return. Ventura Publisher would try to reformat the footnote frame which would push the footnote reference to the next page leaving white space in the footnote frame. You can see how you could get stuck in an endless loop. The only workaround for documents that are footnote intensive is to manually create the footnote references and footnote frames and work with the sizing of the frames manually. While this may be cumbersome, it is the only way to get around the white space problem.

27. *How can you superscript the footnote reference within the footnote frame?*

There is a workaround for less than 10 footnotes. In Paragraph mode, select the Z_FONT # tag. In the Paragraph menu select Special Effects/Set Font. Select Big First Character, reduce the point size, and use Shift Up to position the number in the desired superscripted position. Since Character Big First only works on one character, this can only be used for footnotes 1 through 9.

28. *Is there any way the footnote algorithm can be altered to prevent large white spaces at the bottom of the page?*

    No.

INSERT / REMOVE PAGE

29. *Can I have more than one underlying page format in a single chapter?*

    Yes. The settings for the first underlying page are saved in the style sheet and settings for subsequent underlying pages are stored in the chapter file. Each subsequent underlying page is created each time you add a new page. All you need to do is change the margins and columns for the new page format.

30. *I have a page that I'm trying to delete but it won't go away. How do I get this thing to delete?*

    If there is something on the page, such as graphics, the page cannot be deleted. Remove all objects from the page before attempting a page delete.

CHAPTER 6

Frame Menu

The Frame menu is the real superhero of Ventura Publisher. Frames really bring life to the software. Their purpose is to hold text and graphics. A frame has its own internal margin and columns and even displaces text away from its borders. If a frame can't hold all of a text file, it will remember where it stopped flowing text. When the text is attached to another frame, Ventura Publisher will continue flowing text at the point where it left off. The number of frames that can be attached to one continuous text file is limited only by your particular configuration.

In version 2.0 the Frame Typography option now holds the spot of the Repeating Frame option in 1.1. Repeating Frames has moved to a position further down the menu. The Frame Typography option in 2.0 has control of the Widows and Orphans formerly of the 1.1 Page menu and the Column Balance which was previously found in version 1.1 Sizing and Scaling option. You will notice that these options duplicate the Chapter Typography options on the Chapter menu. This is Ventura Publishers' effort to develop consistency in the menu structure. The frame settings in this menu have the power to override the Chapter Typography settings for the frame selected.

The other rather obvious change is the last option on the menu, Image Setting. This new option controls the TIFF gray scaling on PostScript printers. It tells the printer which halftone screen to use when printing.

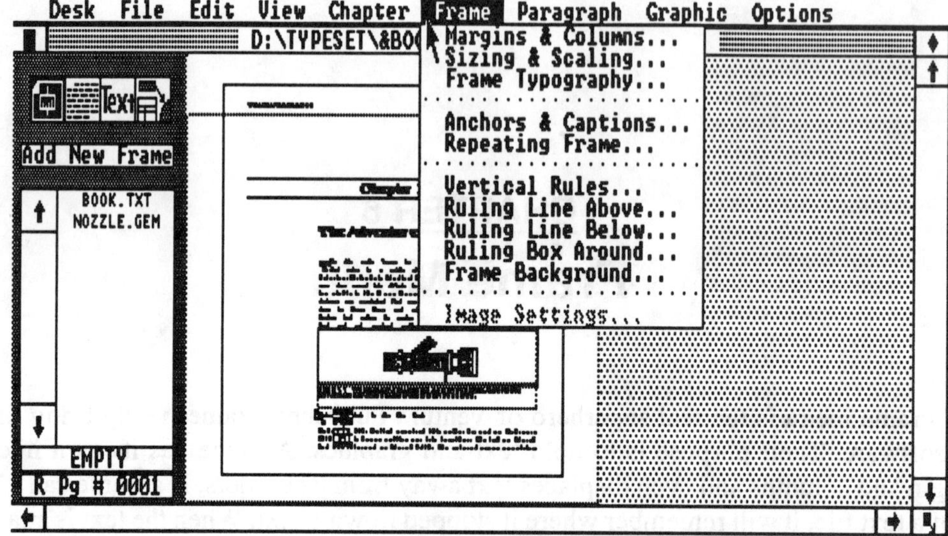

Topic Index

GENERAL

1. *My system lockups when trying to add a new frame after printing a chapter. Why?*

You had set your screen fonts to PSF but did not have that file in your Ventura directory. Settings for screen fonts other than those installed will cause lockups and the error message, "Cannot load GEM VDI screen driver."

2. *I loaded a picture into Ventura Publisher, inserted it into a frame, and scaled it to fit. When I printed the page, the picture did not look right. What is wrong?*

When scaling a picture to fit in a frame, it is advisable to use integers (whole numbers) as the scaling factor. These are easier for the printer to interpret and recreate. Memory limitations within the printer itself may also cause images to distort when printing.

3. *I increased the point size of a line of text within a frame and it disappeared. Why?*

   The size of the frame has a direct bearing on what fonts will fit within the frame. A 48-point headline will not fit in a frame that is only 36 points high and, therefore, Ventura Publisher will not display it. Remember that spacing above and below the text and any ruling lines also affect the final display height of the text. You can place a 24-point headline in a 36- point frame, but if you add spacing above or below or both, you could exceed 36 points and the text will not display.

   If text disappears in this manner, you appear to be stuck, because you cannot grab the text with the Paragraph icon. The way to get around this is to select another line or paragraph on the screen that is in a larger frame. Tag it with the same tag that caused the text to disappear in the smaller frame. Now you can reduce the size of the tagged information so the missing text reappears in the smaller frame. Make sure to return the text in the larger frame to its original tag.

4. *I'm attempting to fill six frames across a page to flow text into so that it will appear to be a column. When I get to the third column it starts to jump around. For example, column two goes away and when I load column four, column one goes away and column two comes back. What's happening?*

   This is a real tricky one because one might think that frames were not drawn in the proper order. The real problem is that you have a tag with an Alignment attribute of Overall Width set to Column-Wide instead of Frame-Wide which you are using for this technique. When Ventura Publisher runs into that tag, it tries to do some strange things. Change Overall-Width to Frame-Wide to solve this unusual problem.

5. *Is frame text measured from the top of the frame where the text is located, or is it measured from the top of the underlying frame?*

   Each frame is its own island and has its own top, bottom, right, and left margin.

6. *Can you tell me what these frames are all about? I don't understand what happens with frames.*

   Frames must be created in sequence, from the first page to the end of the document. For example, text on page six cannot be concluded on page two. The frame that is drawn first will be first in line for text and the frames will be in sequence from first to last.

7. *How can I create identical frames?*

If the same size frame with identical margins, ruling lines, captions, and backgrounds is to be used over and over, make one master frame of the proper size and add the desired margins, ruling lines, and backgrounds. Then copy this frame to the clipboard, go to each page where you want the frame to appear, and paste a copy of the frame on the new page. Pasting a frame onto the page from which it was copied results in two identical frames being placed on top of one another. Merely move one of the frames to another location.

8. *How do I select frames underneath other frames?*

When one frame is placed entirely under one or more frames, you cannot select the frame on the bottom in the normal way. However, if you press and hold the Ctrl key while you select the frame, you can select each frame in succession, starting with the currently selected frame.

9. *How do I achieve precise frame size and placement?*

Frames can be placed and sized precisely using the Sizing & Scaling options in the Frame menu. On the other hand, the mouse provides a much faster way to draw and change the size of the frame. A good way to take advantage of both features is to show Rules and then use the mouse to create and place the frame as closely as your eye and the resolution of the screen allows. Then select the frame and use the Sizing & Scaling option to make exact adjustments to the frame's placement and size.

10. *Why is it sometimes when I place a frame on a page there is a large gap between the bottom of the frame and the next sentence?*

Turn Line Snap Off and adjust frame ever so slightly above and below until Ventura Publisher gives you the desirable appearance. Adjusting padding in your Frame menu Sizing and Scaling option can improve the final outcome.

11. *Is there a maximum number of frames you can place on a page?*

No.

12. *How do I move a frame from one chapter to another?*

Select the frame you want to move. Copy it with the Copy option in the Edit menu. Then open the chapter where you want to place the copied frame, go to the proper page, and press the Insert key. The frame places itself on the page in the same location as the original chapter. To change it, simply move the frame after it appears on the page.

13. *Can Ventura Publisher make text flow around irregular shaped images like circles and triangles?*

While not an automatic process, like flowing text around frames, you can create this effect. First create a frame within a column of text. You will notice that the text flows around the frame. Now select the Graphics mode and draw a circle in the middle of the frame. Select the Frame menu and select the Sizing and Scaling option. Select Text Flow Around Off. You should now see the text flowing inside the frame and the circle. Now select the Add a New Frame box and create a new frame that overlays the top portion of the circle about the height of one line of text. Next create a new frame just under the one you just created that is a just a little wider, reaching just beyond the perimeter of the circle. Keep creating frames until the circle is covered. Size each frame so that it just extends beyond the edge of the circle. These new frames, by default, will cause the text to flow around them making it appear that the text is flowing around the circle. Note: If you are having trouble aligning the frames, turn Line Snap Off in the Options menu. This will give you a finer adjustment capability.

14. *I don't have a mouse. How do I draw a frame using the keyboard?*

The Home key is the same as clicking on the mouse button. The End key is the same as pressing and holding the mouse button. To draw a frame, click on Add New Frame. Bring the cursor on the screen. Press the End key and Ventura Publisher will anchor the upper left corner and display the outline of the frame. Use the arrow keys to enlarge and reduce the frame. Press Home again to place the active frame on the page.

15. *How do I get a document to continue on another page, for example from page 1 to page 4?*

To continue a text file from one page to another, like newspapers do continuing stories on another page, create your frame on the initial page and load the text file. Ventura Publisher will place as much text as will fit in the frame. Now go to the page where the article is to continue and create another frame. From the Assignment list select the same text file again. Ventura Publisher remembers where it left off and continues the text in the second frame. If the frame on the first page is resized, Ventura Publisher automatically pulls text from the second frame to fill the first or pushes text from the first frame to the second frame depending on whether the first frame is enlarged or reduced. If page considerations require that the second frame spill over to another non-sequential page, repeat the process and create the third frame and select the text file again.

MARGINS & COLUMNS

16. *I have a frame with two columns of unequal widths, 1 and 2 inches. Whenever I resize the frame, the columns change back to equal widths, even if the only change I make is in the height of the frame. Why?*

Ventura Publisher automatically recalculates column widths whenever a frame is resized regardless of whether the change is in frame height or width. The default in the algorithm that does the recalculation is to make columns equal widths. This happens in versions 1.0 and 1.1. No workaround exists other than to manually change your column widths back to the original.

17. *Can a 32-column page be formatted inside Ventura Publisher?*

Yes, even though there is an 8-column and 16-tab limitation, the software is versatile enough to accommodate this request. This can be done by using the Vertical Tab option.

18. *Can I create more than four columns of text on the same page?*

Yes. Ventura Publisher allows up to eight columns of text per page or frame. Two frames having eight columns can be placed next to each other on a page to effectively create a sixteen-column layout.

19. *I have placed a small amount of padding around a frame which is imbedded in a paragraph of text. Ventura Publisher seems to have inserted some extra space in the text lines which appear to the upper right and lower left of the frame. Why?*

This is a screen formatting problem which can be fixed by widening the frame to make its margin wider. Maybe only a fraction of a point wider is needed to fix the problem.

20. *How do I move text toward the center of the page; everything is too far to the left?*

Under the Frame menu, the Margins & Columns option allows you to set margins for top, bottom, left, and right. Select this option and adjust the left margin by increasing the value of the space from the side of the page. Selected text can also be moved by adjusting the In From Left attribute of the Spacing option on the Paragraph menu.

21. *Ventura Publisher won't take my margin settings. It keeps changing my settings to something else. Why?*

Two things could be done. First, check your ruler on screen and make sure that it is set to the same increment that you are trying to set. Second, if you are setting something like picas and points, be sure that you are not contradicting your settings. For example, 12 points equals 1 pica, so if you enter 1 pica 12 points, Ventura Publisher will convert it to 2 picas, giving the appearance of a setting jump.

22. *Why do my column widths change from my original settings? I created a 14-pica column and upon returning to the Margins and Columns dialog box, I find the measurement changes to 13 picas, 11 points. Why?*

    Ventura Publisher uses measuring based on 1200 dots per inch to store column and margin measurements. Rounding occurs when these measurements are converted into picas and points, so you will see a small difference.

SIZING & SCALING

23. *How can I crop an image if I don't have a mouse?*

    There are no keyboard provisions in Ventura Publisher for the cropping feature. In order to crop, you must activate the frame and go into the Frame menu Sizing and Scaling option and change the Picture Scaling option to By Scale Factors. Then enter settings in the X Crop Offset and Y Crop Offset options. The picture will redraw at the new location within the frame. To crop with a mouse, you press and hold the left mouse button while holding down the Alt key. You will see a hand appear on the screen; then move the mouse in the direction you would like to crop.

24. *How do I reduce an image in a frame?*

    This is done in the Frame menu Sizing and Scaling option. Set the By Scale Factor and the Scale Width. The smaller the setting, the smaller the image appears in the frame.

25. *How do I prevent the text from printing right against the frame that has a picture inside?*

    With the frame active, click on the Frame menu and select Sizing & Scaling. Put some number in for Padding the Horizonal and Vertical. This will cause a clear buffer space around your frame.

REPEATING FRAME

26. *What is the best way to produce a form letter merge using Ventura Publisher? I'm trying to load files from a database with my customer information (name, address, etc).*

A simple way to do this inside Ventura Publisher is to make a repeating frame at the top of the page for information that will appear in each letter. A frame is drawn at the bottom of the page to contain the body of the letter. These two frames will not touch, and between these two frames is the underlying frame. The underlying frame should be just the size of the text required to show one name and address per letter. This file with the two repeating frames will cause Ventura Publisher to add pages to fit in the text with the repeating frame on each page.

27. *I created a shaded repeating frame with a graphic image in it to run throughout a chapter. I want different text to appear within the frame on each page. The repeating frame will have text flowing around it. How can I do this?*

Creating a repeating frame is not difficult. Shading it and placing a graphic in it is no problem. The problem is when you activate Text Flow Around, you cannot place another frame on top of the repeating frame and display text in it. The Text Flow Around option will not allow it. The solution is to place another frame directly below the repeating frame and shade it in the same manner as the repeating frame (you will have to do this on each page). Now you can type different text into each frame on each page with the appearance that it is all part of the repeating frame.

28. *How do I get text to flow around a repeating frame?*

A repeating frame for the most part acts like any other frame. Select the repeating frame, pull down the Frame menu, click on Sizing and Scaling, and set Flow Text Around to On. This procedure will make the text flow around all frames that repeat from this one.

ANCHORS & CAPTIONS

29. *I can't make a free form caption like it's stated in the Reference Manual. I can't see the end of file marker. Can you help me?*

The Interline Spacing is normally too large when this problem occurs. Reduce the Interline Spacing in the Spacing option of the Paragraph menu and the end of file marker should appear. The Spacing option in the Paragraph menu can also be used to change other spacing settings such as Above and Below. Any of these settings can cause the same results.

30. *Everytime I do an edit I have to move the frames so that they are placed where the text is located. What can I do to speed up the process?*

Use the Anchors & Captions option.

31. *I'm using 1.0 and I would like to anchor a frame with an enclosed graphic to a block of text. This way, when text is added or deleted, the frame moves with the assigned text. Is this possible?*

The ability to anchor frames is a feature of version 1.1; it is not supported in 1.0.

32. *How do I anchor frames?*

This is a two-step process:

    a. Select the desired frame and go to the Frame menu Anchors & Captions option.

       (1) Place a name on the Anchor line to name the frame.

    b. Go into Text mode and click the mouse at the desired location to plant your anchor.

       (1) Pull down the Edit menu and click on Insert/Edit Anchor.

       (2) Type the anchor name you used in the first step on the Frame Anchor Name line.

       (3) Click OK.

Version 2.0 has added a Relative, Automatically at Anchor option which allows you to have these anchored frames move along with the text automatically as you edit. This feature has not been their most reliable feature for long documents, but is somewhat reliable for short documents.

33. *I created a page with four frames and added captions under each frame. When I used the copy function to copy these frames to another page, the figure counters in the captions had reversed. Why?*

This was a bug in version 1.0. You can work around it simply by cutting and pasting again on the page in which they are incorrect. They will again be reversed. This problem has been fixed in version 1.1.

FIGURE COUNTER

34. *I have created several frames and, within the caption box, have turned on the figure counter. However, the figure numbers are out of sequence. Why?*

Ventura Publisher keeps track of frames in the order in which they are drawn. Consequently, the figure counter numbers frames in the order they are created. The frames can be rearranged by cutting them into the clipboard using the Edit menu. Cut the frames in their priority, making sure to cut and replace each frame in its position. When you are finished, each frame will have a new priority based on the one cut previously.

VERTICAL RULES

35. *I want to create a heading section above two columns separated by a vertical rule. I created a ruling line below a tag and then made the tag frame wide to push the vertical rule below the heading information. This pushed part of the vertical rule below the tag but there is still some of it showing in the heading section. How could this have happened?*

Chances are that you have tags placed above the tag containing the ruling line that are only column wide. Check each tag above the ruling line and make sure its alignment is frame wide instead of column wide.

RULING LINE ABOVE

36. *I was attempting to follow the directions of the Tips & Tricks book on Ventura Publisher. It said that the best way to draw a straight line on the page is to draw a frame, then put Ruling Line Above, and then change the size to 0 width. Now I can't get rid of it because I can't select the frame. Can you help me?*

With no width, there is no way that you can select the frame again because there is nothing there as far as Ventura Publisher is concerned. Next time, set the width to a value greater than zero. Straight lines can be drawn in version 2.0 by holding down the Alt while drawing the line.

RULING BOX AROUND

37. *There is a square box around my text file. How do I get rid of it?*

    This sounds like the Frame menu option Ruling Box Around. Look at this feature and change the setting to None and this should correct the problem.

38. *I tried to print a document with a scanned image of a map placed within a frame. There was a ruling box around the frame on the screen, but when I printed the document, the ruling box disappeared. Why?*

    PostScript reserves space on the page for the original size of the scanned image, which in this case fit the entire size of the frame. If you reduce the size of the map, the ruling line will reappear.

39. *I have text inside a frame with ruling box around it. How do I move the text away from the edge of the frame?*

    This can be done by setting a margin for the frame. All frames can have internal margins and columns. Click on the Frame menu and select the Columns & Margins option. You can then set the margin to the desired settings that will move the text away from the ruling line.

40. *How do I set the Ruling Box Around feature around the entire underlying frame?*

    Activate the underlying frame, pull down the Frame menu, and select Ruling Box Around. The settings should be Width = Frame, Color is Optional, Pattern is Optional, Space Above Rule 1 = NN. To move the box down the page, set this number (NN) to .50 inches and the box will start one-half inch from all edges of the page.

41. *What is the easiest way to create a hairline rule one-half inch from the edge of the page all the way around the page?*

    Select the underlying page frame and in the Frame menu select Ruling Box Around. Select Frame for the width of rule, .5 inches for the Space Above Rule One, and .005 for the Height of Rule One. This should produce the desired effect.

NOTE
The effective print field for some printers may not quite reach to within .5 inches of the edge of the page and this effect may not print.

42. *I am developing a chart that needs dashed lines to separate some information that I have entered in Box Text. How do I get this to work?*

To get a dashed line you must use the Ruling box round feature from the Frame or Paragraph menu. For example, draw a frame between the Box Text boxes, then with the frame active, pull down the Frame menu and click on Sizing and Scaling. Change the height of the frame to 0.05 to make a very thin frame. With the frame still active, pull down the Frame menu and choose the Ruling Box Around option. In the dialog box choose the Frame Option and the Color as Black if you are not printing this on a color printer with the pattern set to solid. This will depend on what you need. Click on OK (or press Enter). The screen reappears and you see the dashed line. The Width space between dashes can also be set in this menu. This setting is located directly below the Dashes On and Dashes Off button, in the lower right corner of the dialog box.

Paragraph Menu

If the Frame menu was the superhero of Ventura Publisher, the Paragraph menu is the workhorse. It carries the heavy burden of setting attributes like fonts, spacing, page breaks, indexing, anchoring, and so on, by each group of text. Paragraphs share common names called tags. You can have from one to twenty or more attributes all causing different effects for 128 different paragraphs. Ventura Publisher will only allow a paragraph of 8,000 characters.

In version 2.0 the Paragraph menu has taken on a few new options, including Attribute Override, Paragraph Typography, Paragraph Background, and Update Tag List. When you begin to look deeper into this area of the software, you will agree this is the most changed of all menu areas. Also, the Font option has new responsibilities in version 2.0, letting you set the sizing of fonts in half scales for PostScript printing.

Attribute Override is a new feature that allows you to control the height spacing of Overscore, Strike-Thru, Underline, and Double Underline, which is turned on or off from this menu. To override this menu for individual words, use the Set Fonts button in Text mode. A drastic change in version 2.0 is the on and off switches at the bottom of the screen which can change features for the sentence selected (highlighted black).

The Alignment option has also taken on a new look. It features text rotation which allows you to rotate text 90, 120, and 270 degrees in a frame. In From Right to Decimals allows text to be centered during table and tag development. The Maximum Rotation Height allows you to control the position of text and frame.

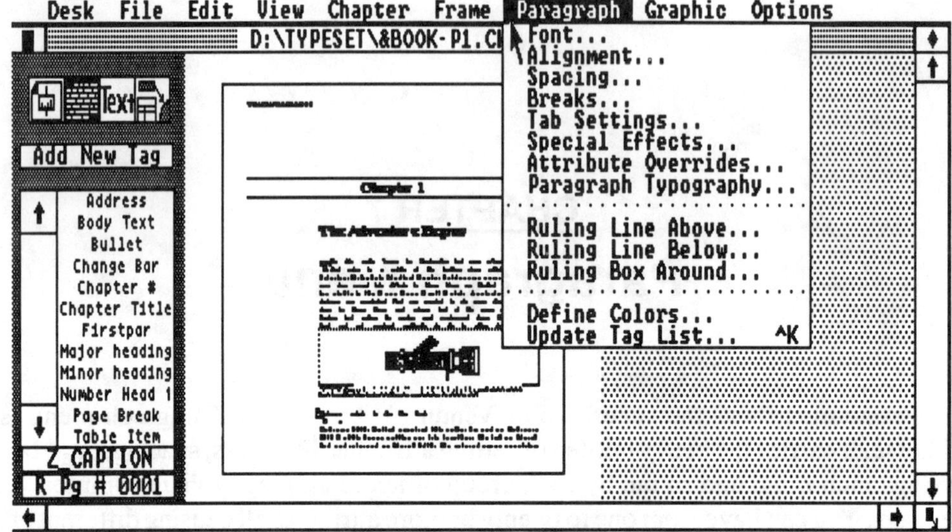

Topic Index

Topic	Questions	Page
Parafilter	1	62
Font	2 - 3	63
Alignment	4 - 8	63
Spacing	9 - 11	64
Breaks	12 - 16	65
Tab Settings	17 - 23	67
Special Effects: Bullet	24	69
Ruling Line Above/Below/Around	25 - 29	69
Typographic Controls	30	70

PARAFILTER

1. *I can't seem to get the parafilter to work. The tag is showing on the screen. Can you help me?*

When you see a tag on the screen (@parafiltr is a tag) this means that the tag is not active. The reason for the tag not activating was the presence of a left margin. When Ventura Publisher processes tags internally and rewrites the file, it ignores margins; but when you place the tags manually, the margin is sometimes understood as a space, thus ignoring the @parafiltr tag. A word to the wise: when editing documents outside of Ventura Publisher, the left margin should be zero.

FONT

2. *The headline in one of the sample style sheets reads Logo for two lines of text. The first line is large (24-point type), but the second line is smaller (10-point type). Why can't I make the second line look like the first, when they are tagged with the same tag?*

The second line probably has an attribute setting. Whenever text within a paragraph tag appears in a different font from the other text with the same tag, it is a pretty good bet that an attribute has been set for that block of text. The attribute can be removed by placing the text cursor at the beginning of the word or block of text which is different. Using the Left and Right Arrow keys, move the text cursor until the words ATTR. SETTING appear in the current selection box at the bottom of the Assignment list. Press Del and all the text within the tagged paragraph should now look the same.

3. *I was using the Shift: Up & Down in the Paragraph menu Font option while in the Text mode. The manual states that the value <Jnnn> may range from - 127 to + 127. However, when I viewed my text file in the word processor, the values were out of range. I had <J181> if I shifted up a quarter of an inch, and <J226> if I shifted up one tenth of an inch. I want to know why the values were not as stated in the manual?*

There was an oversight in the manual on the Shift Up values. They were not converted back to the ranges stated. However, they still perform correctly and can be entered in the text editor following the instructions in the manual. The Shift Down values are translated correctly in the text editor. However, the Shift Up values will always be displayed as a larger number in the text file. To determine the correct value once the number has been written back to the word processing file, you can subtract that number from 256. For example, 181 from 256 yields +75, or shifted up one-quarter of an inch.

ALIGNMENT

4. *How do I turn off the Hyphenation Dictionary for the whole document?*

Hyphenation is turned off paragraph by paragraph. If you want to turn it off for the whole document, you must turn off the option for each paragraph. This is found in the Paragraph menu Alignment option.

5. *My foreign language document is not hyphenating properly. Why?*

A minor bug in foreign language hyphenation was discovered in the initial release of version 1.1. It was corrected in Patch 1 to version 1.1.

6. *I have created a page with two columns: a minor column of about one and a half inches on the left side of the page and a major column of about five inches on the right. I have created titles which I want to outdent from the major column into the minor column. My problem is that once I have outdented the titles, I cannot access them any longer with the paragraph tag or the text cursor. What can I do to access these titles?*

Normally you can outdent text beyond the edge of a column without a problem. In this case the text was outdented so far that it lost touch with the major column (all text and returns were beyond the edge of the major column) and could not be edited or tagged. By adding spaces to the end of a line of text so that the paragraph end stays within the column, you can keep it in touch with the column of origin so you can access it for editing or tagging.

7. *My text is ignoring the margins and columns on the page and going all the way across all the columns. Why?*

Go to Paragraph menu Alignment option and change the settings for OVERALL WIDTH to "Column-wide" not "Frame-wide." Frame-wide is used in instances such as headlines or titles.

8. *How do I do a hanging indent?*

Go to the Paragraph menu and select the Alignment Option; Indent\Outdent. Select First Line: Indent In/Outdent Width:xx.xx In/Outdent Height: xxx Lines. The xx.xx stands for entry number where the line is indented or outdented from the left margin.

SPACING

9. *How do I do vertical tabs? I cannot seem to understand the fundamental rules.*

The first thing to understand is that you are attempting to place individual paragraphs in different areas on the same line. So the text must be prepared with each paragraph having an individual paragraph return. Only press a Return at the end of each paragraph. After the text file has been prepared, develop a tag name scheme and add the tag names using the Add New Tag option. Next, you need to work in the Paragraph menu, using the Spacing and Breaks options. Always do the spacing settings first. If you do not, the paragraphs overwrite each other and are very hard to handle. Select the first tag on the line and select the Spacing option from the Paragraph menu. For the first paragraph, In From Left should be set to 0 and In From Right should be set to a number that will tell the line how far away from the right margin to begin word-wrapping. For example, an In From Right setting of three inches will keep the paragraph three inches away from the right margin. The next paragraph will need an In From Left statement slightly greater than the last character of the preceding paragraph. The inside paragraphs are set so that they also meet these settings. After this is done, the Breaks option from the Paragraph menu is next. Set the Line Breaks so that they allow all the paragraph desired to be on the same horizonal line. The only rule is that the first paragraph has to have Line Breaks set to Before, and the last paragraph in the line has the Line Break set to After, while the ones in the middle have their Line Break set to NO.

10. *I am trying to import a WordStar file into the &TDOC-P1.SYS style sheet and my text is three inches from the left side of the page. I have tried to reset the margins in WordStar but I can't get the text closer to the left side of the page. What can I do?*

In this style sheet, Body Text, the default tag, has an In From Left setting of one and a half inches. You can change the margin setting or In From Left to properly position your text.

11. *I can't get any spacing to show up between two paragraphs in my document. I've set inter-paragraph spacing at .45 inches for the first and .35 inches for the second. Why isn't there spacing?*

Inter-paragraph spacing should be used for spacing between paragraphs with identical tags. Use Spacing Above and Below to space between different paragraph tags.

BREAKS

12. *How do I do page breaks?*

Go into Paragraph mode. You can either place an empty paragraph return on the page or tag a paragraph of text. Pull down the Paragraph menu, choose the Break option, set the Page Break option, and set the Page Break settings to After or the desired setting. Ventura Publisher will then break the page each time it encounters this tag.

13. *I would like to move a heading from the bottom of page one to the top of page two. What is the best way to do this?*

Under the Breaks option in the Paragraph menu there is a selection that allows you to determine when a page break will occur. By selecting Before for a tag, a page break will be inserted before the tag each time it occurs.

14. *I am setting up a heading block for a newsletter. I want the name, address, and phone number of the company on the left of the heading against the left margin and the volume and issue of the newsletter against the right margin. I want the first line of the name and address block to line up with the first line of the volume and issue block. For example:*

<table>
<tr><td>XYZ COMPANY</td><td>Volume 1</td></tr>
<tr><td>123 First Street</td><td>Issue 01</td></tr>
<tr><td>Tulsa, Oklahoma</td><td></td></tr>
<tr><td>(918) 555-1234.</td><td></td></tr>
</table>

There are two ways this could be done. Each method requires that a tag be created for the block of text on the left and another tag for the block on the right. Within each block the lines must be linked together into one block of text. To do this, type the first line of the left block followed by a line break (press Ctrl Enter). Follow each line with a line break until the last line has been typed. The last line should be followed by a paragraph end (a normal return). Now follow the same procedure for the right block. Create a new tag for the block on the left and establish the appropriate font size. Alignment for this tag should be Left. Now create a new tag for the right block and assign font properties. For this tag change the Line Break attribute to occur after the tag instead of before (this will place both tags beginning at the same vertical position on the page). Next select Alignment and make this tag align from the Right. You should see the text on the right side of the page with the end of each line against the right margin.

15. *I would like to create a document with titles for each paragraph appearing to the left of the paragraph. I would also like to have a larger typeface for the titles, but I want the top of the titles and the top of the main text to align with each other. How can I do this?*

To place the titles on the same line as the text, you must use two tags, one for the title and one for the text. These two tags will allow you to establish two typefaces, one for the title and one for the text. The title tag should be set for the appropriate font size and the normal default alignment, spacing, and break attributes. The text tag should be set for the desired font size. Spacing for the text tag should be In From Left enough to allow the titles to appear as if in their own column, and Line Break should be set for After the text, placing the text on the same line as the title. With both tags on the same line, the title and the text will not align along the top because of the difference in type sizes. To move the title down, select the Text Editing mode and highlight the title. Select the Set Font box directly above the Assignment list. Choose the Shift Down selection, and you should see that your title has moved down by the measure you indicated. You can fine-tune the alignment by adding to or subtracting from the Shift Down measurement.

16. *I'm trying to follow one of the examples in the training guide. I cannot figure out how to change the address from three centered lines, to one line. I want the street on the left, the city in the middle, and the phone number on the right. How is this done?*

   Assign each of the three lines of the address a unique tag. Leave the font style identical on all three tags but set the Alignment and Line Break attributes differently. On the first line (the street), set the Alignment to Left with a Line Break set Before the line. For the second line (the city), set Aligned Center with No Line Breaks. In the third line (the phone), set Alignment to Right with the Line Break set After the line.

TAB SETTINGS

17. *How can I create a numeric list with the numbers aligned by the period?*

   Create two tags, one for the numbers and one for the text. Set the text tag for In From Left spacing about one inch. Set the Line Break for this tag to come Before the text #. Set the number tag for In From Left spacing at zero. Now set a tab for the second tag. The tab should be decimal and positioned at one-half inch. Set the Line Break for this tag to After the text. This should provide the desired effect. The In From Left spacing can be adjusted for either tag to fine-tune the effect.

18. *I placed a tab at the beginning of a paragraph and it pushed the text beyond the edge of the right-hand column. What caused this?*

   Tabs are not designed to be used to indent paragraphs, they are designed to format tabular data. Use the fixed indent in the Alignment dialog box under the Paragraph menu to set indents for paragraphs.

19. *How are the tab measurements oriented? I can never seem to figure out where the tabs will appear on a page.*

Each tab measurement begins at the margin. For example: a left tab, first tab, set at one inch will appear one inch from the left margin. Tab two set at three inches will appear three inches from the left margin, not three inches from the end of tab one.

20. *I'm trying to design a form with vertical tabs with a paragraph tag that doesn't have any text. These paragraph tags are in part of the Auto-numbering menu and I'm expecting it to number each of my paragraphs, but when Ventura Publisher loads, the paragraph markers have been deleted. Why?*

This is caused by the parafilter being in the file. It is designed to delete any paragraph return that does not have any text associated with it. The parafilter should be the first line of the file. It looks like:

@PARAFILTR = .

21. *I am attempting to use a decimal tab, but the tab will not move the text. Why?*

Check to make sure that the paragraph isn't justified. This will stop Ventura Publisher from moving text if a tab is applied. Ventura Publisher will present a warning "[THE TABS YOU HAVE DEFINED FOR THIS TAG WON'T SHOW UP SINCE THE TAG IS MARKED AS JUSTIFIED. TO MAKE THEM SHOW UP, CHOOSE LEFT ALIGNED IN THE ALIGNMENT DIALOG.]"

22. *I'm using the tab feature but it is not working. What am I doing wrong?*

In the tab location setting (Tab Location: xx.xx inches), the xx.xx equals the distance from the left margin. Check the ruler to see if the tab setting is less than where the text is located. For example, suppose you want to set a tab in the sentence and the word that requires the tab is located at the three-inch mark. With the tab location setting at two inches, the tab will not move the text at all.

23. *How many bytes does each Tab key occupy in a Ventura Publisher chapter file?*

The amount of memory cannot be determined with any accuracy. The Tab key is given a line element status by Ventura Publisher and Ventura Publisher will only allow 725 line elements per frame. Every line of text counts as two line elements. A leader character counts as six line elements. The number of paragraphs has no bearing on the line elements in the frame. This is a way to determine line elements: [tab] = four elements; with leader characters add two more for a total of six. If you exceed 725 line elements, Ventura Publisher displays the error message: "This frame is too complex to format."

SPECIAL EFFECTS: BULLET

24. *I have assigned a bullet to a paragraph title which appears in the margin to the left of my text. I tried to shift the text down to align the top of the title with the top of the text, and when I do, the title moves but the bullet doesn't. How can I move both?*

    A bullet is a system generated character and is not easy to edit or shift. Try replacing the bullet with an ASCII 195. This is done by holding down the Alt key and typing 195 on the numeric pad. This will produce the same character and will allow you to move it with the rest of the text.

RULING LINE ABOVE/BELOW/AROUND

25. *How do I create the effect of white text on a black background?*

    There are at least two methods. One method is to select Solid Black as the background fill pattern for a frame. All text within this frame, even if tagged as black text, will automatically be shown as white on black.

    A second method is to create a ruling line above the text that equals or exceeds the height of the text. Next move the cursor down to the selection labelled Space Below Line Three and press Enter the same measure as you did for the line itself. Next to this entry, select the box with the minus in it and then select OK. When the screen redraws, the text will seem to have disappeared. Now go to the Font option and select White as the color of the text. It may be confusing when you return to the screen, because you will see black text on a white background and you may think that the effect did not work. Remember that paragraphs which have been selected are shown in reverse video. Move the paragraph icon off the paragraph and press the left mouse button and you should see the desired effect.

26. *I placed a ruling line above a block of text. When I tried to place a ruling box around the same tag, the measurements for Ruling Line Above show up in the Ruling Box Around dialog box. Why?*

    Ventura Publisher does not allow Ruling Box Around to be active in the same tag with Ruling Line Above or Ruling Line Below. So instead of issuing an error, Ventura Publisher merges the settings.

27. *There is a line around my frame and I can't get rid of it. It is not a Ruling Box Around; I checked that and it was off. What is it?*

   There is more than one way to generate a Ruling Box Around; you must check both the Paragraph menu and the Frame menu. Also check for a graphic box or line.

28. *I sent a document to the typesetter and when it printed, the ruling lines were inconsistent in width.*

   This happens if you try to produce ruling lines that are extremely thin (.05 fractional points). The minimum thickness should be .24 fractional points or greater.

29. *How do you get a double underline to be shown?*

   From the Paragraph menu select Ruling Line Below. Use the following settings: Width = Text, Color = Black, Pattern = optional, Height of Rule 1 = your setting, Height Of Rule 2 = your setting. This will give you a double underline for each line in the paragraph.

TYPOGRAPHIC CONTROLS

30. *I have placed an underline on a word through the Text mode. That underline is now too close to the word. How do I shift the line down a bit so that the line is not touching the word?*

   This can be done through the Typographic Controls option. The settings for the underline attribute are in this format: Underline 1 Height NN.NN Shift By xx.xx Inches. The "xx" needs to be changed to shift the underline down.

CHAPTER 8
Graphic Menu

The Graphic menu is Ventura Publisher's way of giving the software the ability to develop forms and charts. By using the Graphic features you can develop bar, pie, and line charts. Ventura Publisher's graphics are dependent on frames and will attach themselves to any frame that is active at the time the graphic is created.

The Graphic menu controls all the graphics when in the Graphics mode. It controls how the boxes and lines appear, also the shading, thickness, and color of the graphics. It allows graphics to be selected as a group for copy or cut and paste operations. Graphics prepared with a little imagination can be very useful in the all around appearance of the document.

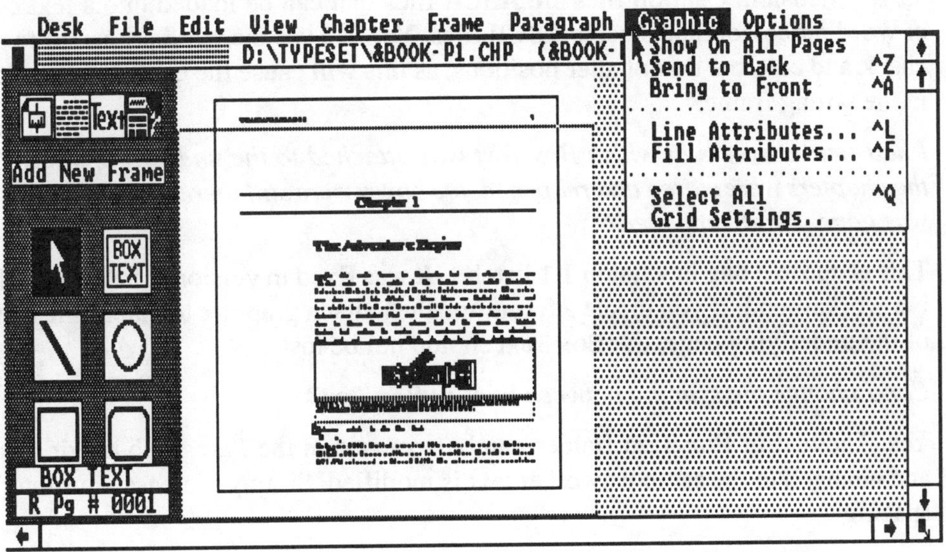

Topic Index

GRAPHIC MODE

Box Text

1. *When I type into a frame or Box Text, where is that text being stored?*

   The text is stored inside a caption file of the same name as the chapter file with a
   .CAP extension. Caption files are ASCII files that can be loaded into a text editor
   or word processor that accepts ASCII files. You can use the word processor to spell
   check and edit, but do not alter positions, as this will cause the caption to be placed
   in the wrong frame.

2. *I had four chapters in which Box Text was attached to the underlying page. After
   the chapters were stored and reopened, the boxes were still there but all the Box Text
   was gone. What happened?*

   This is due to a bug in version 1.1 Patch 1. It was fixed in version 1.1 Patch 2. There
   is a workaround: If you create a frame and then attach graphics to that frame instead
   of the underlying page, the Box Text should not be lost.

3. *Can I change the spacing between lines in Box Text?*

   Yes. The text in Box Text frames can be accessed in the Paragraph tagging mode
   and changed in the same way other text is modified. Simply increase your interline
   spacing.

4. *I created a Box Text frame and it is repeating on every page. The repeating frames setting is turned off; why is this happening?*

   Box Text is a graphics feature of Ventura Publisher. All graphics are "anchored" to frames. If no frame is created to anchor a graphic, it defaults to the underlying page and will repeat on subsequent pages. If there are no frames created specifically to receive text on a page, you can still draw a small frame anywhere on the page (preferably outside the margins of the underlying page, so as not to interfere with text flow) to anchor graphics and prevent them repeating on every page. This feature has been taken out of Ventura Publisher 2.0. Ventura Publisher 2.0 now gives you the ability to make graphic drawings repeat or not.

5. *How do I get a Box Text frame on screen?*

   Box Text frames are created by selecting the Graphics mode, pointing to the Box Text selection, and pressing the mouse button. This activates Box Text. Now move the cursor to the point on the screen where you would like the upper left corner of the box to anchor. Press and hold the left mouse button. Move the mouse to the right until you have created a box of the desired size, then release the mouse button. You have now created a box with the words "Box Text" inside.

6. *Can I change the spacing between lines on my Box Text?*

   Yes. The text in Box Text frames can be accessed in the Paragraph tagging mode and changed in the same way other text is modified. Simply increase your Interline spacing in the Paragraph menu Spacing option.

Grid Setting

7. *How do I get my grid setting to work?*

   Normally, if Grid Snaps don't work correctly, the best thing to do is to delete the INF files in the VENTURA directory.

Perfect Circle or Square

8. *How can I make a perfect circle or square, instead of an ellipse or rectangle?*

   Turn on Grid Snap with the Horizontal and Vertical units the same, for example each at 0.250 inches. If you are drawing a square, watch to see that it snaps to the same number of units horizontally as vertically. If you are drawing a circle, it will be contained within a squared-off set of selection handles. Once you have the selection handles arranged in a perfect square, with the height = width, the ellipse inside it will be a circle. In version 2.0 this has been simplified. You simply hold down the Shift key during the creation of boxes or circles.

Graphic Selection Box

9. *In Graphics mode there are six function boxes to be selected. I've noticed the upper left box (the arrow) doesn't do anything. Is it for future use? Or, does it do something now and I just don't understand how it is used?*

This is a mystery. Ventura Publisher has never documented this area of the package. In the Ventura Publisher Reference Guide it is called Graphic Selection Box. I have heard of no future use as of publication date.

Line Draw

10. *How do I draw a lot of lines on a page?*

Use the Line tool in Graphics mode. In versions 1.0 and 1.1 it's best to use the grid setting to help you space them. This allows you to draw straighter lines. In version 2.0 pressing the Alt key while drawing the line will develop perfectly straight lines.

Copy

11. *How can I copy a Ventura Publisher graphic from one page to another?*

In the Frame mode, select the frame on the originating page to which the graphic is anchored, then change to the Graphics mode and select the graphic itself. Now use the Edit menu, Copy Graphic option (keyboard shortcut is Shift-Del) to move a copy of the graphic to the clipboard. Once this has been accomplished, go to the destination page, and select a frame to anchor the copied graphic. If there are no frames on the destination page, you can create a small one in a margin so that it does not interfere with text flow. Once a frame is selected, change to the Graphics mode and, from the Edit menu, select Insert Graphic (keyboard shortcut is pressing the Insert key). The graphic will appear on the page and can then be repositioned if necessary.

Shading

12. *I would like my tables to be shaded within my chapter. How do I accomplish this?*

You can use a rectangle created in the Graphics mode to overlay the tables. Select the desired shading using Fill Attributes and make sure you select Transparent so that tables will show through the rectangle or square you create. Be sure to create a frame to anchor the graphics, or they will default to the underlying page and be repeated in the same place on every page.

Fill Attributes

13. *I'm using Ventura Publisher graphics with several different shapes using the same fill pattern (#3 for example). They don't all print out with the same pattern on the HP LaserJet II; why?*

To conserve printer memory, Ventura Publisher uses the printer's built-in shading capability wherever possible, instead of building a bit pattern itself and sending it to the printer. Printer internal patterns are available only for rectangular shapes; any other shapes Ventura Publisher has to build a pattern. The problem is that Ventura Publisher doesn't build patterns that match the printer patterns. As a result, rectangular graphics get one pattern, and rounded graphics get another, even though the same pattern was selected.

Repeat on Several Pages

14. *How can I get my graphics to repeat throughout the document?*

When drawing or creating repeating graphics, be sure to select the underlying page before creating the art work.

GRAPHIC LINES

15. *I have a graphic line on my screen that I can't click on or select in the Graphic menu Select All option. How do I get rid of it?*

This is one of those problems that will cause you to pull your hair out. This particular problem was caused by using the RED LINE feature in WordPerfect. Deleting this feature in WordPerfect caused the line to go away.

16. *I used frames to draw a large white box and then draw a smaller box inside the first frame and set it to solid. When printed on a PostScript printer, the smaller solid box was ignored. Why?*

This worked correctly in versions 1.0 and 1.1 but not in 1.1 Patch 1. It was repaired in Patch 2.

17. *Is there an easy way to create a form with multiple graphic lines that will be used for fill-in-the-blank entries?*

If all of the lines are the same length, you can use the Copy Graphic feature to make multiple copies of the line. First draw the line using the Ventura Publisher graphics capability. Once the line has been drawn to the proper length and you have released the mouse button, hold down the Shift key and press Del. This creates a copy of the original graphic. Now press the Insert key, which will place another copy of the graphic directly over the original. Select the new graphic by pressing the left mouse button and "dragging" the graphic until it appears in the proper position on the screen. Release the mouse button and the graphic has been placed. Pressing the Insert key again will create another copy of the graphic, which can be repositioned, and so on.

18. *Why is it in graphic line drawing mode, when I put my cursor in one place, the line starts above or below my cursor and not on the line?*

This is because the grid setting is on and the lines are trying to go to the closest grid position. If you go to the Graphic menu Grid Settings option and select Grid Snap Off or reduce the distance between grids, you will find the line appearing closer or directly on the cursor.

Line Attributes

19. *I drew a line using Ventura Publisher graphics and wanted to place an "arrow" symbol on the left side of the line. I selected Line Attributes in the Graphics menu and the arrow symbol in the left column, but when the screen came back, the arrow was on the right side of the line. Is this a bug?*

The Line Attributes dialog box contains two columns of line end attributes. The left column will change the originating end of the line and the right column will change the terminating end of the line. If you drew the line beginning on the right of the screen and ending on the left, the left column will define the originating (in this case the right side of the line) and the right column will define the terminating (in this case the left side of the line) end.

20. *I've drawn little boxes in a frame but now I can't activate or see them. But when the screen redraws, I see them for just a moment. Why?*

You had frames hidden behind other frames and attached to other frames. Remember what frame is active before going into Graphics mode. This will save you a lot of grief.

CHAPTER 9
Options Menu

The Options menu is the setup menu of Ventura Publisher. It is used to set the way you want the software to be displayed. Most options in this menu are simple toggle switches that turn options on and off. The wording is a bit confusing at times. A simple rule to make things easier is, when looking at the pulled down Options menu, whatever the menu says is what will happen if that choice is clicked on.

The Options menu also contains the ability to perform multi-chapter operations. This is Ventura Publisher's way of developing publications and transporting files from disk to disk and system to system.

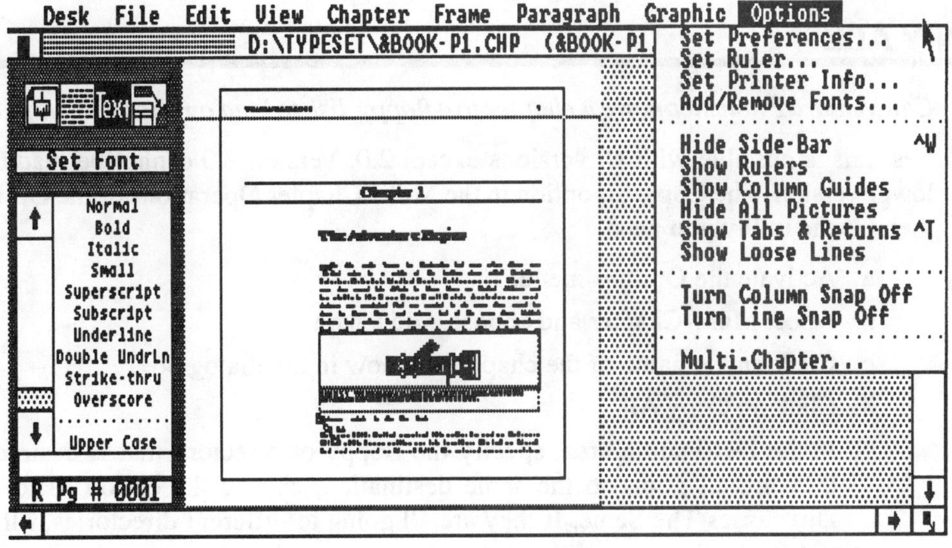

Topic Guide

Topic	Questions	Page
General	1 - 2	78
Copy All	3 - 4	78
Multi-Chapter, TOC	5	79
Set Printer Info	6	79

GENERAL

1. *I loaded Ventura Publisher and I don't have a side panel displayed. What happened?*

   To restore the side bar, go to the Options menu and select the Show Side Bar (Ctrl-W) option.

2. *I loaded my backup text file (filename.$XT) as my original text file by mistake and continued to work with backup on. This resulted in losing both the new and old backup file.*

   You should always rename the backup file to another name without the backup file code "$" in it before using it as a text file.

COPY ALL

3. *Can Ventura Publisher move a chapter to a floppy disk to load on another computer?*

   Yes, this is possible with all versions except 2.0. Version 2.0 cannot be read by a lower version. The Copy All option in the Multi-Chapter Operations of the Options menu is the utility you need.

   a. Activate the Options menu.
   b. Select Multi-Chapter and choose Add Chapter.
   c. Click on the name of the chapter file now in the dialog box.
   d. Click on Copy All.
   e. In the Destination area, specify the floppy or directory that is desired. If they are all going to the same destination, choose the option Make All Directories The Same. If they are all going to different directories, fill out the destination area as desired.
   f. Click on Ok. The program will copy all the files to their chosen areas.

4. *Why can't I get a chapter that was developed on one computer and copied to a floppy disk with Copy All to load on another computer?*

This is a problem that requires the two computers to be configured correctly with similar buffers and files in the CONFIG.SYS file. Also, check the memory with the DOS CHKDSK command to see if the computers have the same amount of memory.

MULTI-CHAPTER, TOC

5. *Is there a way to put the generated TOC inside a publication? When I do a Copy All on a publication, I would like to be able to have that TOC file copied also.*

The TOC file must be placed inside a frame in a chapter. It should be its own chapter named TOC.CHP. You can then save the chapter as part of a publication in the Multi-Chapter Operations in the Options menu.

SET PRINTER INFO

6. *I have a two-page document that I want to print to a file, how can I do it?*

Go to the Options menu and Set Printer Info Output To option to a filename. Go to the File menu and click OK. Ventura Publisher will allow you to name the file by showing an Item Selector. Type in the name on the Selection line. Do not enter anything in the extension area. Ventura Publisher will give it a C00 extension.

CHAPTER 10
Load Picture Option and Graphic Packages

This chapter addresses questions about using one of Ventura Publisher's most advanced features. The Load Picture option on the File menu allows Ventura Publisher to import text and graphics from other software packages, combining both text and graphics into one document.

There are two types of graphics file formats that are compatible with Ventura Publisher: the line art format and the image format. The line art format is usually graphics that contain a lot of line drawings, for example, HPGL, CGM, GEM, AutoCAD, and Macintosh graphic files (the files contain mathematical statements). The image format is usually graphics that contain more artistic drawings, for example, PC Paintbrush graphic files (the files contain bit-map graphics). This chapter discusses the various requirements or limitations Ventura Publisher has with importing files from different software packages.

Topic Guide

Topic	Questions	Page
General	1 - 14	82
Arts and Letters	15	85
Number of Pictures on One Page	16	85
Mentor Graphics	17 - 18	85
Harvard Graphics	19	86
PC Paint	20	86
Lotus Freelance	21 - 22	87
HPGL	23 - 26	87
GEM	27 - 28	88
AutoCAD	29 - 36	88
Macintosh	37 - 39	89
Paintbrush	40 - 44	90
Screen Capture	45	91

GENERAL

1. *What are the limitations of the CGM files?*

   All fonts are converted to Helvetica. Colors are converted to patterns as shades.

   Fill patterns are converted based on the GSS CGI definition.

2. *I cannot see the pictures I have loaded in my document. Why?*

   Check the Options menu to see if the Pictures option is set to Hide Pictures. If so, select this option and change the setting by pressing the mouse button. You should now be able to see the pictures you have loaded.

   NOTE

   It takes the system longer to redraw a screen with pictures displayed. Once you have determined that you have positioned your pictures correctly, you can speed up the screen redraw time by choosing the Hide Pictures option.

   Remember that many PC Paintbrush and scanned image files cover a large part of the page and have a large amount of white space. If you draw a small frame and load a large picture, you may only see a corner of the image and it may be white, leading you to believe the image has not loaded correctly. Solution: Make the frame larger or use the Alt key and mouse to pan the image into view.

3. *What are the limitations of Video Show conversion?*

   Ventura Publisher converts General Parametric Video Show files. Color is not converted; instead, it's turned into shades of gray. Polygons with more than 128 vertices are truncated.

4. *I can't load my picture file, even though it loaded great just a short time ago. Why did it load then and not now?*

   The disk has filled to the point that Ventura Publisher cannot store the information to the disk .TMP file. The way to fix this is to free up disk space using the DOS File Ops option in the File menu. You can delete unnecessary files from the directory so you don't have to lose your work. However, be very careful when using this option, because the default is set to C:*.*. If you click on the choice DELETE ALL MATCHING FILES, you could erase every file in your root directory, so please watch out for this one.

5. *How do you load graphics from graphics software?*

Click on the File menu and click on Load Text/Picture. For Type of file, select Line Art for those files produced by line drawing products such as AutoCAD, Lotus PIC, HPGL, etc. Select Image for files produced by paint programs such as PC Paintbrush and GEM. Click OK and you see an item selector. Select your file and click OK. Ventura Publisher loads the file to the list or to an active frame.

6. *I would like to incorporate an image created by a graphics package that is not currently supported by Ventura Publisher. I have left a blank frame on a page in the precise location that the graphic will print from the graphics package itself. Can I inhibit page eject after printing the Ventura Publisher page so that I can call up the graphics package and print the graphic into the frame?*

Page eject is not a feature that can be turned on and off within Ventura Publisher. The workaround would be to insert the page back into the printer and then call up the graphics package to print the image.

7. *Can the generated IMG file that Ventura Publisher makes from the original PCX files be used in the frame instead of the PCX?*

Yes, that is what Ventura Publisher is using when it does the conversion. You can remove the file from the frame through the Edit menu with the Remove Text\Picture option. Then load the IMG file using the Load Text/Picture option in the File menu. The original file can be deleted off the disk if you desire.

8. *What are the key limitations in importing Encapsulated PostScript (EPS) files?*

EPS files do not display on screen. A large "X" appears in the frame area where the picture is located. It can also only be printed on a PostScript printer. Ventura Publisher can produce a pseudo EPS file that can only be read by Ventura Publisher by printing an EPS picture to a disk file and then loading the C00 as a PostScript file.

9. *Can Ventura Publisher use the print drivers in Windows now that Ventura Publisher runs under Windows? I would like to use the DeskJet printer driver.*

No. Ventura Publisher will not use the Windows print drivers for any printer.

10. *I'm attempting to load a picture into multiple frames using the multiple frame selection mode but it doesn't work. It only loads into one frame. Why not all?*

The multiple frame feature doesn't work in that way. If you need the same picture or graphic in multiple frames, you must load them one at a time.

11. *I scanned in images using the Xerox Kurzweil scanner. When the images were printed with Ventura Publisher, they had vertical bar-like scan codes in the images. Why?*

This problem applies to all scanned images. The closer the scan image remains to a l-to-l ratio in Ventura Publisher (compared to original size) the less problems there are with lines at print time. To help the problem, you can turn off Line and Column snaps in the Options menu. In the Frame menu Sizing and Scaling option, change from Fit In Frame to By Scale Factors and leave on Maintain Aspect Ratio or change to Distorted, as desired. If you do these things when the image is first imported, you can then read the actual original size of the image, displayed as the Scale Width and Scale Height in Sizing & Scaling. Best results are obtained if you don't change the size at all. If you do change it, multiply or divide both the scale height and width by an even number.

12. *Does Ventura Publisher load AutoSketch files as line art?*

No, not directly. That package can be converted to some CAD programs such as AutoCAD.

13. *Can I save a graphic drawing so that I can use it in more than one chapter where it's already cropped and magnified?*

This is possible if you develop a Library Chapter File where you have already developed frames and done the cropping and magnification. These frames can be copied away from the LIBRARY.CHP file and into any desired file by choosing NEW, then OPEN Chapter. Load the chapter desired, go to any page and press the Ins key, and the frame, with its graphic in tow, will come into this new chapter cropped and ready.

14. *Can Ventura Publisher edit pictures?*

Ventura Publisher can change the size of pictures and can crop images. To actually edit the picture itself, use the original graphics program (e.g., AutoCAD, Mentor Graphics, Lotus 1-2-3, PC Paintbrush, etc.) You can also use the Ventura Publisher built-in Graphics mode to overlay additional graphics on top of pictures for callouts, etc. By placing a box with White Solid fill pattern over a portion of the picture, you can also selectively eliminate portions of the picture on PostScript printers.

ARTS AND LETTERS

15. *How do you load letters from Arts and Letters?*

There are two ways of completing this task.

Workaround # 1:

Art & Letters can save files to CGM format. In Arts & Letters, everything is considered a symbol (text/graphics). The default color for symbols is solid dark blue. Any other solid dark color is incompatible with Ventura Publisher. The solution is to change the color in Art & Letters to a light (white/yellow) shade. The symbol will still have an outline to make it visible. The resulting CGM file can then be imported into Ventura Publisher.

Workaround # 2:

Print to filename using HP (Plotter) as the output device to produce HPGL Format. Within MS Windows, modify the configuration file WIN.INI to add another port called OUTPUT.PLT (reference MS Windows handbook).

NUMBER OF PICTURES ON ONE PAGE

16. *Is there a limit to the number of pictures I can place on one page?*

Page description languages such as PostScript can support virtually as many pictures (either images or line art) as you want on a page. Other laser devices, such as the Xerox 4045, JLaser board, and LaserJet are restricted by processor bit buffer size to a limited number of images on each page. The 4045 and LaserJet will support about four images per page and the JLaser will support six. Line art is not restricted by memory in any of these devices.

MENTOR GRAPHICS

17. *What version of Mentor Graphics is Ventura Publisher compatible with?*

Mentor Graphics runs on a Unix-based computer. They have developed a basic front-end type product that will run on an IBM-AT called an Entry Level System. This system provides a schematic screen-capturing software utility which can be read by Ventura Publisher.

18. *When I try to retrieve a Mentor Graphics sample file that came with Ventura Publisher, I get a message that the file is not in the appropriate format. Why?*

This is an error with the sample file. The sample files provided by Ventura Publisher do not contain true Mentor Graphics files. The file filter used to retrieve Mentor Graphics images is *P* and the default subdirectory is TYPESET. Using this filter the system selects a publication file as satisfying the criteria for the filter search. Of course, this publication file was not in Mentor Graphics format and that caused the error message.

HARVARD GRAPHICS

19. *How do I bring a Harvard Graphics drawing in as HPGL?*

Before entering Harvard Graphics version 2.0, you must invoke the program that captures the output to LPTl by typing at the prompt LPT=<<filename>>. Then go into HG and configure the plotter by choosing from the Main menu Setup, then Plotter. In the plotter configuration menu, choose HP7550A as the plotter, and LPTl as the output. With the chart or drawing loaded, choose from the Main menu Produce Output, then Plotter, and finally, Draft or Standard quality. In Harvard Graphics version 2.1 you no longer have to invoke the LPT.COM program. Select Import/Export, select Export Picture, and then select HPGL. This produces a PLT file with the same name as the chart or drawing. Using the HIGH quality seems to produce files with very fat lines. In order to see patterns when using an HPGL file, you must make sure the fill style is set to pattern, not color or both. This is done by selecting Enter/Edit Chart from the main menu, which gives the Chart Data Screen. Select F8 to get the Chart Title and Options Page. Then change the fill style to pattern.

PC PAINT

20. *I can't get my PC Paint files to load into Ventura Publisher. Why?*

PC Paintbrush is the product that is compatible with Ventura Publisher. The name similarities between PC Paint and PC Paintbrush frequently cause confusion.

LOTUS FREELANCE

21. *How do you load Lotus Freelance files into Ventura Publisher?*

    Select Load Text/Picture from the File menu and use the Line Art: CGM format filter.

22. *I had a logo that was developed in Lotus Freelance. Now in the version 1.1 Patch 2 software, the cross hatching area has turned solid black. What's happening?*

    Ventura Publisher's 1.1 Patch 2 was supposed to fix most graphics problems but it caused more then it fixed. The only way around these problems is to restore the versions 1.0 or 1.1 Patch 1.

HPGL

23. *Are there any problems loading HPGL files?*

    Yes, there have been some problems with Ventura Publisher versions 1.0 and 1.1, converting HPGL files. Fonts are all converted to Helvetica. Colors are not converted. Filled areas are made up of vectors; gaps may appear in the fill patterns.

24. *I cannot get my HPGL file to load into Ventura Publisher. Why?*

    Ventura Publisher identified a problem with the converter for HPGL files in Ventura Publisher 1.1. The converter was improved in Patch 1 to version 1.1 and further improved in Patch 2.

25. *I can't get Patch 2 to translate my HPGL file. It keeps telling me that it can't translate the file. Why?*

    You need to have at least two megabytes of disk space for Ventura Publisher to do its translation. The only other problem might be that the file is not in a true HPGL format.

26. *I am loading an HPGL file from a floppy disk. When Ventura Publisher presents the dialog box saying that it is loading the file, it returns to DOS. Why?*

    Perform a DOS CHKDSK command on the floppy disk. This problem could be caused by a bad sector area on the disk. Copying to another floppy or the hard disk will clear up this problem.

GEM

27. *When I import GEM line art (for example, GEM Draw) into Ventura Publisher, why does text below 12 points default to Courier? I am using Patch 2.*

There is a bug in the HP LaserJet Plus drivers (both 150 and 300 dpi) in Patch 2 which causes this to happen. This bug causes any text below 12 points in an imported GEM line drawing to default improperly to Courier 12. Corrected drivers are available from Xerox. The HP drivers (PD_HPLH5.SYS and PD_HPLMS.SYS) both have the date 3/4/88 if they are the corrected versions.

28. *I'm importing a GEM 3 file into Ventura Publisher, but when Ventura Publisher imports this information, it crushes the text all together. Why?*

This sounds as though GEM 3 is attempting to import its fonts into Ventura Publisher. If this is the case, Ventura Publisher will not be able to space the fonts correctly due to not having a proper width table for these fonts. What you need to do is import the graphics file without the labels. From inside Ventura Publisher, the labels can be retyped using the Box Text feature in the Ventura Publisher Graphics menu.

AutoCAD

29. *There is a new version of AutoCAD (version 10). Are there plans to incorporate the new file format?*

Yes, in Ventura Publisher version 1.1 Patch 2.

30. *I can't seem to get an AutoCAD 9 SLD file to load.*

Not until Ventura Publisher 1.1.2, known as Patch 2, was AutoCAD 9 able to load into Ventura Publisher. All of the previous versions of AutoCAD load with no problems.

31. *I have just purchased the latest version of AutoCAD and my DXF and SLD files will not load. Why?*

Version 9.0 of AutoCAD incorporates changes in the formats of SLD and DXF files which make them incompatible with Ventura Publisher version 1.1 and version 1.1, Patch 1. Version 1.1 Patch 2 can read AutoCAD 9.0 SLD files, but cannot read DXF files. An alternative to DXF and SLD for AutoCAD is to try HPGL.

32. *When I read an AutoCAD SLD file, the lines appear thicker than when the file was created in AutoCAD. The lines also print thicker. Why?*

    This is actually a screen resolution issue. As Ventura Publisher creates the lines on the screen, the thickness of a given line may fall between two pixel widths. If Ventura Publisher adds a pixel, the line will appear thicker; if it drops a pixel, the line will appear thinner. The printed output will reflect what is displayed on the screen.

33. *AutoCAD SLD files that loaded with Ventura Publisher version 1.1 Patch 1 will not load correctly with Patch 2. Can you tell me why?*

    You need to delete the VENTURA directory before installing the patch. Ventura Publisher will load AutoCAD SLD files correctly when the patch is installed correctly.

34. *Since AutoCAD slide files are bit-mapped files, why are we importing them as vector graphics?*

    Slide files are not bit-mapped files. They are vector graphics files which are saved by AutoCAD at screen resolution.

35. *Can Ventura Publisher export AutoCAD files?*

    No.

36. *How do I import the DXF-formatted CAD file from my CAD program?*

    Drawing Interchange Format (DXF) files can be converted and imported by using a utility provided by Ventura Publisher. The file is found on the #11 disk in version 1.1 and the #5 disk in version 2.0. Place the Utilities disk in the A drive. Go to the directory where the C00 file is located and type A:DXFTOGEM *filename*. Press Enter. If the file does not have an extension, the DXF extension is assumed.

MACINTOSH

37. *I have loaded a MacPict file and the text appears much larger than in the original document.*

    The preliminary release of 1.1 did not properly size the text from MacPict files. This problem was somewhat reduced by Patch 1, though not completely eliminated.

38. *I am having difficulty loading a MacPict file into Ventura Publisher. Why?*

    The preliminary release of 1.1 was unable to convert MacPict files larger than 32K. This problem has been fixed by Patch 1 for version 1.1.

39. *Can any Macintosh or Apple graphics be imported into Ventura Publisher?*

Graphics files from Mac cannot be imported directly in version 1.0. The files can be transferred as standard ASCII files using a Mac Link or communications program. Versions 1.1 and 2.0 provide the capability to read MacPaint and MacDraw files.

PAINTBRUSH

40. *The new PC Paintbrush Plus (versions 1.6 and 1.7) have gray scale information in the PCX files which Ventura Publisher cannot read. Will there be a patch to fix this?*

Ventura Publisher will probably not be supporting gray scale PCX files directly through the PCX file. However, quite a number of mini-applications now exist which convert between various formats (for example, The Graphics Link from PC Quik Art or Hijaak from Inset Systems).

41. *Can I use PC Paintbrush Plus with the Xerox Full Page Display?*

Yes. PC Paintbrush Plus comes with a driver which supports the Xerox Full Page Display.

42. *I can't get a PC Paintbrush file to load in Ventura Publisher. I load the picture but it won't display in the frame. Why?*

Make sure the frame has been selected when you load the Paintbrush file. If it hasn't, select it and then select the Paintbrush file from the assignment list. The file should now load into the frame. Also, make sure you are using PC Paintbrush version 2.5 or greater and that you are using PC Paintbrush and not PC Paint. PC Paint is not compatible with Ventura Publisher.

43. *I created an image in PC Paintbrush, yet when I load it into Ventura Publisher, it does not even resemble the original. What could be wrong?*

Check to see that the monitor selection for the PC Paintbrush program matches the screen driver for Ventura Publisher. This has been the most frequent mismatch which has led to less than satisfactory results. Make sure PC Paintbrush is configured for the same type of screen resolution and driver as you have installed for Ventura Publisher.

44. *I am using version 1.0 and cannot load certain PC Paintbrush files. There doesn't seem to be any logical pattern as to which will or will not load. Why?*

ZSoft changed the way they created the header record in PC Paintbrush files. In some cases the header formats in a manner that version 1.0 cannot read. Version 1.1 has been altered to correct this problem.

SCREEN CAPTURE

45. *How can I do a screen capture with Sidekick?*

   a.   Load Sidekick, if it is not already loaded, by typing SK and pressing Enter.

   b.   Bring up the screen you want to capture.

   c.   Activate Sidekick by pressing Ctrl-T.

   d.   Press F2 to activate Sidekick's notepad feature.

   e.   Press F3 to create a new filename.

   f.   Erase the default filename NOTES and enter a name for your screen file (example SCR.TXT).

   g.   Press F4 and the Sidekick notepad screen will disappear, leaving a cursor in the upper left-hand corner of the screen you are capturing.

   h.   Press Ctrl-KB (the cursor will change shape becoming taller and thicker).

   i.   Use the Down Arrow to move the cursor down the screen highlighting the number of lines you wish to capture.

   j.   Use the Right Arrow to move the cursor to the right highlighting the total screen area to be captured.

   k.   Press Ctrl-KK. (the Sidekick notepad screen now reappears).

   l.   Press Ctrl-KC. (Sidekick reads the screen and writes it into the notepad window).

   m.   Press F2 to save the file to disk and press Esc to exit Sidekick.

   n.   Place the Ventura Publisher Utilities Disk in drive A.

   o.   Change logged drives to drive A by typing A:.

   p.   Type TXTTOPCX C:filename.txt (SCR.TXT in this example).

   q.   You should not have Sidekick memory resident when Ventura Publisher is loaded. This will affect the size of the files you can load in Ventura Publisher. You should deactivate Sidekick prior to loading Ventura Publisher by pressing Ctrl-Alt-Del to reboot your system.

Monitors and Graphics Boards

Since its introduction into the microcomputer software market, Ventura Publisher has written drivers for users of different monitors. Now that it is the top selling desktop publishing software, the attitude of the developers has changed. After the 2.0 release, Ventura Publisher is attempting to get the display manufacturers to write the drivers if their monitor is to be used with Ventura Publisher. However, for version 2.0, Ventura Publisher did add more drivers than in past releases.

There are a couple of these drivers that are not working correctly. The Paradise and Wyse monitors are two with driver problems. The Wyse now uses VGA screen fonts, preventing it from displaying a full screen. If you are experiencing this problem, you need to set up Ventura Publisher as an EGA machine by doing a partial install. First, rename the original VP.BAT file so that it doesn't get overwritten. Then reinstall Ventura Publisher, answering "NO" to the question, "Are You Installing For The First Time?" This will allow you to reinstall without overwriting all the program files. You then install Ventura Publisher for any EGA monitor. Ventura Publisher will write EGA screen fonts to the VENTURA directory instead of the VGA. After this is done, delete the new VP.BAT file and rename the old VP.BAT file to its original name. After this is done, Ventura Publisher will use EGA fonts with the Wyse and the display will return to the normal full screen. Be sure to delete the VGA fonts that were left.

Before you decide to go with a display not listed on the install list, call the manufacturer to see if they have written a driver compatible with Ventura Publisher for this monitor.

Topic Guide

Topic	Questions	Page
General	1 - 7	94
CGM	8 - 11	95
Monitors		96
Viking	12	96
Verticom 2	13 - 14	96
SummaGraphics	15	96
AMDEC 1280	16	96
Sigma Designs	17 - 19	97
Paradise	20	97
Genius	21	98
Wyse 700	22 - 23	98
Xerox Full Page	24 - 25	98

GENERAL

1. *Which graphics boards does Ventura Publisher support?*

   The IBM Color Graphics (640 x 200), IBM Enhanced Graphics (640 x 350), Hercules Monochrome (720 x 350), or Xerox HRC (640 x 400).

2. *Which full page displays does Ventura Publisher support?*

   Ventura Publisher supports the Xerox full page display, the MDS Genius, the Wyse WY-700, and the Hercules monochrome graphics card with appropriate full page monitor. Additional full page displays may also work if appropriate drivers are provided by the manufacturers. Sigma, Conographics, and DBM are examples of vendors who provide 19-inch monitors and drivers to run with Ventura Publisher. These drivers are supported by the manufacturer.

3. *Does the 3270 driver in Ventura Publisher include the APA (All Points Addressable) capability?*

   No!

4. *Do I need to display in color in order to print in color?*

   No. Color information is always stored even if your screen can't display it. You can create color documents on a monochrome monitor.

5. *What do I need to display Ventura Publisher in color on a Xerox 6065?*

You need to add the color graphics adaptor board, part number W45. This board will provide three additional 640 x 400 bit planes and software-controlled lookup tables. This board also provides the ability to display 16 colors, eight of which are supported by Ventura Publisher (white, black, red, green, blue, cyan, yellow, magenta). In the earlier versions, these basic colors could be combined with different patterns to give a toned-down shade of the color. Version 2.0 has expanded this element of the program to display and print 256 different colors and define different custom blends of colors. However, when you add a custom color, you lose the use of a base color, because Ventura Publisher can only hold eight colors (what the menu has room for). Actually you have six, because the colors black and white cannot be altered or replaced.

6. *The screen fonts are shown with how many dots per inch and then printed with how many dots per inch?*

A graphics board having 640 x 350 resolution (such as the Hercules card or EGA), displayed on a standard PC screen, has an effective resolution of about 75 dots per inch. Printer resolution is determined by the printer being used (for example 300 dots per inch for lasers).

7. *Will the 640 x 480 driver included for PS/2 work with other PC graphics cards which support VGA at 640 x 480?*

No. PS/2 is the only 640 x 480 graphics card supported.

CGM

8. *Whose CGM driver is Ventura Publisher's based on?*

Ventura Publisher's CGM filter is not based on any particular CGM driver. However, the guidelines used include the ANSI CGM specification and specifications from several other vendors who generate CGM files.

9. *Does Ventura Publisher read color from CGM?*

Ventura Publisher will translate colors from CGM files.

10. *Which monitor selection is used for the Compaq portable?*

Select "A," the IBM Color Card.

11. *I have a Compaq portable with a gas plasma screen which offers a screen resolution of 640 x 400. Which screen driver should I select to run Ventura Publisher?*

Try the Xerox 6065, AT&T, driver. Articles in recent trade publications have indicated that other software products providing drivers for the 6300 were tested with the Compaq display and worked quite well.

MONITORS

Viking

12. *Is there a driver for the Viking monitor?*

The Viking monitor requires a different driver for 1.1 and 2.0, each available from Viking.

Verticom 2

13. *What can you tell me about the Verticom 2-page monitor?*

It has its own drivers, but it uses the Ventura Publisher EGA Screen Fonts. It will not function if another EGA card is available.

14. *Unless my Verticom 2-page display has an A switch of /A=28, I get distorted screen fonts. Why?*

You have installed the Lasermaster Cap Card and have run out of memory. Install a mouse that requires no MOUSE.COM and it will fix the problem.

SummaGraphics

15. *Any problems with the SummaGraphics 1201 graphics board?*

The SummaGraphics 1201 graphics board, which has an active area of approximately 12", will not access the lower 1- 1/2" of The Xerox Full Page monitor or the lower 2" of the MDS Genius monitor. When used with the Verticom 2-Page monitor, the lower 3" of the monitor could not be reached.

AMDEC 1280

16. *I am using an AMDEC 1280 monitor. When I move the mouse across the screen, it leaves a trail or smear on the screen. Can you tell me what is causing this?*

AMDEC claims that this is a characteristic of the monitor, it appears we must live with it.

Sigma Designs

17. *I am trying to get a Sigma Designs Color 400 graphics board to work with Ventura Publisher. Can you help me?*

    It might be best to check with the manufacturer to find out if your device is on the current list of Ventura Publisher supported products.

18. *My system locks up when using a Sigma Designs Laserview. Why?*

    This may appear after adding screen fonts or otherwise altering memory usage. Make sure that the only screen drivers present are those for the monitor in use. The vendor for the add-on monitor may specify which monitor is installed on Ventura Publisher first. After Ventura Publisher is installed, a second installation program must be run to add the drivers for the Sigma monitor. The monitor installation program will not delete the first set of drivers. If they are still present, it can cause problems when Ventura Publisher is running. Check that original drivers are not present. If they are present, delete them and cold boot.

19. *I am trying to get a Sigma Designs Color 400 graphics board to work with Ventura Publisher. It works with GEM but when I modify the GEMSETUP.TXT file on Disk # 3 to appear exactly as it does on the GEMSETUP.TXT file provided with GEM, it does not work. Why not?*

    GEMSETUP.TXT is a file that is read by Ventura Publisher during installation. Changing this file does not guarantee that the driver for the device is compatible with Ventura Publisher. Ventura Publisher will generally not work with drivers not specifically created for it, even those that work with other GEM programs. This is true for displays and even more true for printer drivers. Ventura Publisher Software is currently working with a number of manufacturers of graphics boards, screen displays, and printers who all want to be compatible with Ventura Publisher. You might check with the manufacturer to find out the status of your device if it is not on the current list of Ventura Publisher supported products.

Paradise

20. *Will Ventura Publisher still support the Paradise monitor with the 2.0 version?*

    Yes. But with the 2.0 version, some users are having trouble using the monitor's driver provided by Ventura Publisher.

Genius

21. *I installed an MDS Genius full page display which works great in full page mode within Ventura Publisher. But when I exit Ventura Publisher, it loses the full page mode. Why?*

    You need to add "VHR.MDS" as the last line of the VP.BAT file to retain full page mode after exiting Ventura Publisher.

Wyse 700

22. *My Jlaser (AT-2) on my AT clone with WYSE 700 prints black blocks where the text should be. Why?*

    The Jlaser will work if the WYSE 700 isn't used and the WYSE 700 works if the Jlaser isn't used. Both Tall Tree and WYSE say you can have one or the other.

23. *I installed Ventura Publisher on a WYSE 700 monitor with an MS Bus Mouse. When loading VP.BAT the system locked up. Why?*

    There could be an interrupt conflict between the WYSE 700 monitor and the MS Bus Mouse. Check the IRQ (interrupt) jumper settings on your hardware cards to be sure two cards are not set to the same interrupts. The Bus Mouse should be set to 5.

Xerox Full Page

24. *My Xerox Full Page display monitor gets garbage on the screen. I have a Video 7 EGA card.*

    You were trying to drive the Xerox Full Page monitor with the wrong EGA card. You need to get the full page controller card.

25. *Is the Xerox Full Page display compatible with the Microtek scanner and GEM software?*

    Yes and no. There are no screen drivers written to drive the full page display. When installing the Microtek software, use the CGA option which will use the upper third of the full page screen. The resolution will not be the same quality as Ventura Publisher, but you will be able to drive the scanner.

CHAPTER 12
Mice

Ventura Publisher is dependent on a mouse in many areas of the program. If the mouse becomes inoperative, Ventura Publisher can be operated without a mouse using the keyboard cursor arrow keys. Operating Ventura Publisher without a mouse will cost you both speed and mobility. Without a mouse, Ventura Publisher has the slowest reaction I have ever noticed in a software package using keys to move the on-screen pointer. It runs even slower on a 386 machine than on a 286.

Ventura Publisher operates using a serial, bus, or keyboard mouse. If you are having a hard time installing due to lack of memory, you might consider using a serial mouse. Ventura Publisher can port directly for the serial mouse. This setup eliminates the need for a mouse control driver in the CONFIG.SYS or the AUTOEXEC.BAT files, thus saving memory. Ventura Publisher can also use a sketch pad and pen, or stylus.

Topic Guide

Topic	Questions	Page
No Mouse	1	100
SummaSketch	2 - 3	100
SummaMouse	4	101
LogiMouse	5 - 7	101
Microsoft Mouse	8 - 14	102
Mouse on IBM PS/2	15 - 18	103

NO MOUSE

1. *Can Ventura Publisher operate without a mouse?*

   It is possible but not recommended. The software is designed to take advantage of the mouse (drop-down menus, point and drag graphics, and frame manipulation). The software will function using the cursor keys to move about the screen, but it is not efficient.

SUMMASKETCH

2. *I can't get my SummaSketch 1201 pad to work with Ventura Publisher. It worked fine under AutoCAD. When I tried booting up Ventura Publisher and then went into AutoCAD, the SummaSketch would not work until I powered the system down. Why?*

   Like Ventura Publisher, many programs have their own built-in drivers for the SummaSketch; AutoCAD happens to be one of them. These types of programs change the default setting of the 1201, which can often prevent another package from setting the 1201 correctly. The result is that, until the 1201 is reset to its default parameters, a particular package may not work. Evidently Ventura Publisher still resets some of the 1201's parameters. There are several ways to reset the SummaSketch 1201. You can reset the 1201 to its default parameters by unplugging its power pack, thus clearing the 1201's memory. Another way to reset the 1201 is to send a reset code to it. All it takes is to send a NULL character to the proper port. It is also important that interrupts are set properly. Most people will not tinker with interrupts, but you may want to verify the settings.

   SummaSketch Plus incorporates a driver which allows it to emulate a MicroSoft bus mouse. SummaGraphics can also supply this driver to SummaSketch (non-Plus) users for a fee.

3. *The SummaSketch 961 and 1201 are supported by Ventura Publisher but most of us have not had much opportunity to work with them. How does it work?*

   The SummaSketch 961 and 1201 are also called the MM Series. The MM stands for the data tablet. The hardware components of the SummaSketch consist of a tablet and a stylus cursor. The tablet is a flat surface which can tilt or lie flat. The MM 1201 has an active area of 11.7" x 11.7" The 961 has an active area of 6" x 9".

The stylus cursor is a hand held device which is used with the tablet to locate points. The stylus has two buttons: one on the outside of the barrel and one inside the barrel, activated by pressing the refill tip.

To use the SummaSketch, place the stylus cursor on the tablet and look at your monitor to note the location of your cursor as you move the stylus cursor around the tablet. When you want to plant the cursor at a certain spot, press one of the buttons on the stylus cursor.

SUMMAMOUSE

4. *I bought a SummaMouse 420 and it does not work on my system. Why not?*

This new model mouse uses a different driver than the original SummaMouse. Contact the manufacturer and ask them to send you a driver which will allow you to simulate operation of the original model.

LOGIMOUSE

5. *I installed Ventura Publisher with a LogiMouse, using selection B for PC Mouse, and it worked fine. Then I installed PC Paintbrush and installed LogiMouse for PC Paintbrush and it worked fine. Now the mouse does not work with Ventura Publisher Why?*

LogiMouse is unique in that it can emulate several types of mice. When installed as a LogiMouse, using the driver which comes with the mouse or using the LogiMouse selection in PC Paintbrush, the mouse will emulate a Microsoft serial mouse. The Microsoft mouse driver was still loaded when you brought up Ventura Publisher. Ventura Publisher was expecting a PC Mouse protocol. To correct this problem, either reinstall Ventura Publisher and select the Microsoft serial mouse, or reinstall PC Paintbrush and select the PC Mouse.

6. *I have tried several times to get my Logitech mouse to work with Ventura Publisher. I have installed it as a PC Mouse and a MicroSoft serial mouse but it will not respond. Why?*

The following instructions will configure the LogiMouse:

    a. Use CLICK.SRC which comes packaged with your LogiMouse.

    b. Insert a line for Ventura Publisher as follows:

        VP 1200 150 5B(tab arrow); Ventura Publisher

    c. Modify the AUTOEXEC.BAT by inserting lines as follows:

        MOUSE 2
        MENU
        CLICK.SRC

7. *I am trying to load Ventura Publisher with a Logitech LogiMouse but I am having difficulties. Why doesn't the mouse respond?*

The LogiMouse can emulate several different mouse devices. Make sure that you understand which mouse selection requires a mouse driver in the AUTOEXEC.BAT file. The LogiMouse works without a driver in emulating certain mice and with a driver when emulating others. It could be that you have selected a mouse which does not require a driver (PC mouse) and you have a driver installed on your system. If you are sure your selection is correct, try powering the system off immediately after finishing the VPPREP program and then turning it back on and bringing up Ventura Publisher.

MICROSOFT MOUSE

8. *When installing Ventura Publisher, what choice do I select for a MS bus mouse?*

Choose the "C" or edit your VP.BAT file and make the /M=XX [XX indicates mouse type] code /M=32. This is the setting that Ventura Publisher needs for the bus mouse.

9. *Why is my Microsoft serial mouse leaving a trail of dots across the screen on my MDS Genius monitor?*

Check your hardware. Make sure all the jumpers and switches are set correctly. This problem is a result of a wrong switch or jumper setting.

10. *I purchased an enhanced graphics card for my PC and now my Microsoft bus mouse is not working. Why?*

Check the mouse controller card and possibly change the jumper settings or the DOS interrupt levels to correspond to the type of graphics card and monitor you are now using. Refer to your Microsoft mouse user's guide or your dealer for the correct settings.

11. *Which MS mouse product is compatible with Ventura Publisher?*

    All versions of MS mouse are compatible with Ventura Publisher (bus, serial, and serial for the IBM PS/2 system). The serial mouse for the PS/2 system must be installed as a bus mouse.

12. *I can't get my bus mouse to work with Ventura Publisher. I have tried every setting that I can try, but Ventura Publisher won't recognize it. It is a Human Interface mouse.*

    The Human Interface mouse is a mouse that requires a MOUSE.SYS in the CONFIG.SYS file to operate inside Ventura Publisher.

13. *I installed Ventura Publisher on a Tandy TX with CGA display and Microsoft bus mouse. I selected "C" in the installation program. However, the mouse did not respond in Ventura Publisher. Why?*

    The Tandy TX is a pseudo-XT clone with an XT-type bus but 80286 (AT) processor. The interrupt must be changed from 2 to 3.

14. *When moving a PC mouse around on its pad, the movement in Ventura Publisher is jerky. Why?*

    Turn the pad 90 degrees and try it. Optical mouse pads often have two different colors of lines.

MOUSE ON IBM PS/2

15. *How do I install the IBM mouse on the PS/2 System?*

    The mouse for the IBM PS/2 system is considered a bus mouse. The DRMRGR string in the VP.BAT file should have a /M=32 directly after the screen driver code. In Ventura Publisher 2.0 or Professional Extension (VPPROF.BAT) the statement should read /M=3:.

16. *I just installed Ventura Publisher on a PS/2 computer, but I can't get my mouse to work. How do you get an MS serial mouse to install?*

    The PS/2 system will only accept a bus mouse. Make sure that the mouse is an MS serial mouse with the PS/2 system adapter. Install the adapter which will make the serial mouse a bus mouse. Then install the mouse in Ventura Publisher as a bus mouse. Or, edit the Ventura Publisher batch file and change M=XX to M=32. The XX stands for your previous mouse number.

17. *My new Microsoft serial mouse, with the special adapter that plugs into a special round mouse port on the back of my PS/2, is not working with Ventura Publisher. Why?*

Installing it as a "C—bus Mouse" will make it work.

18. *My new Microsoft serial mouse is installed on an IBM PS/2 Model 80 and it is not responding. Why?*

Microsoft has released a new version of their serial mouse which has a special PS/2 connector that plugs into the special mouse port on the back of the PS/2. It appeared at first that this mouse installation was proving unusable with Ventura Publisher.

However, it turns out that it will work after all. A warm boot (Ctrl-Alt-Del) will not correct the problem, but a COLD BOOT after installation of Ventura Publisher will, provided AUTOEXEC.BAT activates the proper MOUSE.COM.

CHAPTER 13

Printers: General Printers

This chapter is devoted to questions concerning the installation and operation of printing equipment that will operate with Ventura Publisher. Ventura Publisher supports a number of assorted devices that can be used to help you produce professional looking documents.

Topic Guide

Topic	Questions	Page
General	1 - 8	105
Printers Supported	9	107
Print Spooler	10	108
Laser Printer Compatible	11	108
Plotter	12	108
AST TurboLaser	13	108
Linotronic	14	109

GENERAL

1. *When I print graphics, a portion of my image shifts. Why?*

   You have an accelerator board in your computer. Take out the accelerator board and it will work.

2. *What are the resolutions of the different printers, both for text and for graphics?*

   Most laser printers are supported at full 300-dots-per-inch resolution for both text and graphics. However for the HP LaserJet is 300 dpi for text, but only 75 dpi for graphics. With the Xerox 4045 Laser, the size of the graphic which can be printed is dependent upon the amount of memory resident in the 4045. Epson dot matrix resolution is 120 x 140 dots per inch. Xerox 4020 ink jet color resolution is 120 dots per inch.

3. *Can Ventura Publisher output to a parallel printer?*

Yes.

4. *Can you print an 11 x 17 inch sheet on a Dataproducts printer using the manual feed for inserting paper?*

Manual feed capability to override the paper tray size was only corrected in Ventura Publisher 1.1 Patch 1 for HP printers. Version 1.1 Patch 2 enables PostScript manual feed selection to override the paper tray size, so the above application should work with 1.1 Patch 2 and 2.0.

5. *I have a VP000.$$$ file in my Ventura directory and I want to know what is in the file.*

These files are created during print time. If the print is successful, they are automatically deleted. However, if the printer locks up or the system crashes or reboots during print, this file is left on disk. You can delete these files without causing any problems.

6. *I am attempting to print to an 11 x 17 inch page in landscape mode. The output is printed in portrait mode with text being lost from the left and right sides of the page. What am I doing wrong?*

This sounds like a bug in PostScript which reversed the print selection when printing to an 11 x 17 inch page. Portrait would print in landscape and landscape would print in portrait. Determine what version of PostScript is resident on the printer. With 38 or higher you should be OK.

7. *Can I send a document to another location via disk or network?*

Yes. You can print to a disk file and this file can be sent to a production printer or typesetter.

8. *Do I need to have a printer which will print on 11 x 17 paper in order to successfully create and print an 11 x 17 document?*

Yes. A printer which handles 11 x 17 paper is mandatory. It is extremely difficult, due to printer register considerations, to split an 11 x 17 page into two separate 8½ x 11 pages which can then be pasted together to form an 11 x 17 page.

PRINTERS SUPPORTED

9. *Can you give me a list of printers supported by Ventura Publisher?*

Supported printers are listed in the manual. Others are noted for guidance as to the proper choice for installing them, but as untested hardware. Their full compatibility with Ventura Publisher is not guaranteed.

Dot Matrix Printers:

> Epson MX-80, FX-80, RX-80
>
> IBM Proprinter
>
> Other dot matrix printers with Epson MX/RX-80 emulation (emulation is not always perfect) Epson LQ 1500 (with wrong aspect ratio, 2.0 only)
>
> Toshiba 24 pin (2.0 only)
>
> Hewlett Packard Inkjet (wrong aspect ratio)

Laser Printers:

> Hewlett Packard LaserJet with 92286F font cartridge (select FONT Standard).
>
> Hewlett Packard LaserJet +, 150 dpi or 300 dpi and Series II and various laser printers with LaserJet Plus emulation (select Hewlett Packard LaserJet Plus) Laser printer emulation is not always perfect. Some emulators may not have a printer buffer with sufficient memory to support font downloading.

PostScript Printers:

> Apple LaserWriter and LaserWriter Plus
>
> Texas Instruments Omnilaser
>
> DEC PrintServer 40
>
> IBM 4216
>
> Data Products LZR2660 & LZR2665
>
> QMS PS 800, 1200, & 2400
>
> Linotype Linotronic or any compatible PostScript printer.

PRINT SPOOLER

10. *Is Ventura Publisher compatible with a print spooler?*

    No.

LASER PRINTER COMPATIBLE

11. *Is the QMS PS 800 Laser printer compatible with Ventura Publisher?*

    There are a number of laser printers on the market today. Ventura Publisher is compatible with the Xerox 4045 and 4020, the Hewlett Packard LaserJet and LaserJet Plus, the Apple Laserwriter and Laserwriter Plus, and the Epson MX 80 and FX 80 printers. Ventura Publisher also supports the PostScript document description language and the Tall Tree Systems JLaser board. If a laser printer manufactured by any company is PostScript compatible or compatible with the JLaser board, or if it emulates one of the printers listed above, then it will be compatible with Ventura Publisher. If it does not satisfy the above criteria, it will not produce satisfactory results. The QMS 800 is a PostScript printer and is compatible with Ventura Publisher.

PLOTTER

12. *Is Versatec plotter supported by Ventura Publisher?*

    No. Plotters are not supported.

AST TurboLaser

13. *Is the AST TurboLaser compatible with Ventura Publisher?*

    AST has developed a driver which is compatible with Ventura Publisher.

LINOTRONIC

14. *Printing an 11 x 17 page to a Linotronic 100 results in no page being output. Why?*

The Linotronic 100 may not be able to print an 11 x 17 page at 2540 dpi resolution. Try printing at a lower resolution like 1270 dpi.

CHAPTER 14

Printers: Dot Matrix /
Ink Jet/ and Compatible

Even though dot matrix printers are a dying breed, Ventura Publisher has not deserted users with dot matrix printers. You can add 24-pin printers to the list of devices that Ventura Publisher supports. The Epson and the Toshiba 24-pin dot matrix printers have been added in the 2.0 version of Ventura Publisher. The NEC 24-pin printer driver is provided by the NEC Corporation and is not included with Ventura Publisher.

The ink jet printer is coming into its own, which is good and bad when using Ventura Publisher. The good part is the print resolution of the ink jet printer. The bad part is to get the ink jet printer to print at higher resolutions, the printer will require more disk space to produce the output. Currently, Ventura Publisher requires 2Mb of hard disk space free at all times. It will use more space if the rastorization is done on the hard disk like it is done for the earlier 9-pin printers.

Topic Guide

Topic	Questions	Page
General	1 - 8	112
Epson Printers	9 - 10	113
Epson JX	11	114
Epson LQ	12	114
Epson MX-80	13	114
Print to File	14	115
Limitations / Capabilities	15	115
Epson Width Table	16	115
Dot Matrix 24 Pin Printer	17	115
NEC 24-Pin Printer	18	115
Toshiba 24-Pin Printer	19	116
HP Deskjet	20 - 22	116
Color Printers	23 - 25	116
Cordata	26	117

GENERAL

1. *I was using my dot matrix printer and I noticed that I get an extra line feed at the top of some pages. This happens on Epson and Epson-emulating printers. Why?*

   The extra line feed occurs, specifically, at the top of the first page of any chapter. The succeeding pages of the chapter should be positioned properly. If you have a multi- chapter publication consisting of a series of single-page chapters, the extra line feed occurs on each page printed. In this situation, the successive pages of the publication gradually walk downward until they no longer stay on the sheet.

   This is a software bug which is present in both Ventura Publisher 1.1 and 1.1. Patch 1 versions. This problem was fixed in versions 1.1 Patch 2 and 2.0.

2. *How do I send a print file created by Ventura Publisher to the printer?*

   In DOS you can use the COPY command to send the file to a printer. For example, COPY filename LPT1: (be sure to include the colon). This instruction will work only with output devices that are connected with a parallel cable. For serial printers please refer to the instructions in the Ventura Publisher Reference Manual.

3. *Can fonts be added to Ventura Publisher for use with my dot matrix printer?*

   There is not a method for doing this in the Ventura Publisher Reference Guide. However there is a way in the 2.0 version that it can be done using Bitstream Fontware.

   The steps are as follows:
   a. Install Fontware for Epson.
   b. Generate the desired fonts and a width table using the Fontware instructions.
   c. Use Add/Remove Fonts to merge the new width table into a copy of the standard Ventura Publisher Epson width table. The status of the added fonts should be Download, even though Epson fonts are not downloaded in the sense of a laser printer.
   d. In Paragraph/Typographic Controls set Tracking as necessary to get the character spacing to look right.

4. *Are there any known problems with Patch 1 when printing with an Epson emulator to a wide bed printer specifying the double page size?*

   The Epson driver is only designed to print 8½" wide. It will never access the full width of a wide carriage printer no matter how good the emulation.

5. *Can codes be pre-downloaded to a dot matrix printer in order to access the resident Courier font and then print that font through Ventura Publisher?*

   No. Ventura Publisher accesses dot matrix as a graphics system. It cannot access the text mode of the dot matrix printer.

6. *How do I extract a chapter file from a C00 file?*

   This cannot be done. A C00 file is a printer language print file that cannot be separated.

7. *How do I add spaces inside a document that will not be stripped away by Ventura Publisher?*

   Hold down the Ctrl key and press the Spacebar. This will place a space in the document that Ventura Publisher will not remove.

8. *How do I get a C00 file?*

   First click on the Option menu and select the Set Printer Info option.

   Click on Filename in the Output line and click on OK. Go to the File menu and select To Print option. After making sure that the settings are correct inside this menu, click OK. Ventura Publisher will offer you an Item Selector. Notice the Directory line; this is where Ventura Publisher will place the C00 file. Put a name in the Selection area and click on OK. Ventura Publisher will display screen description boxes like all other print jobs. This will produce the C00 file desired.

EPSON PRINTERS

9. *Can you give me a list of supported Epson printers?*

   The following printers are supported by Ventura Publisher. Their full compatibility with Ventura Publisher is not guaranteed.

   Epson MX-80/FX-80

   Epson LQ series (2.0 only)

   Other dot matrix printer with Epson MX/RX-80 emulation. Emulation is not always perfect.

10. *I have added software to my computer that required the /A=32 setting in Ventura Publisher's VP.BAT file. Now my Epson printer will not print. Why?*

The fact that the Epson is affected by the /A switch needs to be noted. The Epson driver has to create a graphics image of the page to send to the printer. Given the resolution required, the internal memory required to print can be extremely large. This printer is definitely affected by the /A switch. If this is the only printer installed in Ventura Publisher, you need 1.3Mb of hard disk space.

Epson JX

11. *I am using an Epson JX-80 with a number of computers. The Epson emulates FX-80 mode which is compatible with Ventura Publisher. On a Leading Edge machine running MS-DOS, the software and the printer work fine. However, I have a PC-XT and an AT running PC-DOS and the Epson is inserting extra line feeds when driven by either one of these machines. What is causing this?*

This is probably being caused by the different BIOS in the two operating systems. Try changing the dip switch settings (check Epson operating manual for settings) on the Epson when cabled to the PC-DOS machines.

Epson LQ

12. *I'm having problems printing with my Epson LQ printer. Can you help me?*

There is a 24-pin driver for Epson LQ emulating printers. The program is called LQ PATCH and is available from M/A/P/ Systems, Inc, 1120 NASA Rd #1, Suite 320, Houston, Tx. 77058. If the printing is being done from a high speed system (286 or 386) with switchable processor speeds, the clock speed may need to be set to the slower speed. The problem occurs when the parallel port is not operating at the same speed as the processor. Since Ventura Publisher is passing information to the parallel port at processor speed, some bits will be dropped when the parallel is not operating as fast. This occurs quite often in Compaq 286 and 386 systems.

Epson MX-80

13. *I have an MX-80 printer and I was trying to get it to work with Ventura Publisher. I was getting garbage and a bunch of line feeds and page feeds. This printer does not have a Graftrax board and, therefore, I can't use it with any other graphic based program. Can you help me?*

Epson MX-80 will not function with Ventura Publisher until you buy the Graftrax option. The MX-80 without Graftrax can only output "character graphics" and cannot output bit-mapped graphics.

Print to File

14. *Is there anyway to export a bit-map from Ventura Publisher besides printing to file using an Epson or Xerox 4020 drivers?*

    No. These two printers are the only ones in which Ventura Publisher rasterizes the image and lets you print to file.

Limitations / Capabilities

15. *What special capabilities and limitations are required when using an Epson serial printer?*

    Your resolution must be 120 x 144 dpi. If an Epson- emulating printer deviates from this resolution, aspect ratio and final dimensions of the printed document will be affected. Twenty-four-pin dot matrix printers are not supported.

    Any computer which successfully runs Ventura Publisher and has a parallel interface should operate satisfactorily with an Epson-emulating dot matrix printer.

Epson Width Table

16. *I printed to a diskette to be printed out on an IBM Pro-Printer on another system. The file was created using the Epson width table. The document is two pages long, but only half of the first page prints. What is wrong?*

    When copying print files to either an Epson or Epson compatible, use the /b option since these are binary files and may contain a Ctrl-Z in the text (which is interpreted by the printer as an end of file marker). The /b option prevents this from happening.

Dot Matrix 24-Pin Printer

17. *How do I install Epson's 34-LQ or NEC's P12 and P32 printers?*

    Install for the Epson MX-80 for all three printers. You will have to set your 34-LQ in the alternate mode for it to function properly. On the P32 you will want to reset the fourth switch on switch bank 2 to the off position.

NEC 24-Pin Printer

18. *Is there an NEC 24-pin driver to use with Ventura Publisher?*

    NEC 24-pin driver was developed with help from Ventura Publisher. It is available by bulletin board together with the fonts.

Toshiba 24-Pin Printer

19. *Is there a driver available for the Toshiba 24-pin printers?*

    It is available from their bulletin board service. The filename is VENTURA.EXE. When executed, the file will un-archive itself automatically. In version 2.0 this printer is compatible.

HP Deskjet

20. *Is the HP DeskJet supported by Ventura Publisher?*

    The DeskJet is an inkjet printer designed for laser-like quality at 300 dots per inch (dpi). It uses a version of "PCL," the HP Printer Command Language used for the HP LaserJet printer series. The DeskJet is not supported by Ventura Publisher at this time. You can buy an extra-cost cartridge for Epson emulation that might work, but that would be a rather expensive way to achieve dot matrix quality.

21. *My computer locks when I try to print to an HP DeskJet with an Epson emulation board installed. Why?*

    This is the same as having an HP Laser that prints like an Epson dot matrix printer. So like the HP printer, it must have enough memory installed. In your case the printer board needs more memory installed.

22. *Can Ventura Publisher use the DeskJet printer driver from Windows now that Ventura Publisher runs under Windows?*

    Ventura Publisher will not use the Windows printer drivers.

Color Printers

23. *Can Ventura Publisher handle color printers?*

    Yes. Ventura Publisher supports eight colors and can print to the Xerox 4020 color inkjet printer.

24. *Do I need to display in color in order to print in color?*

    No. Color information is always stored even if your screen can't display it. You can therefore create color documents on a non-color monitor.

25. *Does Ventura Publisher support color printers other than the Xerox 4020?*

Not at this time. Version 2.0 supports the PostScript color printers.

Cordata

26. *When attempting to print a Ventura Publisher document, my Cordata LP300X prints only blank pages. Ventura Publisher behaves onscreen as if it has printed successfully. What is happening?*

The problem is caused by failure of the Cordata adapter board to initialize properly at boot-up. Here is what to watch for and what to do if you run into this problem:

During Boot-up:

You will see on the screen: LLD: Cordata LP300X Low level Driver—Version 1.31 Copyright (etc.) LLD: Initializing the Laser Printer Mechanism... The "initializing" message should stay on the screen for several seconds if it is initializing properly. Then it will be followed by:

LLD: Installed successfully.

The computer should complete its normal boot-up. If the "initializing" message appears only momentarily and then is immediately followed by the "installed successfully" message, the initialization has actually failed.

To fix the problem:

    a. Shut down both computer and printer.

    b. Cold boot the computer with the printer remaining off.

    c. Wait until just before the "LLD" messages are about to appear. At that moment, flip on the printer switch. This may take a few attempts to get the timing correct, but keep trying.

Printers: Interpress / PostScript

Since PostScript is a recognized standard Page Description Langauge (PDL) from Adobe, Ventura Publisher outputs in the PostScript-compatible language. The code can be understood by most PostScript printers processing in batch mode. Ventura Publisher has been keeping up with the latest versions of PostScript. Numerous printer questions are located in this chapter because of their association with PostScript. Ventura Publisher also supports the PDL langauge developed by Xerox which is similar to PostScript known as Interpress. This chapter also gives detail on the Interpress type of output.

Topic Guide

Topic	Questions	Page
DESCRIPTION LANGUAGES	1	120
EPS	2 - 3	120
Apple Laserwriter	4 - 10	120
Interpress	11 - 14	122
Install	15 - 16	123
Print	17 - 19	124
Compatibility	20 - 23	124
Linotronic	24 - 27	125
NEC	28 - 33	127
QMS	34 - 35	128
Texas Instruments OmniLaser	36	129
Typesetters	37 - 38	129
PostScript	39 - 41	129
Printing	42 - 46	130
Thick Lines	47 - 48	132
Print to Disk	49	132
Point Sizes	50 - 51	132
Graphic	52	133
No Output	53	133

DESCRIPTION LANGUAGES

1. *What page description languages does Ventura Publisher support?*

   Version 1.0, PostScript only. Version 1.1 supports PostScript and Interpress page description languages. Interpress is supported only in context with a PC-on-the-net type Ethernet setup. Ventura Publisher creates an Ethernet master print file; then the operator exits Ventura Publisher and sends the print file to the Interpress printer operating on the network.

EPS

2. *Which graphics packages produce Encapsulated PostScript files which can be displayed in Ventura Publisher?*

   Adobe Illustrator and The Curator (a Macintosh program from Solutions) produce Encapsulated PostScript files with an embedded TIFF bit image to display on the screen.

3. *How do I create an Encapsulated PostScript file?*

   First print to file, then insert the following lines at the beginning of your PostScript disk file:

   ```
   % ! PS-Adobe-1.0
   %%Title: Ventura Publisher Document
   %%Creator: Ventura Publisher
   %%Pages:  (atend)
   %%BoundingBox: 0   0   611   791
   %%EndComments.
   ```

APPLE LASERWRITER

4. *I have an older LaserWriter and experience lockups in printing. Can you help me?*

   Apple Laserwriters version 2 operated under version 23 of PostScript. This version had a bug which can sometimes cause printers to lock up. The solution is to copy a file called PS2.PRE from the Ventura Publisher Utilities Disk #11 into the VENTURA directory.

5. *I tried to print an 8½ x 14 landscape page to my Apple Laserwriter Plus. The output was garbled starting at the left margin and stopping at 11 inches. Why?*

Ventura Publisher has identified a problem with the version 1.0 PostScript driver which will cause this to occur. This was corrected in 1.1 Patch 1.

6. *I have an Apple Laserwriter Plus and, after downloading DTR.TXT in order for the printer to function with DTR handshaking mode, I was not able to get other software packages to function with the printer. Why?*

Most software packages communicate using XON/XOFF handshaking protocol. To convert DTR.TXT into XON.TXT requires editing the number four (4) in line two of the DTR.TXT file to a number three (3). This change, when downloaded to the printer, will reset handshaking to XON/XOFF protocol. Create a batch file containing the following:

```
Line 1 = serverdict begin o exitserver
Line 2 = statusdict begin 25 9600 4 setsccbatch end
Line 3 = <Ctrl-Z>.
```

7. *I'm trying to print to a legal sheet of paper on an Apple Laserwriter Plus but it only prints regular sheets. Why?*

You need a legal-size tray.

8. *Is there any difference in fonts between the Apple Laserwriter and the Laserwriter Plus?*

The Apple Laserwriter Standard Model includes only Helvetica, Times Roman, Symbol, and Courier Fonts. Laserwriter Plus contains the above plus ITC Avant Garde, ITC Bookman, Helvetica Narrow, Palatino, Century Schoolbook, Zapf Chancery, and Zapf Dingbats.

9. *I printed a multiple-page document to my Apple Laserwriter Plus and it stopped printing after the second page. I can print the third page by itself but it will not print after the second page if I select All to be printed.*

Remove GEMPRINT.SYS from your CONFIG.SYS file. This is apparently an old driver used by GEM for the Laserwriter, and it introduces the XON, XOFF problem in which the printer and the processor don't properly exchange ready indications back and forth. When this driver is removed, the file should print completely.

10. *A document was printed to a Laserwriter and looked fine. The chapter was taken to a typesetter and the last paragraph on a page was moved to the top of the next page. Shouldn't PostScript output be the same on all printers?*

    Yes. But the PostScript versions of Ventura Publisher may be different. Version 1.1 unpatched had different spacing than 1.0 due to a bug. Patch 1 of 1.1 fixed the bug. Now depending upon which version you have and which version of PostScript the printer has, there could be a spacing discrepancy.

INTERPRESS

11. *What are the limitations of an Interpress printer?*

    The resolution is 300 dpi for all current Ethernet Interpress printers. The fonts used for printing via Interpress must be resident in the network print server. They are not downloaded to the printer by Ventura Publisher on a job-by-job basis. Interpress fonts are discrete-sized bit-mapped characters. They do not scale in the manner used by PostScript.

12. *Is there some way to get Ventura Publisher Interpress documents to a 9-track tape and from there into the 9700 for printing?*

    At the current time the 9700 stand-alone with tape input does not support Interpress formatted documents. Xerox is working on an Interpress Interpreter for the 9700 stand-alone. The minimum configuration for an Interpress 9700 requires an 8000 server with the FPS (Formatting Print Service) software connected to the 9700 in an Ethernet environment. The File transfer may be done by a PC connected to Ethernet with XNS-PC software and a 3-COM PWA or from a 360K bytes disk to a Xerox 6085 with a DOS option package.

13. *What are the requirements for Interpress?*

    You need 640K bytes of memory for Ventura Publisher version 1.1 to load. If a combined CONFIG.SYS file is used which will satisfy both Ventura Publisher and XC-80 requirements, Ventura Publisher will have about 70K bytes less working space than normal to work with. Interpress printing requires use of XC-80 network software and the XC-80 adapter card. If any conflict between the XC-80 adapter card and mouse or display card is encountered, you can change the interrupt used by the XC-80 adapter board. A jumper can be moved to change the interrupt used. Available interrupts on the XC-80 board: 2,3,4,5,6,7.

14. *Does a 3700 use Interpress language?*

The 3700 formerly was not supported for Interpress printing from Ventura Publisher due to inadequate graphics capabilities. However, the latest version, called the "3700 Plus," can be used for Interpress printing of Ventura Publisher files over an Ethernet system.

Install

15. *Are there any special procedures for installing Interpress?*

Printing a chapter via Interpress printer:

    a. Load Ventura Publisher. Make sure Set Printer Info reads:

        Device Name: Interpress
        Output To: Filename
        Width Table:\VENTURA\INTERPRS.WID (X=Disk Drive)

    b. Print chapter to filename. The easiest way to keep track of Interpress print files is to give the print file the same name as the chapter. You should also override the .C00 extension with the extension of your liking.

    c. Exit to DOS and copy the Interpress print file to the name and location which will be accessed by XPRINT (the network printing program). Normally XPRINT looks for the Interpress master print file to be named XPRINT.IP, located in the root directory of the drive on which the network is installed. (sp)X:\DIR\filename.IP(sp)Y:/XPRINT.IP (sp stands for space).

    d. To print the file via the network print command, log onto the root directory of the network drive and enter: XPRINT(sp)-M<cr>.

16. *I'm installing an Interpress printer. What are the CONFIG.SYS and AUTOEXEC.BAT files supposed to contain?*

CONFIG.SYS: XC-80 software requires the installation of several device drivers by way of the CONFIG.SYS file in order to operate:

    device=pro.sys
    device=buf.sys
    device=eth.sys
    device=idp.sys
    device=spp.sys
    device=cou.sys
    device=rip.sys

buffers=8
files=20

The seven device drivers use up about 70K bytes of memory. Ventura Publisher requires that the buffers line be altered to read, "Buffers=15."

AUTOEXEC.BAT: All versions of XNS PC 80 network software create an AUTOEXEC.BAT file which loads the network automatically at boot-up. Ventura Publisher will load and operate properly with XC80 in the background. However, memory shortage noted in question 12 may have an impact, causing slower processing due to having to spool a larger part of files onto disk instead of holding them in RAM.

For Ventura Publisher's Installation:

The proper printer selection is: "F" INTERPRESS and determine the printer port selection.

Print

17. *I'm trying to print using Interpress and it prints blank pages. Why?*

The font selected in Ventura Publisher is not available on the system. Check with your system administrator for a listing of currently loaded fonts.

18. *I am trying to print with Interpress and all I get is slugs (filled-in small squares) printing instead of characters. Why?*

This problem occurs if the font does not contain the requested character.

19. *What are the available Interpress fonts in Ventura Publisher?*

The available Interpress fonts are as follows:

Titan, 10 Normal, Bold, Normal Italic, Bold Italic.
Titan 12 Normal, Bold.
Modern, sizes 6, 8, 10, 12, 14, 18, 24, 30, 36 Normal, Bold, Normal Italic, Bold Italic.
Classic, sizes 6, 8, 10, 12, 14, 18, 24 Normal, Bold, Normal Italic.
Symbol, 6, 8, 10, 12, 14, 18, 24 Normal, Bold, Normal Italic.

Compatibility

20. *Can you give me a list of supported printers that use Interpress?*

These printers are listed in the manual for Interpres printing, but may not be fully compatible with Ventura Publisher: Xerox 8700, 9700, 4045, 8044 series. Any Interpress-compatible printer or typesetter must be equipped with Interpress version

2.0. Interpress printers are supported only via network, by way of printing to a disk file. No direct printing to Interpress printers is supported.

21. *What software level of Interpress is available for Ventura Publisher?*

XC-80 can use any of the DOS levels acceptable to Ventura Publisher.

22. *What compatibility is the Interpress Printer Language?*

Interpress files can be printed only by sending them via Ethernet to a network printer. Only Interpress version 2.0 is supported by Ventura Publisher. The computer must be compatible with both Ventura Publisher software and XC-80 (or XNS-PC) network software and hardware. XPRINT does not work on 286-level computers unless a math co-processor is present. With XC-80 version 1.2, XPRINT works on ATs without having to install a math co-processor.

23. *What version of Interpress is compatible with Ventura Publisher?*

Interpress version 2.0 is compatible with Ventura Publisher.

LINOTRONIC

24. *I have a Linotronic 300 and I'm unable to access all the fonts I have on my hard disk. I installed them using the Adobe downloader for the PC. Can you help me?*

There is not a version of the Linotype downloader for the PC yet. When you used the Linotype downloader from your Mac, all the fonts could be accessed and all was fine.

NOTE
The typesetter had to download from a MAC environment,
then transfer to the PC.

25. *I tried to print a broadsheet (18" by 24") landscape document on a Linotronic 100. Since the Linotronic 100 is limited to a maximum paper size of 18"x 12", the printing had to be done by choosing the Strips feature, which is only supported on typesetters. Why doesn't this work?*

Since the document is 18" high and 24" wide, one would expect that the 3 strips by Ventura Publisher would each be 18" high and 12" wide—one for the left side, one for the right side, and one for the middle overlap area, so that the final pasteup for camera-ready copy could be complete. What happens instead is that three landscape strips emerged, 1 each 12" high and 18" wide. These covered the top half, the bottom half, and a middle overlap area...but only for the left ⅔ of the final page. The right-hand 6" of the page was lost altogether. There is an error in the PostScript driver—it will correctly do broadsheet printing only for portrait. This was corrected in versions 1.1 Patch 2 and later.

26. *I'm attempting to print to Linotronic 300 Film for color stripping. I need to set some portions of text to black on black solid background so they would disappear. The text to be printed (in red eventually) would be white on black background. Can you help me?*

Ventura Publisher will allow text stripping only as a function of printing white text on a white background. Funny, but Header, Footer, and Graphic Caption text will disappear when background is set to black; box and frame text will not. The following batch files cause the printout to reverse video at the printer.

Hidden text must be set to white on white. Normal text will appear at the printer as white on black. Two batch files are needed, one to turn on reverse video, and one to turn the effect off.

The following commands are required to reverse video at the printer:

Rev-On.ps Serverdict begin O exitserver<R> Statusdict begin<R>
True setdefaultmirrorprint<R>
True setdefaultnegativeprint<R>

The following commands are required to return to Normal at the printer:

Rev-Off.ps Serverdict begin O exitserver<R> Statusdict begin<R>
False setdefaultmirrorprint<R>
False set default negativeprint<R>
End.

Steps necessary to print stripped file on Linotronic 300:

    a. Print Ventura Publisher document to disk file (filename.C00).

    b. Exit Ventura Publisher and copy the correct batch file to printer, ie, COPY REV-ON.PS COM(n): (N= COM 1 OR COM 2) or COPY REV-ON.PS LPT(n) (n= LPT1-(P+4). Then copy Ventura Publisher print to disk file to printer.

    c. Copy REV-OFF.PS to turn the effect off.

27. *Can the Linotronic print in broadsheet? In landscape?*

The L100 and L300 printers can print up to 12" wide but you must print in strips. The L500 can print up to 18" portrait only. Ventura Publisher 1.1 Patch 1 and Patch 2 do not currently support broadsheet landscape printing.

NEC

28. *My NEC Silentwriter LC890 PostScript printer is having problems with the outline of circles. Can you help me?*

The PostScript version number of this system is 47.0. This problem is directly due to the update of the PostScript code. Upward compatibility of PostScript versions has been an ongoing problem, not limited to Ventura Publisher. All levels of Ventura Publisher up through 1.1 Patch 1 were designed for earlier versions of PostScript and may encounter this problem. Version 1.1 Patch 2 is designed for PostScript 47.0 and should solve this problem. When all choices are made, simply press Online again to return to an online state. First select Software; your options include HP, PostScript Batch, PostScript Interactive, and Diablo 630.

29. *How do you install the NEC LC800 Series printer in Ventura Publisher?*

NEC has several printers; they are the LC850, LC860 Plus, and the LC890. The model most widely used by Ventura Publisher users is the LC890. This printer can emulate PostScript and Hewlett Packard. The LC850 is a line printer but is compatible with Ventura Publisher. The LC860 Plus emulates Hewlett Packard. The LC890, however, is a more versatile, complex printer. The emulation and other parameters are set on a menu panel on the printer. These settings fall into three basic categories: Software, Hardware, and Miscellaneous. The menu panel is quite easy to manipulate. To begin, touch Online; it is a toggle which should toggle the printer to On/Offline. Next, press the menu, which will display the various categories described above. Selections are made by pressing Next until the desired selection is found.

30. *On my NEC 890 PostScript printer, pages with text and graphics usually come out only text. The graphics disappear. Why?*

You were printing with Ventura Publisher 1.0 or 1.1 through a switchbox. When you connect directly to the printer, the problems will go away.

31. *Can you help me get my NEC LC890 to print with Ventura Publisher?*

The NEC printer seems to be very sensitive when printing from Ventura Publisher via a parallel interface. The NEC printer will display "Online processing," then when Ventura Publisher has completed the print job, will drop back to "Online Idle" without printing anything. Printing to filename and copying to LPT# works sometimes. If you are having the above problem and the printing is being done from a high speed system (286 or 386) with switchable processor speeds, the clock speed may need to be set to the slower speed. The problem occurs when the parallel port is not operating at the same speed as the processor. Ventura Publisher is passing information to the parallel port at processor speed. Some bits will be dropped when the parallel is not operating as fast. This occurs quite often in Compaq 286 and 386 systems.

32. *What is the tray selection for the NEC LC 890?*

The NEC LC 890 has two adjustable hoppers (not really trays). Either hopper will print letter size or legal size. The key to which it will print is in the menu setup. The hopper must be set up for legal size if that is the type of output desired. If default is chosen in Ventura Publisher for the printer paper tray, the printer will use the hopper that is currently selected in the printer's Setup menu. If hopper one is currently selected in the Setup menu, it will be accessed by choosing default as the paper tray in Ventura Publisher (as mentioned above). If "Alt1" or "Alt2" is chosen in Ventura Publisher, the printer will use hopper two. This does not work in the reverse. When hopper two is the hopper selected in the printer's Setup menu, the Alt2 choices in Ventura Publisher do not produce any output. After saying OK to send output from Ventura Publisher, "Online Processing" appears for a short time on the printer display window. No output is produced however, and the message "Online Idle" soon displays as if the print job has been completed. While "Alt1" or "Alt2" doesn't function when hopper two is the chosen printer tray, selecting Default in Ventura Publisher will produce output from hopper two. Once a hopper is selected, the paper length also must be indicated.

33. *My Compaq 286 with NEC 890 printer goes from "online processing" to "online idle" without printing anything. Why?*

Switching the Compaq 286's clock speed from 12 to 8 mhz will fix this problem.

QMS

34. *My QMS Jetscript PostScript board in my computer is not printing through the parallel connection. Why?*

Check the CONFIG.SYS file; if BUFFERS= 10 or smaller, then increasing your buffers to 15 will solve the problem.

35. *Is the QMS PS 800 Laser printer compatible with Ventura Publisher?*

Yes, provided the level of PostScript on the printer is not higher than that for which the version of Ventura Publisher was designed. PostScript has upward compatibility problems, so a new QMS 800 may experience some when used with Ventura

Publisher 1.0 or 1.1 (unpatched). The more recent the version of Ventura Publisher, the more likely it is that it will support the level of PostScript on a given printer.

TEXAS INSTRUMENTS OMNILASER

36. *My Texas Instruments 2115 PostScript printer is printing only text. Graphics of any kind come out as blank frames. Why?*

On the front panel of the T.I. 2115 is a display. One of the options available on this panel is PostScript INTERACTIVE/BATCH. The BATCH option for PostScript must be engaged in order for the printer to print graphics.

TYPESETTERS

37. *What typesetter does Ventura Publisher drive?*

Ventura Publisher can drive PostScript compatible typesetters, such as the Linotronic 100 and 300. The APS-5 and Compugraphics 8400 typesetters are not supported at this time. Interpress compatibility is also available in version 1.1, which creates an Interpress master file for transmission via Ethernet to a network Interpress printer.

38. *My file sent to the typesetter (L-300) prints garbage. The typesetter has my file but it does not have Ventura Publisher. I also got garbage when copied to a printer. Why?*

Check to make sure it's a C00-extension file inside Ventura Publisher and not a chapter file.

POSTSCRIPT

39. *Can Ventura Publisher read PostScript files?*

PostScript creates a non-revisable form of the document. Ventura Publisher can create PostScript files and can load Encapsulated PostScript files. It cannot read non-Encapsulated PostScript files and, because of the nature of PostScript, will not be able to edit a PostScript image.

40. *Does Ventura Publisher use a 150-line-per-inch default in PostScript?*

PostScript has a default graphic coordinate system measurement of approximately 72 dots per inch which Ventura Publisher modifies to create graphics at 300 dots per inch.

41. *What level of PostScript is supported with which version of Ventura Publisher?*

PostScript compatibility is an ongoing problem, because new versions of PostScript are frequent and upward compatibility of PostScript versions has been poor up to now. PostScript compatibility in Ventura Publisher so far is:

Ventura Publisher Version—Patch	Date	PostScript Version
1.1—Unpatched	5-13-87	38.0
1.1—Patch 1	7-16-87	43
1.1—Patch 2	4-20-88	47.0
2.0	9-11-88	52.0

Due to upward compatibility problems in PostScript, some problems can be encountered when using 1.1 Patch 1 with PostScript 47.0, such as: wrong font prints, defaults to Courier, or won't print at all. Patch 2 will correct these problems on a 47.0-level PostScript printer if PostScript compatibility is the problem.

Printing

42. *My page layout is set for legal (8.5 x 14). When it is printed to a PostScript printer, the print area is truncated, as if printing on an 8.5 x 11 page. Why?*

Ventura Publisher 1.1 unpatched had this limitation. If you have that version, get Patch 1.

Ventura Publisher 1.1 Patch 1 still will not print legal-size paper unless the printer has a legal-size paper tray. The patch to allow manual selection of legal paper with a letter-size paper tray applies only to the HP LaserJet Plus driver.

43. *When printing from Ventura Publisher to a PostScript typesetter, is it possible to achieve a resolution of 1500 x 1500?*

With PostScript the output is limited only by the capability of the output device. If the typesetter can print 1500 x 1500, then that is the resolution you will receive.

44. *I created a PostScript file and printed a draft on my printer. Then I sent it to a typesetter and the line endings came out different. The print service is using the same version of Ventura Publisher as I am, so why the difference?*

When you created the chapter, you had a large user dictionary for hyphenating words. You used Copy All and sent the chapter to the print service, who didn't have that dictionary. As a result, when the chapter was printed on the typesetter, the line endings were different. When a print file (.C00) was used, the line endings were the same on the typesetter as on the draft printout.

45. *How can I speed up printing on my PostScript printer?*

There are subroutines called Prologue which must be in the PostScript printer or typesetter before a print operation can be carried out. Normally Ventura Publisher downloads these routines at the beginning of each print job. However, these can be permanently downloaded prior to loading Ventura Publisher. The basic information about this is given in the Ventura Publisher Reference Guide, p. F-22. In order to make the process automatic, it is suggested that the following alterations be made using DOS:

    a. Delete the file PS2.PRE from the VENTURA directory.

    b. Copy the file PERMVP.PS from the POSTSCPT directory on the Ventura Publisher Utilities Disk #11 into the VENTURA directory.

    c. Insert the following command into the VP.BAT file ahead of the commands created by Ventura Publisher software installation:

        COPY/VENTURA/PERMVP.PS COM1.

46. *I printed a PostScript chapter on a laser printer which had all fonts resident that were needed for the chapter. It printed in a few minutes. Then the same chapter was printed out on a typesetter which had to download some of the fonts. The chapter printed fine but took longer (several times as long). Why?*

PostScript handles font downloading much differently from the HP LaserJet or the 4045. For most laser printers, Ventura Publisher downloads all the fonts needed for a given page and then accesses them as it works its way through the page. When it goes to the next page, it still has those fonts and only adds extra ones if needed at that point. Thus, once the initial font downloading is done, the print process tends to be pretty fast. PostScript manages its memory differently and does not download fonts in the same manner. If PostScript needs a downloaded font to print a certain part of the page, it downloads it and prints that part of the page. As soon as it sees a change where that font is no longer in use, it dumps it. If a short distance further down the page it needs that font again, it downloads it again, and so on. The net result is a page with quite a few font changes, even if it is only back and forth between a couple of fonts, can take a long time to print out.

Thick Lines

47. *Why are PostScript boxes still coming out with different line thicknesses in the same box?*

    This problem has been fixed in the version 2.0 PostScript driver.

48. *It appears that on some printers, balancing the dimensions of columns and gutters with ruling lines is done by adding thickness to the lines (PostScript); in others (4045) it seems to be done by adding thickness to the gutter, varying thickness of ruling lines across the page and horizontal to vertical differences. Why?*

    This problem was solved in Ventura Publisher 1.1. There was a math calculation error in the line width for inter-column as well as horizontal ruling lines in 1.0. PostScript now has a minimum line thickness of 1/300th of an inch.

Print to Disk

49. *I have printed a file to disk using PostScript. When I took it to another machine to print it out, it didn't work. Can I use the DOS COPY command to output a PostScript print file?*

    Yes, it is possible to use the DOS COPY command to output a PostScript file, but first set up the mode command to set COM1: to 96,n,8,1 and then route LPT1: to COM1. Finally, copy the file to LPT1:. If this does not work, you should copy the DTR.TXT file, which is contained on the utilities disk, to the PostScript device.

Point Sizes

50. *Can I print characters larger than 72 point on a PostScript device?*

    Yes. If using version 1.0, you must use the procedure outlined in Appendix K for creating or changing a PostScript width table. For example, look at the USRPOSTS.LST file as displayed in the Reference Guide. To add a larger point size to TIMESBLD.VFM, you simply add a space after the 2 in 72 and then the point size you are adding (90 for example). Ventura Publisher will print the 90-point characters but will display only 72 point on the screen (in normal view). Ventura Publisher provides a maximum screen font size of 72 points in normal view for PostScript devices.

    Version 1.1 eliminates the need to use the above procedure. PostScript font sizes are selectable online from 1 to 254 points.

51. *Can I use point sizes in PostScript that include half points in the measurement (9.5 points)?*

    In Ventura Publisher 1.1 Patch 2 and earlier, PostScript supported only whole numbers. Version 2.0 has a newer version PostScript and half sizes are supported.

Graphic

52. *How can I determine the graphic capability of my PostScript printer?*

    You can print CHANEL.IMG scaled to various increasing sizes until an error message occurs.

No Output

53. *I get no output at all from my printer. Activity light may or may not flash but nothing ever prints. Why?*

    Verify correct cable configuration to VP. Ventura Publisher 1.1 and above requires the DTR configuration in order to function with serial PostScript devices.

    Copy DTR.TXT from VP Disk #11 in the POSTSCPT Directory to your root directory. Then copy DTR.TXT COM(n) <cr>.

    Verify communications channel to printer by creating a FF.TXT file with the following commands:

```
COPY CON FF.TXT <cr>
SHOWPAGE<cr>
<Ctrl-Z>
MODE COM(n): 96,N,8,1,P<cr>
COPY FF.TXT COM(n)<cr>
```

The words "SHOWPAGE" will print if the printer is on line.

Printers: JLaser / LaserMaster Internal Boards

This chapter is about printing using internal add-on boards. Currently, there are only a few major suppliers of these boards, or cards, but more are joining the game every day. These cards are an affordable solution to someone who wants PostScript quality without the cost or lack of speed. These cards are fast, reliable, and a fraction of the price of a PostScript printer. These cards just plug into the computer through an add-on port and must be connected to any Canon-engine printer. Their speed is attributed to the ability to move fonts from disk to controller card faster than any other way of printing to a printer. Different cards have different ways of dealing with communicating with the printer.

The JLaser board is a large memory board and laser printer driver which plugs into the PC expansion slot. It works with most Canon-based printers, including most versions of the HP LaserJet. It dramatically increases printing speed by bypassing the slow serial or parallel printer connections and having information transferred directly from the hard disk to the printer memory. The LaserMaster Cap card is a true controller card with full functionality. It has a separate memory for page setup and fonts development. The on-board coprocessor adds to the speed. The downloading of 12-point fonts takes about a second using the Cap card, where it will take about one minute without the card. The printer's internal controller is bypassed and the card communicates directly with the printer's video switch. The Cap card also supplies a utility to change HP printer font formats to the QDL font format. Converting to the QDL format will download faster from disk; this will also add to the speed of the LaserMaster.

Topic Guide

JLASER

1. *I am having problems trying to print graphics through my JLaser. It is installed on my Compaq 386. Can you help?*

   The Compaq 386 cannot use the standard JLaser card. It must use the JLaser stand-alone card with no memory on the card. The JLaser will make use of the computer's expanded memory. It is not clear how much memory is needed on the computer before the JLaser is fully usable.

2. *Can I print to file using a JLaser?*

   No. Ventura Publisher does a direct memory transfer to the JLaser which is functionally different from the way information is sent to a printer.

3. *Can I print a document on a JLaser and a PostScript device?*

   It is possible to output a document created in Ventura Publisher to more than one type of printer. Make sure, however, that the appropriate width table is used to achieve the desired result. Using a JLaser width table to print to a Xerox 4045, for example, could cause certain alignment problems and affect the way graphics are displayed.

Fonts

4. *Can I obtain additional fonts for the JLaser board?*

   Yes. Contact Tall Tree Systems for a conversion utility which they have developed with support from Ventura Publisher Software. This will allow you to convert Hewlett Packard LaserJet Plus-compatible soft fonts for use with the JLaser.

5. *I added over 180 fonts to the Ventura directory and now my JLaser is taking 10 minutes to print ¼ page of text. Why?*

Every time you see on the screen "Loading Fonts," Ventura Publisher is taking every screen font and spooling it into a temporary file. With this many fonts in the directory on a slow access drive, it takes a long time. To help this problem:

    a. Increase buffers to 25 or 30.

    b. Set up a separate directory to hold fonts that are not actually needed on a particular document, and set up batch files to copy needed fonts into (and later delete from) the VENTURA directory.

Lockups

6. *I am printing to a JLaser board. After printing one page, the system appears to lock up and will not print anymore. Why?*

This occasionally happens with the JLaser board. The processor will beep and you will see lines across the screen because JLaser is trying to send a message back to the screen. To resume printing, you will have to respond to the message JLaser is sending. Without knowing the message, it is difficult to know which response to give, but one of the following letters should work; "R," "D," "I."

7. *JLaser will only print one page from Ventura Publisher, then it locks up. Why?*

This problem is due to a bug in the JLaser software. It is supposed to be fixed by a new software release. Before going into Ventura Publisher, access drive A in some manner. For example, put a disk in drive A and do a DIR on it. Then you should be able to load Ventura Publisher and print successfully using the JLaser.

Printing

8. *I am getting garbage when printing to my JLaser-driven HP LaserJet. There are bars across the page and letters are incomplete. Why?*

Check for the interrupt setting in your CONFIG.SYS file. It could be that the interrupts for the JLaser board and your enhanced graphics adaptor are in conflict. The enhanced graphics board has a typical interrupt setting of 10. If the JLaser is also set at 10, this could be your problem. You can also check the memory paging settings on the JLaser board itself.

These are physical settings, changed by shunts on the JLaser card. Changing the position of the shunts could also solve your problem. If in doubt, call Tall Tree Systems for further technical assistance.

9. *My JLaser is able to print 8½ x 11-inch letter size in both portrait and landscape but cannot print legal 14-inch lengths. Why?*

   Your CONFIG.SYS may have the command DEVICE=JDRIVE.BIN 720k. This statement effectively removes about 25% of the JRAM PWA memory from your RAM disk. Removing this statement will cure the problem and the JLaser will be able to print legal as well as letter-size documents.

10. *The JLaser is printing a separate page for the footer.*

    Check the footer frame bottom margin. If it is set to zero, change it to .25 and it will print correctly.

11. *With my JLaser, my pages fail to print properly, I get garbage text, the fonts are improper, and my graphics are misplaced. This happens on every page printed out. Can you help me?*

    This problem may be caused by insufficient disk space needed to create all of the temporary files required to format the document. This is especially likely if the system has been working fine until recently.

    Or, you may have an old printer software driver. For JLaser you need JLASER.BIN or JLASER3.BIN file.

12. *My margin shifts on JLaser-printed documents. Why?*

    The left margin can be adjusted within the JLaser by adding an "H" command to the CONFIG.SYS JLASER3.BIN device driver. The command is preceded by a forward slash-as in DEVICE=JLASER3.BIN/H=NNN. The numbers following the equal sign are expressed in 300 dots per inch. For example H=150 would be one-half inch from the left margin.

13. *My JLaser prints blank pages. Why?*

    Several things can cause this to happen:

    - CONFIG.SYS should not contain a "JRAM" or "GEMPRINT.SYS" driver.

    - JLaser board could have a problem. Check this by running JLaser diagnostics, according to the manual provided. If the board is okay, it should print a page which is blank except for a large "X."

    - The Ventura Publisher installation could be bad. If this is suspected, try to reinstall Ventura Publisher.

Hewlett Packard

14. *I have a JLaser board with a Hewlett Packard LaserJet. Can I purchase additional Hewlett Packard fonts for my printer and use them with the JLaser?*

    If you have Ventura Publisher version 1.0, no. If you have version 1.1 or 2.0, yes.

LASERMASTER

15. *I have a LaserMaster Cap card and I'm using slanted text with Patch 2. Why does it print funny?*

    Slanted text is one of LaserMaster's special effects features. Slanted text rotates the words 60 degrees in Patch 1. Patch 2 rotates each letter 60 degrees. LaserMaster has redone their driver. The new driver asks for Version 3.5.

Printers: Laser Printers HP / Xerox / Others

This chapter is all about the house that Jack built. If there were no laser printers, there would be no desktop publishing. Now, due to desktop publishing, the popularity of the laser printers has skyrocketed, soon to replace the dot matrix printer. Ventura Publisher and other desktop publishers have forced the manufacturers of laser printers to keep up with this new popularity. This has allowed a whole new computer card called the printer enhancement card to enter the market, such as LaserMaster's Cap card. At this time they are just add-on cards but soon they will find a way to place that speed inside the printer. Then you will see a breakthrough in the laser printer world. In this chapter you will find common problems with the Hewlett Packard series, Xerox 4045, and other non-PostScript laser printers.

Topic Guide

GENERAL

1. *During printing of a large publication, my Quadram QuadLaser (HP LaserJet emulator) stops printing at some point. On smaller print jobs it goes through okay. What's wrong?*

   There is a timeout problem on the QuadLaser that can cause this effect when printing a large publication. Try breaking up your publication into smaller ones.

2. *I hooked up a clone printer and did a partial install for the HP LaserJet Plus 300 dpi. Now my kerning isn't working. For example, a 36-point masthead looked spread out at print time. Why?*

   The HP LaserJet Plus does not have 36 point. Look at the Set Printer Info and check to see if you have the Epson width table installed. Ventura Publisher does not respond well to mismatched width tables. The way to check is to look inside the Set Printer Info box at the top of the screen. The word Ultimate or Draft will appear; Draft will cause this problem.

3. *I'm trying to print on a Canon LBP with Lasertwin emulator. It emulates HP LaserJet Plus when large fonts such as 18-24 pt. are used, but the top 1/5 of each character is cut off. Why?*

   This is almost certainly a printer emulation problem.

CORDATA

4. *Which Cordata printer is compatible with Ventura Publisher?*

   The Cordata LP300X is compatible with Ventura Publisher.

5. *I am attempting to print a Ventura Publisher document, but my Cordata prints only blank pages. One blank sheet is ejected for each page of the actual document, Ventura Publisher behaves onscreen as if it has printed successfully. What's happening?*

   First, make sure your printer is the Cordata LP300X. If there is no "X," it is not supported by Ventura Publisher. Second, make sure the printer is installed correctly. The CONFIG.SYS contains the command line "DEVICE=LLD.SYS." The AUTOEXEC.BAT contains the command line "RIM" and does not contain a command that reads "LPX (something)." If the printer is installed correctly, the problem is probably the failure of the Cordata adapter board to initialize properly at system boot-up. Here is what you should watch for and also what to do if you run into this problem. During boot-up you will see the following lines on the screen: "LLD:Cordata LP300X Low Level Driver — Version 1.31 Copyright (etc.) LLD: Initializing the Laser printer Mechanism..." The "initializing" message should stay on for several seconds, even on a 386 computer, then be followed by the message: "LLD:Installed successfully." If the initializing message appears momentarily and then is immediately followed by the "installed successfully" message, the installation has actually failed. This is how to get it to initialize correctly:

   a. Shut down both the PC and the Cordata.

   b. Turn the PC on with the Cordata still turned off.

   c. Wait until just before the "LLD" message is about to come up; then turn the Cordata printer on (you may have to boot up a few times to get the timing right).

This is not a Ventura Publisher problem but a problem with the Cordata printer initialization.

6. *How do I install a Cordata printer?*

Printer selection is H for Cordata.

Select: Printer Serial Port 1 (if mouse is not connected to COM2) or Printer Serial Port 2 (if mouse is connected to COM1).

7. *I can't get my Cordata LP300X Laser printer and the SummaSketch Mouse to work.*

These two devices use the same area in memory for the drivers to allow them to operate. If the mouse is loaded first, its driver will be overwritten by LLD.SYS and or RIM.EXE programs. You can have a printer or you can have the SummaSketch mouse but not both at the same time.

8. *I am getting a garbled line at the top of each page whenever I print to my Cordata printer. It is installed with two monitors, an EGA and LaserView.*

The hardware configuration for your system includes a 2-monitor setup, creating an interrupt level conflict which caused the garbled line. The system configuration was an IBM AT with EGA card, Sigma Designs LaserView monitor and card, PC mouse, and the Cordata printer. The conflict came from the location of each device driver in memory. Memory locations are referred to as pages. Cordata allows for installation to either the "C" page (default) or the "D" page (optional). The LaserView is normally installed to the "D" page, but Sigma Designs can provide you with a driver which will position the LaserView on the "A" page. The EGA card addresses the "C" page. To resolve the conflict, the addresses of the Cordata and the

LaserView must be changed. Install the Cordata to the "D" page and the LaserView to the "A" page, leaving the EGA on the "C" page.

AST TURBOLASER

9. *What are the special capabilities and limitations of the AST TurboLaser?*

The AST TurboLaser can operate in several different modes, including 630 emulation. These modes are set up by the software which comes with TurboLaser instead of by DIP switches.

The maximum number of images per page is four pictures. Rotated text on the page will not print correctly. It prints white text on a black background. It prints text under graphics with the text visible. It can print 6 through 24-point fonts.

It may require a Mode Com statement to prevent timeout while printing long documents.

10. *My AST TurboLaser printer was fine yesterday. Today it prints blank pages. Why?*

Perform a CHKDSK on the hard drive to show the amount of memory and disk space available. You need approximately 2Mb of disk space and 575K bytes of free memory.

11. *AST TurboLaser would not print using the standard Ventura Publisher setup. It prints multiple blank pages or pages with garbage in one corner. Why?*

You have an outdated version of the AST software (version 1.02). Write to AST for an update to 1.21G. Right now AST no longer sells the version of the AST TurboLaser directly supported by Ventura Publisher. Two versions and an upgrade kit are now available. Version 1 - AST TurboLaser EL, comes with 512K memory and two software printer emulation drivers: ASTJEL.LNG for HP LaserJet Plus emulation and ASTDEL.LNG for Diablo 630 daisywheel emulation. The EL Language Upgrade Kit upgrades the printer to 2Mb and supplies the ASTLASER.LNG driver for Ventura Publisher. It also supplies an extended character set driver for Diablo emulation, as well as Epson, and the HPGL plotter language. Version 2 - AST TurboLaser PS is a PostScript-only printer. It will have to be driven by the Ventura Publisher- supplied PostScript driver, not the AST driver.

12. *Why is my AST TurboLaser taking 1.5 hours to print 11 lines on a page?*

The best print speed is obtained by installing the AST TurboLaser to the COM2 printer port. When you installed a new software package, the number of files and buffers was modified in the CONFIG.SYS. Change the number of files and buffers to 15 in your CONFIG.SYS. This will correct the problem.

13. *Is the AST TurboLaser compatible with Ventura Publisher?*

There are now three versions of the TurboLaser:

- The original TurboLaser, which has its own adapter card with imaging memory on it. It is compatible with Ventura Publisher version 1.1 but not directly with 1.0. Drivers were available from AST to support the TurboLaser in version 1.0.

- TurboLaser EL emulates HP LaserJet Plus. Install in Ventura Publisher as HP LaserJet Plus (not TurboLaser).

- TurboLaser PS used for PostScript only. Install in Ventura Publisher as PostScript (not TurboLaser).

XEROX

14. *What hardware is required to print to Xerox equipment on a network?*

Any network printer accessible via Xerox XC-80 network software (also known as XNS—Xerox Network Services). Examples are Xerox 9700, 8700, 4050, and the 8044 series. Printing on the Xerox 2700 is not supported. Interpress files are highly memory intensive at the network print server. Ventura Publisher may well create files which will create memory-related print problems. If so, the printer will issue an error message "Page Too Complex..." This is especially true of graphics. As one benchmark, a print server with 1.3Mb of memory will be unable to print more than 16 square inches of scanned pictures on a page (equivalent to one 4" x 4" image).

Your PC must be connected to network via Ethernet cable. Either standard-size or thin Ethernet (RG-58) cable may be used. A network adaptor board must be installed in the PC.

8700

15. *Is the Xerox 8700 printer compatible with Ventura Publisher?*

No. That is not one of the compatible printers.

3700

16. *I understand that you can run a 3700 printer with Ventura Publisher. I can't get it to work. Why?*

   You must purchase the 3700 driver from Xerox to drive the printer and fonts. Your system needs at least 1Mb of memory. It will also operate with the 4045 fonts.

17. *What are the Xerox 3700 laser printer hardware and software requirements?*

   A 3700 must satisfy two criteria to support Ventura Publisher. One is hardware, the other is printer software.

   a. Printer memory: Must have 1Mb memory board (called IGA board). If it has the smaller 256K IGB board, Ventura Publisher is not supported.

   b. 3700 Software: Must be at least level 2.4-09 or higher. The version currently available is 2.4-10. If you have a lower level of 3700 software, you can get a patch to upgrade to 2.4-10 by calling the Xerox Software Library.

   c. 3700 Driver Disk: In order to use the stand-alone 3700 with Ventura Publisher, a 3700 installation disk must be purchased from Xerox. It is available from Software Telemarketing. Setting up to run the 3700 from Ventura Publisher involves the following general steps:

   (1) Install Ventura Publisher for the Xerox 4045.

   (2) From the 3700 install disk, copy the 3700 printer driver and width table into the VENTURA directory.

   (3) Using the 3700 install disk, run a batch file that permanently downloads 4045-type Ventura Publisher system fonts to the hard disk of the 3700. This is a one-time procedure; the fonts are thereafter on the 3700 hard disk, so there is no further downloading required. This greatly speeds up printing.

   (4) Enter Ventura Publisher. Using Set Printer Info, select "Device Name = Xerox 3700, 300 dpi" and use Load Different Width Table to select XRX3700.WID. Then use Add/Remove Fonts to change all 3700 fonts to resident.

   (5) Follow setup instructions that come with the 3700 install disk.

4020

18. *Does Ventura Publisher 1.1 support color printers other than the Xerox 4020?*

   Not at this time. Ventura Publisher 2.0 supports color output from a PostScript printer.

4045

19. *I have a Xerox 4045 with 128K bytes of memory. Can I use it with Ventura Publisher?*

No. Ventura Publisher requires at least 512K bytes of installed memory in order to print Ventura Publisher-generated documents. The reason is that each page is formatted in the printer's memory before it is transferred to the printer's drum. The more complex the document, the more memory needed to format it. This is why you may occasionally see error messages that indicate that the printer did not have enough memory to handle a complex page.

In terms of memory, there are now three basic categories of the 4045 in the field. Each category is distinguished by its motherboard electronics or firmware level. Each of these, in turn, has different ranges of available memory, as follows:

Model	Latest Firmware	Min RAM	Max RAM Model
Model 10	2.1.1	128K	512K
Model 50	3.1.1	512K	1.5Mb
Model 150	3.2	1Mb	2Mb

The Model 10 is not supported unless it has its maximum available RAM, 512K. If the firmware level is 2.0, it should be upgraded to 2.1.1. The Model 50 can support Ventura Publisher with the built-in memory, but for full function, memory should be added to bring the total to 1.5Mb. With either model, 512K gives only very limited graphics capability.

20. *Are there bugs in the 3.0 version of the 4045 firmware?*

Yes. Printing duplicate pages when only one copy was requested is one. Another problem is printer lockup. Now 3.1.1 is available and will correct the known graphics bugs in 3.0 firmware.

21. *Tell me about memory in the Xerox 4045 Model 10?*

It comes with 128K bytes memory built-in. You can add 384K additional memory, which must be installed for Ventura Publisher to be supported on this model 4045. The amount of installed memory can be determined from the "Bytes Available" entry on the configuration sheet. Produced at power-up, this gives the amount of memory available after the 4045 has used a portion of the memory to handle its operating system. If 2.0 firmware is installed, the entry will be one of the following: 65520 Bytes Available DRAM not installed; 458736 Bytes Available DRAM is installed.

Ventura Publisher is supported, though graphics will be limited. If 2.1 or 2.1.1 firmware is installed, the corresponding entries will be slightly lower because the printer's operating system uses a little more memory.

22. *My added 4045 fonts print garbage all over the page. Why?*

You installed the Optima family of fonts. The fonts printed garbage along with scattered letters. You must rename your portrait fonts to landscape and your landscape fonts to portrait before font installation. The X45P1ON.XFN portrait fonts have filenames X45P???.XFN. Landscape fonts have filenames X45L???.XNF. Renaming the files after width table creation will also work.

23. *What is the maximum point size for the Xerox 4045 and is this a hardware or software restriction?*

Currently 36-point type is the maximum point size supported on the Xerox 4045 and it is a hardware limitation. However, there is also an additional limitation for added 4045 fonts that is imposed by the current Ventura Publisher font conversion utility for the 4045. Large 4045 fonts (about 14 points and larger) are segmented so that no segment is larger than 64K, due to the way the 4045 font memory works. When fonts segmented this way are converted with the Ventura Publisher utilities, Ventura Publisher accesses only the first segment. The result is not all characters of the font are accessible. The Ventura Publisher software is hard-coded to circumvent this for the system fonts that come with Ventura Publisher (Swiss and Dutch), but not for added fonts.

24. *How is the 4045 Model 10 configured?*

Model 10 configuration sheet shows Revision #2.xx This model is no longer in production, but many remain in the field. Model 50 configuration sheets shows Revision 3.xx. This is the model currently in production.

25. *I have a document which uses the same tag in numerous places throughout the document. The tag has a 36 fractional point ruling line below, and when I print it out using my Xerox 4045, the line varies in size from one appearance to another. Can you tell me why?*

This document was printed out using the 150 dpi selection for the 4045. At 150 dpi resolution, a line of this thickness may vary if it borders between pixels. In one instance it might take an extra pixel and in another instance it might not. When printed at 300 dpi, the page will print without variation in line size.

26. *I upgraded from version 1.1 to 2.0 and now when I print documents with ruling lines and graphics they shift on the page when printing on my 4045.*

There is a bug in the 2.0 4045 driver. If you have upgraded from version 1.1, the old 4045 driver will work with 2.0. To fix the problem, 1.1 users need to reinstall 1.1 software. Ventura Publisher will ask "are you installing for the first time?" You must type N for no. Then install for 4045 printer as normal. This will only change the 4045 driver.

HEWLETT PACKARD

27. *Can you give me a list of supported HP Laserjet Printers?*

Hewlett Packard LaserJet W/92286F ("F" cartridge only)
Hewlett Packard LaserJet Plus
Hewlett Packard LaserJet Series II

28. *How many graphics per page will an HP Laserjet print?*

In 1.1 the maximum graphic images per page were:

LaserJet Plus: 4 images (loaded as files into frames)
LaserJet Series II: 8 images (with expanded memory)

In 2.0 you're limited only by memory configuration.

29. *Are there drivers for the HP PaintJet or DeskJet to work with Ventura Publisher?*

Not by Ventura Publisher Software. Atech Software provides support for the DeskJet in their Publisher's PowerPak. Digital Research may have a driver for the PaintJet which is compatible with VP.

30. *Hewlett Packard has announced a new printer called the DeskJet. What is it, and is it supported by Ventura Publisher?*

The DeskJet is an inkjet printer designed for laser-like quality at 300 dots per inch (dpi). It uses a version of "PCL," the HP Printer Command Language used for the HP LaserJet printer series. However, it is not compatible with the LaserJet for Ventura Publisher purposes, because the DeskJet is a line printer, not a page printer. That is, the DeskJet uses a small print buffer to enable it to format and print one line at a time. By contrast, a laser printer, such as an HP LaserJet, formats the entire page before it prints. Since the laser printer processes the whole page before it starts printing, it can organize graphics and text in combination on a page. A line printer such as the DeskJet cannot do that.

31. *What are the special capabilities and limitations for the HP Laser?*

Resolution: 300 dpi for text, 75 dpi for graphics, Fonts: Cartridge HP 92286F only. No landscape fonts on supported cartridge. Character Set: Some characters included in the Ventura Publisher character set will not print on the LaserJet because they are not included in the font cartridge. The printable characters can be determined by printing the sample chapter CHARSET.CHP in the TYPESET directory. Maximum number of fonts printable per page: 8 MODE commands: The MODE commands normally used in setting up a serial printer for Ventura Publisher are as follows:

    MODE LPT1: = COM1:
    MODE COM1 96,N,8,1,P.

The first command redirects the printer from the parallel port installed in Ventura Publisher to the serial port (assumed to be COM 1: for illustration). The second command sets the baud rate to 9600, no parity, 8 data bits, with 1 stop bit, so as to agree with the printer switch settings. No special entries are required by HP LaserJet in your CONF1G.SYS, and AUTOEXEC.BAT files.

32. *What does GSS and HPGL stand for?*

GSS stands for Graphics System Software outputs to CGM format.

HPGL stands for Hewlett Packard Graphics Language used by plotters.

33. *Can the HP LaserJet printer print multiple copies of the same document?*

The HP LaserJet series II can be set from the front panel menu to print from 1 to 99 copies of the documents being received. It is much faster to set the Series II for multiple copies than it is to allow VP to print 12 copies of each document.

Hardware Requirements

34. *What hardware is required and memory configuration is needed for an HP LaserJet Printer?*

The most basic model of the LaserJet series uses memory of 128K bytes built in with 59K available to you. The memory is not expandable. Any computer which successfully runs Ventura Publisher and has a serial interface available should operate satisfactorily with the HP LaserJet printer. The HP LaserJet must use a serial port. If a serial mouse is used, at least two serial ports must be available.

35. *How much hard disk space is required to install an HP LaserJet printer.?*

If this is the only printer installed in Ventura Publisher, 1,180K bytes (1.18Mb) will be taken up by installation. If this is a second or additional printer installed: Add 220K bytes to the installation space required by other printers.

Landscape Printing

36. *My text in the leftmost column of a landscape printout on a HP LaserJet Plus II is missing. The whole column of text may be missing or only certain paragraphs. Everything looks fine on screen. What's happening?*

   Check the margins and In From Left settings on the text in the leftmost column. If the first character in any line of text is supposed to begin in the non-printing area near the edge, the entire line of text will be lost. If the left margin is set within the unprintable zone, and if all the text in the first column starts at the margin, the whole column will be lost. If some lines or paragraphs are indented past the non-printing zone, they will print.

   This problem is most often found in unpatched version 1.1, since the non-printing zone at left and right is about 0.5 inch in landscape orientation with that software.

Font

37. *After loading an image file on a page, all fonts on that page print as Courier using HP LaserJet II. When the image file is removed, the text prints fine. Why?*

   Your CONFIG.SYS file contained no BUFFERS or FILES. Edit your CONFIG.SYS and insert the following commands:

   ```
   FILES=20
   BUFFERS=20
   ```

   These statements are essential for font downloading when a graphic is present.

38. *Can I use fonts other than Hewlett Packard fonts on my LaserJet Plus or LaserJet II?*

   If these fonts are guaranteed by the manufacturer to be compatible with downloadable fonts for the LaserJet, you can follow the font conversion process for Hewlett Packard fonts detailed in the reference manual. Please note that these fonts are provided for the printer only. Ventura Publisher provides screen and printer fonts for the typefaces which are included in the standard package. So there will be no corresponding screen fonts for Ventura Publisher to load. Ventura Publisher will try to match, as closely as it can, the font size on the screen, but the screen characters will not be identical to the printed output.

39. *Can LaserJet Plus fonts reside in a directory other than the Ventura directory?*

   Not with Ventura Publisher version 1.1 unpatched and Patch 1. Ventura Publisher will only look in the Ventura directory for LaserJet fonts. However, Patch 2 and version 2.0 enables LaserJet Plus fonts to be stored in any subdirectory.

Cartridge

40. *Why does the HP with F cartridge not have as many fonts as the HP LaserJet Plus?*

Because the HP printer with the F cartridge has the ability to retrieve Ventura Publisher's downloaded fonts. The HP LaserJet Plus F cartridge is confined to using the cartridge fonts.

41. *How many of the print cartridges for the Hewlett Packard LaserJet does Ventura Publisher support?*

The only print cartridge supported for the LaserJet is the F cartridge.

42. *Can I use a "B" cartridge on my HP LaserJet printer to print from Ventura Publisher?*

No, Ventura Publisher only allows the use of the F Cartridge.

43. *I'm trying to print with an HP LaserJet with the F cartridge. The portrait printing is fine, but when I turn the page to landscape orientation, the print looks grainy and distorted. Why?*

The F cartridge does not contain any landscape fonts. Unfortunately, with that LaserJet, you are restricted to the fonts available on the font cartridge. If the font selected by you is not resident in the font cartridge, the resulting printout will not be of acceptable quality.

Printing Problems

44. *I have a serial LaserJet Series II and it will not print unless I first press the Esc key. What am I doing wrong?*

Check for a resident memory program running in memory which could cause this problem. Remember, it is highly recommended that all memory resident programs be deactivated prior to running Ventura Publisher.

45. *I am trying to print a document to a Hewlett Packard LaserJet Plus. Whether I select 150 or 300 dpi, all lines print on one line of the page. My printer works with other programs. What is wrong?*

Check your LaserJet Plus; you may have an original LaserJet. The device driver for the Plus is not compatible with the standard LaserJet. Once you have obtained the proper hardware to upgrade your LaserJet to a true Plus, the system will print properly.

46. *My PCX image brought into Ventura Publisher prints the Courier font on my HP LaserJet Series II. Why?*

    This usually occurs at 150 and 300 dpi and is due to not having any files and buffers in your CONFIG.SYS file.

47. *My HP LaserJet series II has problems with nearly every occurrence of the combined letters "O" and "P." The word "HOPE" would turn into "HPPE." I reinstalled Ventura Publisher multiple times. Can you help me?*

    Here is another case of "It isn't always the software." In this case changing the parallel cable from a 12-foot version to a 10-foot version will cure the problem. High speed transfer and long cables just don't work too well.

48. *The HP Laserjet Series II printer is shifting the print down ½" on the page. Why?*

    The lines per page (set manually via printer menu) were set to a value less than 60. Setting them to 60 will cure the problem.

49. *I have an HP LaserJet Series II with an IBM Model 50. I installed Ventura Publisher with 589K free memory and 1.7 Mb on my hard drive. When I print, either direct or to file and copied from DOS, the graphics are fine, but there are certain letters in the text that are misplaced. For example, in Book-P1.CHP, the "A" in adventure is next to the "V" and the place where the "A" should appear is blank. The page is exactly the same if printed inside Ventura Publisher or from DOS. What's happening?*

    The key here is the fact that both the file copied from DOS and direct from VP were printing with the same results, and it was an untested new install. The solution is to remove the printer's expanded memory PWA and use only the standard memory inside the printer. The system will function fine after removing the extra memory cartridge.

50. *Why won't graphics print from inside Ventura Publisher to my HP LaserJet II?*

    Run CHKDSK if your system has less then 570K bytes of memory available. Check your CONFIG.SYS file for device drivers. CONFIG.SYS should consist of only the files, buffers, and MOUSE.SYS statements. It is recommended that you keep your device drivers, if needed, in your CONFIG.SYS, to a minimum.

51. *I have Ventura Publisher 1.1 Patch 1 and cannot print 14" legal pages using manual feed on my HP printer. Why?*

Performing the following steps should allow you to print 14" legal with manual feed:

a. Type as follows:

Copy con SETUP.TXT <Enter>
<space>E<space>&184<space>&12H<Ctrl-Z>

press Enter (reports "one file copied")

b. Use debug to modify all space codes (20) to Escape code (1B) using the Enter data command of debug and the Spacebar to move through the file.

Debug SETUP.TXT
-d<cr>
Screen dump of file - first and second line only relative.
-e0100<cr> XXXX:0100 20. 1b <space> 45.<multiple spaces> 20.1b <more multiple spaces> 20.1b <cr>
-w<cr>
writing 000d bytes
-g <cr> Returns to prompt.

c. Now copy this file to the printer from DOS.

COPY SETUP.TXT lpt1: <cr>

The printer manual mode indicator light should come on as the printer activates manual mode.

d. For every file you want to print in 14" landscape with manual feed, you must use Ventura Publisher to print to a filename in the Set Printer Info option. Then use Debug to eliminate the first two bytes of the file. These two bytes will cause the printer to reset the pre-setup you just did.

Debug filename.C00
To eliminate the initial Ventura Publisher escape?
E which would reset the printer
-e0100<cr>
XXXX:0I000 1b.00 <space> 45.00 <cr>
-w<cr>
writing XXXX bytes
-q <cr> Returns to prompt.

52. *I have a three-column page that was printed on a LaserJet. The first two columns print on some pages; on other pages it prints only the lines that are not underlined. Why?*

This is a limitation of the printer memory on the HP LaserJet. Check to make sure that the printer has more then 1Mb.

53. *Every page fails to print properly. I'm getting garbage text, improper fonts, or graphics misplaced, etc, on every page printed out. Why?*

    This problem could be caused by the following:

    Not enough hard disk space to create all of the temporary files required to format the document. This is especially possible if the system has been working fine until recently.

    Problem may be tied to hardware. Some IBM PS/2 users have severe problems with parallel cables causing garbage text. Some users have had to go through several cables before finding one that will work with the HP LaserJet printers.

54. *I tried to print a large graphic on my LaserJet Plus and it came out on two pages with the center of the graphic on one page and the two outside quarters on the second page. Why did it print this way?*

    Typically this type of problem is caused by insufficient memory in the printer. A laser printer constructs the entire graphic in its memory before outputting it to the paper. Large graphics are memory hogs using large amounts of memory. The LaserJet Plus contains about 500K bytes of memory which may not be enough for large graphics. Try reducing the size of the graphic or increasing the memory of your printer. The current printer in this series, the HP LaserJet II, comes with 512K built in. An expansion board can be added containing 1Mb, 2Mb, or 4Mb memory. The most common choice is 2Mb, giving a total of 2.5Mb of printer memory.

55. *Why does the HP Series II only print 8 of my 12 images on one page?*

    Limitation of VP and HP LaserJet Plus driver. Solution: Run paper through printer twice with different pictures on each printing.

56. *My Hewlett Packard II prints the wrong fonts or partial pages. Why?*

    Your problem may be a memory resident program. Always check for memory resident programs before you reinstall for printer problems.

57. *I purchased version 1.1 and I am unable to get my LaserJet to print correctly. I am using the F cartridge as specified in the manual. What is the problem?*

    This is a problem in the device driver in the preliminary release of 1.1, which can cause this type of problem. This problem has been fixed by Patch 1.

Lost Text

58. *I'm losing text when printing to an HP LaserJet Series II on a three-column newsletter document. I have a hard copy of the same document that was printing to within .25 inches of the edge.*

Change to the 150-dpi driver and it will print to within .25 inches of the edge.

Dingbat

59. *Is there a way to print dingbat symbols on the HP LaserJet Plus or HP LaserJet Plus II?*

Yes. Dingbat soft fonts can be obtained for the HP LaserJet Plus from Weaver Graphics. To install them for use by Ventura Publisher, basically copy all of the *.SFP fonts and width tables to the VENTURA directory and merge the new width tables with the current width tables.

Cable

60. *What kind of cabling and switch settings are required for a Hewlett Packard printer?*

LaserJet Plus and LaserJet II have both a parallel interface (36-pin Centronics) and a serial interface (25-pin RS-232).

Parallel interface:

 Cable—HP part No.24542D Serial interface (25-pin RS- 232):
 Cable part numbers: HP No. 15255D (1 meter cable)
 HP Part No. 92219] (5 meter cable)

For connecting IBM AT 9-pin serial port, use method A or B.

 A. Either cable above, plus IBM Serial Device Adapter Cable: IBM Part No. 6450217 or IBM Part No. 6450242.

 B. Special cable for direct connection of printer to AT: HP Part No. 24542G

Switch settings for the LaserJet Plus:

There is a single bank of DIP switches located inside the top rear of the printer. It is reached by first removing the rear cover (4 screws must be removed) and then removing the vertical support bracket at the top.

Switch Settings for Serial:

1 OFF, 2 ON, 3 OFF, 4 ON, 5 OFF, 6 OFF, 7 OFF, 8 ON.

Switch settings for parallel:

1 ON, 2 ON, 3 OFF, 4 ON, 5 OFF, 6 OFF, 7 OFF, 8 ON.

Switch Setting for LaserJet Series II:

The LaserJet Series II does not have DIP switches but rather a menu that displays on an LCD display on the front panel. All interface settings may be accessed from that menu.

CHAPTER 18
Fonts / Width Table

This chapter is devoted to fonts and width tables. These two work hand-in-hand when using Ventura Publisher. The matrix code of all fonts used inside Ventura Publisher must first exist inside the width tables. The width table determines the complete placement of characters. If the fonts are increased in size, the width table decides how much space is required to develop the proper page format. Without a width table it would be hard for Ventura Publisher to reflect a "What You See Is What You Get" (WYSIWYG) screen page layout. Ventura Publisher is famous for this feature that allows you to see what a page will look like before you print. Also, after editing, the page will reformat without the need to print again. This feature allows you to see what's going to print without losing time printing the document.

Topic Guide

GENERAL

1. *Does Ventura Publisher accept soft fonts, other than those supplied.*

   Ventura Publisher supports additional soft fonts purchased from Xerox, Adobe, or Hewlett Packard that can be added to the system. Fonts obtained from other font vendors in these formats can also be used, provided they adhere strictly to the original standards. Resident fonts are supported on PostScript only. In the 2.0 version, Ventura Publisher supplied a way of downloading HP fonts to the printer with the utility HPDOWN.EXE found on the Utility disk.

2. *What fonts are supplied with Ventura Publisher?*

   The fonts supplied depend on the printer. A list of compatible printers is contained in the Setup and Installation section of the Ventura Publisher Reference Guide.

3. *How many dots per inch do the screen fonts display, and how many dots per inch are printed?*

   A graphics board having 640 x 350 resolution, displayed on a standard PC screen, has an effective resolution of about 75 dots per inch. Printer resolution is determined by the printer being used. For example, 300 dots per inch are printed on laser printers.

4. *What letter do I use when setting switches in font conversions to indicate a light typeface?*

   If you do not have a normal weight in that particular typeface, use "N." Actually you can use any of the four letters ("N," "B," "I," or "T"); just remember which letter you used. The purpose of the letter is to tell Ventura Publisher which weight to indicate as available in the Font dialog box. There is no danger, for example, in setting a switch to bold when the face is actually light.

5. *Explain how fonts are used by the printer?*

   Within a graphic printer (such as a laser printer or typesetter), each character in each font is ultimately drawn as a series of individual dots. The printer creates these dot-by-dot drawings from information contained in font files. Font files are stored on either the computer's hard disk or in the printer's memory, depending on the type of printer you may have. Ventura Publisher works with three different types of printers:

Type 1: Printers that manage font files within the printer (e.g., HP LaserJet Plus or 4045)

Type 2: Printers that let the PC manage the font files (e.g., AST TurboLaser, Cordata, JLaser)

Type 3: Printers that use a page description language to generate font sizes from font outlines (e.g., Apple LaserWriter, IBM 4216, other PostScript printer; Interpress printers.)

6. *How many fonts does Ventura Publisher support per page?*

In version 1.0 the maximum number of fonts per page is 16, in version 1.1 the number is 32. However, a lower limitation may be imposed by the printer itself. For example, the HP LaserJet II can print up to 32 fonts per page, but the HP LaserJet Plus is limited to a maximum of 16 fonts per page.

7. *Sometimes when I'm in text mode and I place my cursor in one spot to insert or delete a character, I find that Ventura Publisher inserts or deletes up to several characters away rather than where I wanted. Why?*

This sounds like you selected an odd-numbered printer font and Ventura Publisher is displaying an even-numbered screen font. If you have added a font of an odd size, for example Roman 17, and do not have a Roman 17 screen font, Ventura Publisher will be forced to show you a Roman 14 screen font. It gets confused when attempting to edit and place the cursor. The best thing to do is change sizes to the same as the screen fonts, do the edits, then return the fonts to the proper size.

COURIER

8. *Does Ventura Publisher support 10-point Courier type?*

As a built-in font, Ventura Publisher supports Courier type only in 12 point, except in PostScript. To support other sizes, additional printer fonts must be added as described in Appendix K of the Reference Guide. Font addition in version 1.0 did not work properly for printers other than PostScript, but generally works in 1.1 for all of the printers described in Appendix K. The only exception is the Xerox 4045. Fonts larger than 14 points are divided into segments, and the Ventura Publisher utility accesses only the first segment of added fonts.

9. *How do I get a non-proportionate font in Ventura Publisher?*

The only non-proportionate font in Ventura Publisher is the Courier font.

10. *Can I use a condensed font in Ventura Publisher? What will the screen look like?*

You can use a condensed font, but Ventura Publisher screen fonts cannot duplicate the appearance of a condensed font. Consequently, Ventura Publisher adjusts the space width between words to compress the text. You will see the correct representation of line endings, paragraph endings, etc. on the screen but the words will appear closer together. The printed output will produce the proper character width and spacing.

11. *How can I print font characters different from those in Ventura Publisher?*

You need to purchase fonts from a font supplier which are designed for your particular printer. You can store these fonts on your computer's hard disk or within the printer's memory, depending on the printer type you may have. Once you have this stored, you can create tables which provide Ventura Publisher with information about each individual character in the new fonts. These created tables are called width tables. In addition, width tables also contain information which configure Ventura Publisher's Font dialog boxes to display the font name and sizes correctly.

ADDITIONAL FONTS

12. *Can I obtain additional fonts for my printer?*

Additional fonts may be obtained from the manufacturer for the HP Laserjet Plus and II, Xerox 4045, and the PostScript printers and compatible. Font conversion utilities come with Ventura Publisher and are explained in Appendix K of the reference manual. You can convert HP fonts to PostScript and Xerox 4045 or 4045 to HP fonts.

13. *I have a JLaser board with a Hewlett Packard LaserJet. Can I purchase additional Hewlett Packard fonts for my printer and use them with the JLaser?*

For version 1.0, no; for version 1.1, 2.0, yes. Appendix K of the Ventura Publisher Reference Guide describes procedures to convert HP soft fonts for use with the JLaser, Cordata, and AST TurboLaser.

FANCY FONTS

14. *I made these fonts from Fancy Fonts and they worked great with version 1.1 Patch 1. But now they show but don't print with version 1.1 Patch 2. Why?*

   This might be a bad install of Patch 2. You didn't delete the Ventura directory. This can cause some unexpected results.

SYMBOL FONTS

15. *How do you make the TM symbol in Ventura Publisher?*

   Hold down the Alt key and press 191 from the number pad. This can't work if you press the number from the numbers over the keyboard. Or, hold down the Ctrl Shift keys and press T.

16. *Why won't the symbol fonts display on my Sigma Design Laserview monitor?*

   Assuming that all screen fonts are in the Ventura directory, there must be some problem in the screen driver provided by Sigma Design. Please check with the vendor for assistance.

ADOBE

17. *What is the telephone number for Adobe Font Library?*

   1-415-961-4400

18. *I purchased downloadable soft fonts from Adobe and followed their instructions to install them into the Ventura Publisher program. When I try to use them, the correct font prints but they are spaced wrong both onscreen and printed. What is wrong?*

   Adobe downloadable fonts come with their own Ventura Publisher width tables. The Adobe instructions tell you to merge the width table for each of their added fonts into the Ventura Publisher width table. In most cases that is not actually necessary, since the Ventura Publisher PostScript width table contains most PostScript typefaces already. When the Ventura Publisher Add/Remove Fonts procedure is used to merge in a PostScript width table for a face that is already there, a duplication occurs. Occasionally when this is done, the Add/Remove Fonts program does not deal with this duplication properly, leading to peculiar results like those mentioned above. The solution, when this happens, is to go back to an original, unmerged copy of the Ventura Publisher width table from your original Ventura Publisher diskettes.

19. *Once Adobe has released their PC version of downloadable fonts, how will I incorporate these into Ventura Publisher?*

Adobe will provide you with the utilities to download the fonts to the printer. They will also provide font metric files which you will convert into Ventura Publisher format using the font conversion utilities described in Appendix K of the reference manual.

20. *How do I get the dingbat character?*

First you need a PostScript printer and the dingbat fonts. You can tag the paragraph or change a single word to dingbat through the text mode by using the Set Font button.

WIDTH TABLE

21. *I tried to create a new width table and wound up with a 0 byte file. Can you tell me why?*

Make sure that all your VFM files were created properly. A 0 byte VFM file could cause a 0 byte width table.

22. *Can Ventura Publisher generate PostScript width tables?*

At the current time there is not a method within Ventura Publisher 1.1 Patch 1 or Patch 2 that will allow you to add PostScript fonts to the Ventura Publisher program unless the font vendor has supplied a Ventura Publisher compatible width table for merging.

23. *What is the OUTPUT.WID file that Ventura Publisher makes when you install.*

The OUTPUT.WID file is developed as the default width table. It is developed for the first printer that was installed when you installed Ventura Publisher.

24. *I created a new width table and have no trouble printing the desired typefaces. The problem is with the screen display. When in the normal view, the text appears as if it is being displayed in the enlarged view. Why?*

Check to see if Times and Helvetica 10 point normal were included in the list file when the width table was generated. Although these typefaces are no longer required to successfully generate a width table, they are still referenced to determine screen scaling information. Their absence may be the cause of the screen distortion.

25. *Can you explain the purpose of the width tables and how they are used?*

Every printer or typesetter has a unique method of creating letters, symbols, and spaces in terms of their height and width. Ventura Publisher has calculated how each device it supports outputs characters and spaces and has incorporated those measurements into reference tables called "width tables." These tables are used to generate the screen and print image for each character and space to deliver a true WYSIWYG relationship between displayed and printed text.

Width tables are created at installation by Ventura Publisher for each print device installed. An additional width table called OUTPUT.WID (containing the values for the first print device installed) is also created as the default width table. Width tables are saved in the style sheet and can be changed through the Option menu, Set Printer Info selection. These width tables can be found in the GEMSYS subdirectory in version 1.0, in the Ventura subdirectory in version 1.1 through 2.0. Select the appropriate width table and return to your document.

26. *What should I do when I get the message, "Do you want to save or abandon the changes you made to this width table by removing fonts?[Save\Abandon]."*

If you remove fonts using the Add/Remove Font option in the Option menu, you should save these changes to create a new width table. Select Abandon if you decide not to make any changes.

27. *How many typefaces can be contained in one width table?*

The maximum number of typefaces in one width table for version 1.0 is eight. For versions 1.1 and 2.0, typefaces are only limited by your system configuration and available memory.

28. *Can fonts be added to Ventura Publisher 1.1 for use with my dot matrix printer?*

Fonts can be added using Bitstream Fontware. The steps are as follows:

    a. Install Fontware for Epson.

    b. Generate the desired fonts and a width table for them using Fontware.

    c. Use Add/Remove Fonts to merge the new width table into a copy of the standard Ventura Publisher Epson width table. The status of the added fonts should be Download, even though Epson fonts are not downloaded in the sense of a laser printer.

d. In Paragraph/Typographic Controls set tracking as necessary to get the character spacing to look right.

BITSTREAM

29. *I just installed Ventura Publisher but now I can't get my fonts from Bitstream to print. Why?*

The problem is the old Bitstream, SFP, and SFL extension files had been deleted when you wiped that directory preparing for the reinstall.

30. *I have Ventura Publisher 2.0 and I'm trying to print with a file downloaded to the printer by the Wordperfect Bitstream Fontware package. Ventura Publisher doesn't seem to operate. Why?*

Ventura Publisher's Font Id number is different than the WordPerfect Fontware package. That makes them incompatible.

HP FONTS

31. *I purchased a new font for my Hewlett Packard LaserJet Plus and used the utilities provided by Ventura Publisher to convert it to Ventura Publisher compatible format. However, when I display or print using the new font, the sizing is not correct. What caused this?*

The utility that converts Hewlett Packard fonts to Ventura Publisher format in version 1.0 was inoperative. This utility has been modified to correct this problem and is available in version 1.1.

32. *I'm attempting to make Ventura Publisher provided fonts for the HP LaserJet Plus into printer resident fonts. Can you help me?*

With Ventura Publisher 1.0 thru 1.1 Patch 1, the fonts that Ventura Publisher provides for this printer could not be made resident. They appear to be hard coded into the driver as download only. New fonts added from other vendors can be made resident in the printer. In 1.1 Patch 2 thru 2.0 Ventura Publisher provides a utility named HPDOWN.EXE.

33. *I need to do HPLTOVFM on the SFL fonts.*

You use HPL to VFM only on portrait fonts; the width table assumes that you have an equivalent landscape font of the same name with the .SFL extension. Using HPLTOVFM.EXE, a batch file is mandatory. A shortcut to get all the SFP files spelled correctly into an ASCII editable file is: DIR *.SFP >FONTFILE.BAT. This results in an ASCII file, with all of the filenames correctly spelled, that can be edited to add the rest of the information necessary to create the VFMs. In your font .BAT file, put the following command on each line:

XPLTOVFM <sp> FONTNAME.SFP /F=typeface /D=## /P=pointsize /W=Weight

The following is the parameter definitions:

/F=15 character maximum, font name you would like to see in the Font Selection menu.

/D the Typeface ID # from 15-255 in four groups. Start with the high number and work backward.

49-15 = Serifed Faces,
99-50 = Sans Serifed Faces,
127-100 = Fixed Pitch Faces (monospaced fonts)
255-128 Strange or Symbol fonts.

/P Pitch of the font, always two characters. (ie: 08, 12, 30, etc.)

/W Weight of the font. N = Normal, B = Bold, I = Italics, T = Thick Italics.

34. *I'm trying to use pre-downloaded fonts (not Ventura Publisher supplied) with my HP LaserJet Series II. I used an HP supplied utility to download the fonts and the printer was acknowledging correctly. The width table I created worked fine as long as I was set to download. Can you help me?*

Four things are necessary to use HP resident fonts.

a. The utility or batch file used must make the fonts resident in printer.

b. The utility or batch file used to download must either invoke or otherwise attach a two-digit number to identify the font in the printer.

c. According to the instructions of Appendix K in the reference manual, the HPLJPLUS.CNF file must be modified to indicate both the font ID number (assigned by the utility or batch file) and the font filename, which must be identical to the one used to create the width table.

d. The width table must be set to RESIDENT for those fonts previously downloaded.

35. *My HP fonts don't convert correctly with switches set to lower case. Why?*

The only thing incorrect was that you had not used capital letters for your switches and, therefore, the VFM files had converted to Dutch 14.

36. *After installing HP fonts, should I delete the VFM files that were developed?*

No.

37. *I'm adding HP Soft fonts from Bitstream with the screen fonts. After merging the width tables, the screen appears to be in reduced view for the fonts that are 14, 16, 18, 24, bold, and bold italic. Why do they appear that way?*

This is a problem that is associated with adding the screen fonts. The way to activate is to delete the INF files.

38. *I'm trying to load fonts as in the manual but I can't find the file HPLTOVFM.EXE. Where is it?*

This EXE file is in the Utility Disk #11, in the HP directory. Copy it to the VENTURA directory, then continue the process.

39. *I typed in HPLTOFNT with no filename specified and a screen display came up with the definition of all the switch settings for converting the fonts. Can you tell me how the /D switch works for creating display fonts?*

The /D switch was placed in the HPLTOFNT utility by Ventura Publisher for their internal use. It is not designed for, nor should it be used to, create screen fonts.

40. *Can LaserJet Plus fonts reside in a directory other than the Ventura directory?*

Not with Ventura Publisher versions 1.1 unpatched and Patch 1. Ventura Publisher will only look in the Ventura directory for LaserJet fonts. However, versions 1.1 Patch 2 and 2.0 allow LaserJet Plus fonts to be stored in any subdirectory.

SCREEN FONTS

41. *My screen fonts and the printer are really not printing the proper space between characters. Why?*

When this occurs you should look at the Option menu Set Printer Info option and make sure that the Quality of the print is showing Ultimate. If it is not Ultimate, the printer device needs to be set to the same compatible width table. If the Quality is set to Draft, the printer will produce poor quality printing.

42. *After installing Ventura Publisher, my documents are printing correctly, but when I look at my screen, the 24-point fonts are showing as 14 points. What could be the problem?*

   If your monitor doesn't have screen fonts as large as 24 points, Ventura Publisher will show you the font closest to, but less than, that size and the width that font will need to make the document appear as it appears on the printed page.

43. *I set my screen font to an incorrect value which caused a "Cannot Load Gem VDI Screen Driver" message. How do I fix it?*

   Reset your screen font to CGA or EGA, erase from the Ventura directory all *.INF files, and reboot.

POSTSCRIPT

44. *Is there any way to set a PostScript font to resident from within Ventura Publisher? Or do you know of a way to make a font resident on the PostScript printer from DOS?*

   Currently there is no way that I know of to do it. One problem is PostScript printers do not have unlimited memory, and making fonts resident takes space.

45. *How do I add and modify font choices?*

   Soft fonts are added to the hard disk by creating a special holding directory and copying the fonts into them. This directory is usually called: C:\PSFONTS. If a different directory is to be used instead to hold PostScript fonts, this can be done by editing the POSTSCPT.CNF file in the VENTURA directory.

   Change the line: PSFONTS(C:\PSFONTS\) to the correct directory.

   The added fonts are made accessible for use by changing the status of each and every added font, one at a time, from Resident to Download. This is done by using the Add/Remove Fonts dialog box.

CAUTION

To avoid permanently modifying an existing width table,
always make a copy of it before carrying out the merge.

46. *Can I add any PostScript fonts to Ventura Publisher? Do they have to be from Adobe?*

The only type of downloadable PostScript fonts which can be incorporated into Ventura Publisher are Adobe fonts, created by Adobe Systems.

47. *I have an Apple Laserwriter printer but I can't seem to get the printer to print all the fonts. I have 32 fonts but only the first 13 seem to print. Why?*

Ventura Publisher is set to print the first 13 fonts as resident for all PostScript printers. Since you have more resident fonts then the normal 13 fonts, you must go into the Option menu and choose the Add Remove Fonts option. Under the Style option you see the word DOWNLOAD or RESIDENT. Clicking on this word will change the word from one to the other. Change all of your resident fonts to resident in this area. Then Ventura Publisher will not search for the fonts in PSFONTS directory.

48. *Does Ventura Publisher provide bit-mapped addressing for PostScript? In other words if a font specified is not found as resident, can it be converted into a bit image and printed as requested?*

No. Ventura Publisher does not provide this capability.

49. *Is there a font size limitation in PostScript?*

In terms of point size, the maximum point size Ventura Publisher can handle is 254. In terms of file sizes, the largest screen font Ventura Publisher can load is 35K. There is no limitation to the size of the fonts Ventura Publisher can download.

50. *I have created some new width tables and my QMS PostScript printer is not always printing. Sometimes it prints and sometimes it appears to lock the printer up. Why?*

Check to make sure that when you created your .LST file, all .VFM files were spelled correctly. Also check to see that the typefaces were entered in the correct order, i.e., Normal, Italic, Bold, and Bold Italic.

51. *I created PostScript fonts using ZSoft Publisher's Font Foundry. This font does not appear in the Ventura Publisher width table. How can I use it?*

The font can be named using one of the fonts in the width table, but character width may not be correct. Currently, you are not able to generate a new width table for fonts. Your font vendor must supply the width table capability and compatibility.

52. *Can you tell me what happens if I use the PostScript width table when printing to a LaserJet Plus?*

Ventura Publisher will compare the font ID's being requested by the width table with those that it has available in the device driver. If the font ID's match, Ventura Publisher will download the appropriate font. If Ventura Publisher doesn't find a match, it will download a default serif or sans-serif font, depending upon the type of font requested. Character spacing will not be the same but line, column, and page endings will be correct.

53. *I have been trying to download PostScript fonts and have been unsuccessful. Can you tell me what I am doing wrong?*

You had done everything correctly according to the manual. Unfortunately, the manual tells you to create a subdirectory called PSFONT in which all PostScript downloadable fonts should reside. According to the POSTSCPT.CNF file, which Ventura Publisher reads to determine where to look for downloadable fonts, the directory it is looking for is called PSFONTS. Since the PSFONTS subdirectory does not exist, all text tagged with a downloadable font will be printed in Courier.

54. *My Zapf Chancery fonts will not display with the PostScript width table loaded when I tag a paragraph with this font. Why not?*

Ventura Publisher provides screen fonts for the basic typefaces (Times, Helvetica, Symbol, and Courier) which are displayed with the standard width table loaded. If additional fonts are added, Ventura Publisher will use the basic screen font which comes closest to matching the font you have selected to display on the screen. The Chancery font will print as desired, but will show on the screen as italics. However, Ventura Publisher versions 1.1 and 2.0 have the option of adding screen fonts to match the printer fonts. If these are added, the proper typeface will be displayed on the screen.

55. *Can I use point sizes in PostScript that include half-point sizes?*

Only in version 2.0.

56. *I'm trying to print to a PostScript printer, but I only see four font typefaces when I try to select a font. Although I have 13 resident fonts in the PostScript printer. Where are the other 9 fonts?*

You may be using the wrong width table. To make sure that you are in the proper width table, go to the Option menu and choose the Set Printer Option menu. This will allow you to see if the Quality is set to Draft or Ultimate. If it is not set to Ultimate, you must change it to Ultimate to see the proper fonts in the width table.

57. *I have a typesetting device that can print over 800 fonts. Can Ventura Publisher support all 800 fonts?*

First of all, there is an issue of compatibility. If the typesetter is a PostScript device, it will be compatible with Ventura Publisher. If it uses some other type of document description language, then it is not compatible. Fonts for PostScript that are not already permanently stored in the printer or typesetter are not handled by version 1.0 of Ventura Publisher. Adobe downloadable fonts for PostScript were not on the market when version 1.0 was released. When these fonts are available, there are utilities within Ventura Publisher to convert these into a Ventura Publisher readable format. You will have to use utilities provided by Adobe with the fonts to download them to the output device. Remember that these font tables occupy space on disk and you should be realistic as to the number of fonts you will actually be using.

INTERPRESS

58. *Will I be able to access the Merganthaler font library when the Ventura Publisher Interpress interface is available?*

At this time, it is not clear what information regarding font size and spacing is available for the Merganthaler library. If they provide font metric information, then it may be possible to incorporate these fonts into Ventura Publisher when the Interpress interface is released.

XEROX 4045 FONTS

59. *Is there support for 4045 resident fonts in Ventura Publisher?*

The following is an explanation of the requirements and possible hazards associated with setting the 4045 width table to resident fonts and pre-downloading necessary fonts from DOS.

The most efficient way is to set up batch files. This file would download two Helvetica portrait fonts. Create a batch file with the following commands:

```
Echo > Lpt1:
Echo
(The first two commands get the printer ready to accept font data)
copy c:\ventura\X45PH06N.XFN > Lpt1:
copy c:\ventura\X45PH08N.XFN > Lpt1:
(The above commands transfer the fonts from the Ventura subdirectory to the
printer)
Echo > Lpt1:
Echo
(These last two lines reset printer and output status sheet to you.)
```

NOTE

Do not try to print this batch file; the printer will respond. This is what happens at the printer when the batch file runs:

a. Printer may kick out a status sheet initially.

b. Printer displays "LF" for loading fonts.

c. Printer kicks out status.

60. *I purchased 4045 fonts on disk from the Xerox Font Center and went through the font conversion procedure. The font prints out garbage with letters scattered erratically all over the page. Why?*

The problem is the way the fonts are listed on the font disk from the Xerox Font Center. The 4045 uses fonts originally developed for the 2700, but the two printers feed paper differently. A font which acts as portrait on the 2700 is landscape on the 4045, and vice versa.

Solution: For use on the 4045, portrait fonts are listed as landscape, and vice versa.

61. *I purchased a downloadable font for my 4045. I looked in the Appendix K at the conversion instructions and I could not find a letter which corresponds with the typeface I purchased. How can I convert this font and use it in Ventura Publisher?*

You can convert this font by selecting another typeface name from the list that is similar to the one you will be converting. When you have completed the conversion and created the new width table, just remember that the typeface name you selected from the list is actually the new typeface that you converted.

62. *What are the error codes associated with 4045 font downloading?*

These codes print out on an error sheet that looks like a short status sheet.

(11) Problem detected within font data—font load abandoned. This will cause default font substitution.

(12) Available font memory exhausted—unloaded or partially loaded fonts will be ignored. This means your batch file contains more fonts than will fit in the printer's memory. Good rule of thumb is to calculate memory requirements from the size of the font file on the hard drive. The file will be a little larger than the actual space required in the printer but this difference will keep you out of trouble.

(40) A font assignment attempted to assign an ID to a font not in storage. Command ignored—default font assigned.

63. *I have created a 4045 width table in version 1.0 and some of my fonts are not printing correctly. Can you help me?*

The font conversion utilities in version 1.0 were faulty for the Xerox 4045. However, a temporary interim version called 1.01 was released which used the same procedures given in the 1.0 manual. If this is what you are using, make sure that you have included Ventura Publisher's original Times 10 point Normal and Helvetica 10 point Normal in your .LST file. Also be sure that you have grouped your fonts by family in ascending point size and in the correct weight order. Assuming that all procedures have been followed correctly, the problem could be in the number of fonts you have in the width table. In version 1.0 Ventura Publisher supported 50 fonts in the LaserJet Plus device driver (28 of which were reserved for Ventura Publisher's resident fonts, leaving you only 22 fonts to be added). The 51st font in the .LST file will not print correctly. Version 1.1 eliminates any practical limitation other than disk space and memory.

64. *I have a Xerox 4045 and when I tried to print bullet text, the bullets did not print correctly, I got a "d" instead of a bullet character. Why doesn't the bullet print?*

Make sure the switches are set correctly on your 4045. If the printer is used by other people, someone could have changed the switch settings to use some other software product. Whenever printing looks strange, it is a good idea to check the switch settings.

65. *I'm attempting to download 4045 fonts to a printer and make use of them in resident mode. Of the two fonts that I was using, I could make the normal font work but the bold font text disappeared from the page. Why?*

Looking at the LST file for the VFMTOWID function showed 4 files;

        X45LGO8N.VFM
        X45PGO8.VFM
        X45PGO8B.VFM
        X45LGO8B.VFM

The VFMTOWID function only requires portrait fonts. In this case the bold font last converted was a landscape, forcing the width table to choose landscape for portrait and vice versa. The reason the normal font worked was the fact that the portrait font overrides the landscape selection. An LST file for this function should only contain portrait fonts.

NOTE

One other possible problem here could have been the fonts themselves were named in reverse order. Xerox uses 2700 fonts for the 4045. Xerox sends the fonts with numbers for names indicating that the lowest number is portrait and the highest is landscape. For the 4045 the reverse is true. The lowest number is landscape and the highest number is portrait.

CHAPTER 19

Patch 1 / Patch 2
and Third Party Utilities

Ventura Publisher has been issuing updates since the first release of the software from Ventura Publisher versions 1.0 to 1.1, 1.1 Patch 1, 1.1 Patch 2 and now 2.0. This chapter will discuss some of the differences between versions and their functions. With the introduction of version 2.0 of Ventura Publisher, it has opened a new horizon of software development. The Base, Professional Extension, and Network versions each have their own unique set of problems and solutions. The most commanding problem is the need for memory, and the software's memory requirements are increasing with each release.

Topic Guide

Topic	Questions	Page
General	1 - 3	177
1.1 Unpatched	4	178
1.1 Patch 1	5	178
1.1 Patch 2	6 - 10	178

GENERAL

1. *How can I check my Ventura Publisher version if I can't open the program?*

   The dates of the VP.APP file located in the Ventura directory are as follows:

   VP.APP 5-13-87 1.1 Unpatched
   VP.APP 7-16-87 1.1 Patch #1
   VP.APP 4-20-88 1.1 Patch #2
   VP.APP 9-11-88 2.0

2. *I have a copy of Ventura Publisher that is not like my friend's copy from Xerox. How do I know if my software is from Xerox or not?*

Xerox Software starts with a Serial Number XRX with 6 digits following. There are earlier versions of Ventura Publisher being marketed by other companies. Page Sys is one, PC Craft is another. So be careful when you are purchasing Ventura Publisher via a mail order source. These are sometimes used to unload outdated software.

3. *When installing the patch, do I answer that I am installing the patch for the first time?*

Yes.

1.1 UNPATCHED

4. *I'm using unpatched 1.1 on my IBM PS/2 Model 30 and I'm getting reverse video, white on black instead of black on white. This is a known bug in unpatched 1.1, which is supposed to be corrected by Patch 1. However, I installed Patch 1 and still get the same reverse video problem. Why?*

This problem pertains to Color screens selected in the Frame menu Background option for the PS/2 Model 30. The fix was corrected in the 3½" disk set, but was not correct on the 5¼" disks. This has been corrected in Patch 2.

1.1 PATCH 1

5. *Will chapters developed in 1.1 Patch 1 be usable in Patch 2?*

Yes, Patch 2 is completely compatible.

1.1 PATCH 2

6. *I've just installed Ventura Publisher's Patch 2. The computer gets to the "APP" screen and then locks. Why?*

The first thing you need to do is check the internal memory. Ventura Publisher is a real memory hog and needs much more than most applications. Do a CHKDSK and get the bytes free up to 570K bytes.

7. *I have just loaded the Patch 2 software and the spacing between words has changed. There is a lot more space between the words now than before.*

This is a symptom of a feature that did not work in the 1.1 unpatched version of Ventura Publisher that was fixed in the Patch 1 that you installed. This feature is in the Typographic Control; Normal Space Width option. If this setting was changed in the unpatched version it would be ignored. If that setting was still present after Patch 1 was installed, the patch will honor the settings.

8. *I can't get the Patch 2 program to write to my original Ventura Publisher diskettes.*

You can't patch the original diskettes from Ventura Publisher. They are write protected diskettes. You need to get regular 360K bytes diskettes and make disk copies of all originals.

9. *After installing Patch 2 I'm getting funny looking fonts on the screen. Everytime I print I get a message that the "Gem VDI file Cannot be found." What is going on?*

Check your screen fonts. If they have been altered, this will cause this message to display on the screen. Also check the Set Printer dialog box in Ventura Publisher to see if the screen fonts match your monitor's resolution. Example: EGA monitor = EGA VGA monitor = VGA.

10. *Can the Patch 2 understand extended ASCII?*

Yes. Ventura Publisher with Patch 2 installed can load extended ASCII characters. Only one drawback, Ventura Publisher decided that since Ventura Publisher has its own drawing tools, it will not load ASCII codes that produce line images.

CHAPTER 20

Page Layout Tips

This chapter deals with page layout tips, tricks, and pitfalls. Due to Ventura Publisher's versatility, there are often several different ways to accomplish the same results.

This is one of the major selling points of the program. The most important page layout tip is to think about how you want the document to look before you begin entering text in your word processor. So when it's time to bring the text into Ventura Publisher, the text should be in the proper format for the way you want your page to look. For example, think about how you want to use "Returns" in your text: at the end of each sentence or at the end of a paragraph, etc. Your decisions before entering text will affect your page layout and could save you time in Ventura Publisher during the page layout development stage. If you start a project and decide that the page layout is not working for you, it becomes very time-consuming to reorganize the text file or the chapter. I hope this chapter will help you avoid these pitfalls by giving you possible methods and suggestions.

Topic Guide

Topic	Questions	Page
General	1 - 3	182
Tips	4 - 11	183
Frames	12 - 14	184
Continue on Next Page	15	185
Outline	16	185
Change Caption Font	17	185
Keep Together Text	18 - 19	185
Spaces Disappearing	20	186
Bullet Character	21	186
Printing	22	186

Topic Guide (Cont.)

GENERAL

1. *I'm getting this number in my form that I don't want and when I try to erase it, Ventura Publisher tells me that it can't erase a generated text. Why?*

   You were using a Ventura Publisher style sheet that had an auto-numbering tag installed that generates an index number for all paragraphs that have that name. To correct the problem, you can simply turn off the auto-number feature in the Page menu (1.1) or Chapter menu (2.0).

2. *I was working on a complex table which grew to be fairly large. As I was editing the table, Ventura Publisher started to refresh the screen after each keystroke. Why?*

   This is sometimes caused by column balance being turned on for the frame. Go to the Chapter Typography menu and/or the Frame Typographic menu. Turn the Column Balance OFF for the frame containing the problem. The Chapter Typography menu serves as a central override for this setting and will disable the Column Balance for the entire chapter. The Frame Typographic menu controls the settings for the selected frame.

3. *Will it be possible for a user to extract footnote, index references, 1st match, etc., from frames other than the underlying page?*

   Only index references can be extracted from other frames.

TIPS

4. *How do I move around Ventura Publisher faster when I'm reading, tagging, and editing?*

   There is a great shortcut when editing text and tagging the information. In Text mode Ventura Publisher will go to where the cursor is when going from reduced view to normal. Go to reduced view, then put text cursor at the position where you want to work. Return to normal view and Ventura Publisher will go to text cursor. This can be done with the keyboard shortcut or the mouse. The keyboard shortcut is much faster.

5. *How do I move text toward the center of the page; everything is too far to the left?*

   Under the Frame pull down menu, the line selection for margins and columns allows you to set margins for top, bottom, left, and right. Select this line item and adjust the left margin by increasing the value of the space from the side of the page. Selected text may be moved by adjusting the In From Left attributes in the Spacing options under the Paragraph pull down menu.

6. *How can I create a numeric list with the numbers aligned by the decimal point?*

   First create two tags, one for the numbers and one for the text. Set the text tag for In from Left spacing about one inch. Set the line break for this tag to come after the text. Set the tag for the number to In from Left at zero. Now set a second tag. The tag should be decimal and positioned at one-half inch. This should provide the desired effect. The In from Left spacing can be adjusted for either tag to fine-tune the relationship between the numbers and the text.

7. *I would like to move a heading from the bottom of page one to the top of page two. What is the best way to do this?*

   Under the Paragraph menu Breaks, there is a selection that allows you to determine when a page break will occur. By selecting Before for a tag, a page break will be inserted before the tag each time it occurs.

NOTE

If the tag is used many times throughout the document and you want to use this effect selectively, it would be advisable to create a new tag first; otherwise page breaks will occur everytime the tag appears. Use the same attributes as the original tag, only modify the new tag with the page break turned on. The retagged heading should start on a new page.

8. *Can you put a superscript and subscript code in the text with your word processor?*

Yes, those codes are <^> superscript and <v> subscript. After you have finished what you would like subscripted or superscripted, you must place a <D> to change the rest of the text back to normal.

9. *I would like to put the same text file on the same page; can that be done?*

Yes, just load the text file twice using the load text picture, and load the different files into the frames.

10. *Right now I can't get the pages on the right to mirror the left. Can you help me?*

Go to the Page / Chapter menu and select Page Layout Copy to Facing Page option. This will make the right page mirror the left.

11. *How do I get Ventura Publisher to set all the paragraphs in my chapter to the same format without clicking on each one? There's more than 100 paragraphs.*

There is no feature that Ventura Publisher has to accomplish this.

Frames

12. *My page has two text files in two frames but the text doesn't line up. What is the problem?*

When you have two files as columns of text on one page, their paragraph tags must have their interline space set to have the same devisable number. This setting is made in the Paragraph menu, Spacing option.

13. *I'm trying to hide a frame within another frame. It looks great on the screen but it still prints as if I didn't hide it at all. Why?*

This will depend on the printer that you're using. If you are using an HP LaserJet printer, this will not work, because HP printers look at the information and print it in layers. An HP printer prints everything it sees with limitations. If you are printing on a PostScript printer, the printer is under the control of a program language. The language will omit the commands that you do not print.

14. *How do I display a frame without the selection borders?*

When using any function other than paragraph tagging, a light textured border is displayed around each picture. This border is used to illustrate the placement of the frame and will not be printed. Select the Paragraph Tagging function to display the frames without these selection borders. To add borders that will print, use the Ruling Lines options in the Frame menu, as described in the menu commands chapter.

Continue on Next Page

15. *How do I put a continue on next page message on the end of a page or frame?*

This is what the captions are for when at the end of frame. Activate a Frame, go in to the Frame menu, and click on Anchors and Captions. Type "Continue on next page" on the caption line. After clicking on the OK, the page will display with the caption attached to the active frame with your caption inside.

Outline

16. *Can I number an outline or chapter mixing the types of identifiers I use for the line numbers? Example:*

    1 First Choice
        1.A Second Choice
            1.A.1 Third Choice
                1.A.1.a Fourth Choice

Yes, use the Auto-Numbering selection in the Page menu. The dialog box will appear and the cursor will be at level 1. To recreate the example above, select [1,2] as the first level numbering template. Ventura Publisher will insert [*tag name,1] on the level 1 line. Change the tag name to reflect the name of the tag that you are using for the first level of your outline. Placing a period after the right bracket will separate subsequent level identifiers. Now move the cursor to level 2 and select the identifier for level 2. In the example above, [A,B] was selected. Ventura Publisher inserts [*tag name, A] on the level 2 line. Change the tag name to reflect the second level of the outline. You can identify up to eight levels, each with a different numbering template.

Change Caption Font

17. *How do I make a caption font larger or smaller?*

Captions are the same as any other framed text; they can be changed in the Paragraph mode or by separate words using the Text Set Fonts mode.

Keep Together Text

18. *I have two words that I would like to keep together regardless of where they appear on the page. How can I do this?*

Instead of a normal space between the words, use a non-breaking space (Ctrl Spacebar). This will supercede hyphenation and keep the two words from being separated by a line ending, column ending, or page ending.

19. *Can you tell me how to embed a required (non-breaking) hyphen between two words?*

First, you enter a fixed space between the word, phone number, or whatever needs the required hyphen. Then you add an overstrike character to the required space. The required spaces keep the characters or numbers together and the overstrike prints out to make the hyphen.

Spaces Disappearing

20. *I add space to set something off or indent and when I load it into Ventura Publisher, all of the spaces are gone. What happened?*

Ventura Publisher is seeing this as unused space and is stripping it away. To put spaces inside a line, you must put in a "control space" by holding down the Ctrl key and pressing the Spacebar. This is also referred to as a non-breaking space.

Bullet Character

21. *My bullet character is showing too big; how do I make it smaller?*

This depends on how the bullet was made. If it was created from the Paragraph Special Effects menu, choose the Set Font Properties and change the size of the font. If it was done with the Alt 195 keystroke, you must highlight the bullet in text mode and then choose the Set Fonts button and change the font size.

Printing

22. *Can I print landscape mode on specified pages only?*

Ventura Publisher prints in both portrait (vertical) and landscape (horizontal) orientations. The orientation is constant for any given chapter. To change to a different orientation for several pages, simply format those pages as a separate chapter. Chapters can automatically be combined together into one document and printed as a unit.

LAYOUT

23. *I would like to create a document with titles for each paragraph appearing to the left of the paragraph. I would also like to have a larger typeface for the titles, but I want the top of the titles and the top of the main text to align with each other. How can I do this?*

Placing the titles on the same line as the text is accomplished by establishing two tags, one for the title and one for the text. These two tags will also enable you to establish two typefaces, one for the title and one for the text. The title tag should be set for the appropriate font size. The title tag should have the following modifications to spacing and break attributes; spacing should be In From Left enough to allow the titles to appear as if in their own column. Line break should be set for After the text, instead of the same line. The title and text will not align horizontally along the top because of the difference in type sizes.

24. *Is there an easy way to create a form with multiple graphic lines that will be used for fill-in-the-blank entries?*

If all the lines will be the same length, you can use the Copy Graphic feature of Ventura Publisher to make multiple copies of the line. First, draw the line using the Ventura Publisher graphics capability. Once the line has been drawn to the proper length and you have released the mouse button, hold down the Shift key and press the Delete key. This creates a copy of the original graphic. Press the Ins key, which will place another copy of the graphic directly over the original. Select the new graphic by placing the mouse cursor over the graphic and pressing the left mouse button. This selects the new graphic and it can now be moved by holding down the left mouse button and dragging the graphic until it appears in the proper position on the screen. Release the mouse button and the graphic has been placed. Pressing the Ins key again will create another copy of the graphic which can be repositioned, and so on.

25. *I'm trying to create a hairline rule one-half inch in from the edge of the page all the way around the page. What is the easiest way to do this?*

Select the Underlying Page frame and in the Frame menu select Ruling Box Around. Select FRAME for the width of rule, enter .5 inches for the Space Above Rule One. Enter .005 for the height of Rule One. This should produce the desired effect. The possible print field for some printers may not quite reach to within .5 inches of the edge of the page and this effect may not print.

26. *I want to print text in a frame with shading over it. I overlaid a shaded frame and graphic with shading set to transparent but the text doesn't show. What's wrong?*

PostScript builds graphics in layers. It does not allow material on one layer to show through a shaded layer above it, even if the shading attributes are set to transparent. To obtain the desired result, keep track of the order of the layers you are creating. This can be accomplished as follows:

    a. Create a frame to which graphics can be attached. Make sure it is selected before going into Graphics mode.

    b. In Graphics mode, create the desired shaded, round-cornered rectangle.

    c. Now create a Box Text box that overlays the shaded graphic in the position desired. Set line attributes to None so that the line around the Box Text box doesn't show. Set fill attributes to Hollow and Transparent. It doesn't seem to matter whether it is set to White or Black. Since the Box Text box is the last graphic created, it is on top, and the text will show.

27. *How do you develop a blank document template?*

Different issues of a newsletter or newspaper often use the same layout. Rather than spend the time to place frames in the same place on the same pages for each new issue, you can create and save a complete chapter for your first issue. Then use the Remove File option in the Edit menu to remove each file in the Assignment List from your chapter. For instance, select the first frame on the first page and then select Remove File in the Edit menu. Next, select the Remove from: List of Files option. The file is removed from each frame in the chapter, but the frames, and all the frame settings, remain. After all files have been removed in this way, use the Save As option to save the chapter under a new name. For the next issue, all you need to do is retrieve this blank chapter, load the appropriate text and picture files, place these files in the frames that are already in the chapter, save the chapter under a new name, and then print.

Add in Above

28. *Add in Above in the Paragraph / Spacing dialog box doesn't always work when I'm not at the top of column. Why?*

This function works only when the Paragraph / Alignment dialog box is set for Framewide.

Flow Text

29. *My text will not flow into a page with three columns. The text is not recognizing the column guides. Why?*

The Paragraph menu under the Alignment option is used to override column settings and make a paragraph print across the entire frame. The option is named Overall Width. It can be set to Column Wide or Frame Width. Change the Tags Alignment option to Column Wide and load the text again. This will fix your problem.

Little Bullet

30. *How do I get a little bullet about the same as a period but not on the baseline?*

    Go into Paragraph mode. Select [Special Effects], select [Bullet], and select [Other]. Then type in at [Bullet Char] "183." This will put a period in the place of the bullet. If the bullet needs to be moved up or down, highlight the bullet character with the text cursor, click on command: Set Font Properties in your side panel (side bar), and shift the text up or down using the shift feature found there.

Portrait and Landscape

31. *Can I get portrait and landscape text on the same page?*

    Yes and no, depending on which version of Ventura Publisher you're using. Only version 1.1 Patch 2 will not allow you to do this operation. The command is located in the Alignment menu Text Rotation. In version 1.1 unpatched and Patch 1 it can be done by developing a landscape file with a PostScript driver that can be printed to disk. This file can be loaded into Ventura Publisher as a PostScript file using the Load Text Picture option into a Portrait file and printed. This will give you the file with text rotated as if a graphic. In version 2.0 the operation is now a feature that is supported inside the software.

Newspaper

32. *How do I get my frames to appear the same way as the Fifth Mode newsletter that Xerox sends out?*

    There are a number of ways to get this effect. The best is to draw a frame under or over the area to display the line, then put a ruling line below and above the frame. This will give the effect that you want.

33. *How does a newspaper layout work?*

    Newspapers and newsletters combine a variety of different typographic styles, column widths, and margins. This type of complete layout can easily be generated by placing text into frames. To compose a newspaper layout, first set up the number of columns desired. Use the Margin & Column setting to provide column guides to which frames can be snapped. Activate Show Column Guides if necessary to show these guides on the screen. Use the Frame Setting function to place frames wherever you want text to appear. Then flow text or pictures into each frame by first selecting the frame, then selecting the filename in the Assignment List. The frame can be made larger or smaller to increase or decrease the amount of text it contains.

To continue a text file from a previous frame into a new frame (the new frame can be placed on the current or any succeeding page), select the new frame, and then select the text filename in the Assignment List. The text continues from the first frame. This process can continue with as many frames as you wish, on different pages, until all text from the file is placed in the chapter. Once text is placed in a frame, it can be tagged in exactly the same manner as text placed in the underlying page. All tag spacing is measured from the edge of the frame, not the edge of the page.

Copy-fitting

34. *What is copy-fitting?*

Copy-fitting is the process of making the copy (text) fit a given space. Ventura Publisher provides a tool that can be used individually or together to solve copy-fitting problems. These tools and their applications are described below:

a. Text Editing. The traditional way, and still the best, to get copy to fit a given space is to add and delete text. Ventura Publisher's Text Editing function gives you a word processor that not only lets you add and delete text, but lets you see how the page will look when it is printed.

b. Frame Size. If a frame has been placed on the page, its size can be increased or decreased. As its size is changed, more or less text is placed in the underlying page and text is pushed or pulled from the next page as needed. If Line Snap is turned on, you can easily control the number of lines of text in the underlying page that are pushed or pulled to and from the next column or page.

COLORS

35. *How does color separations work?*

In version 1.1 the color separation process requires a separate page for each primary color. Through the use of style sheets, Ventura Publisher can automatically produce a separate black and white document for each color to be printed. For example, suppose you want to print all paragraphs tagged as a HEADING in blue, and print all paragraphs tagged as a SUBHEADING in red. To do this, Set the font attribute to WHITE for every tag except HEADING. Leave this tag black. Save as a new style sheet called BLUE. Next, set the font attributes to WHITE for every tag except SUBHEADING. Leave this tag black. Save as a new style sheet called RED. Finally, set HEADING and SUBHEADING to WHITE and every other tag to BLACK. Save this style sheet as BLACK. To print separations for any chapter formatted with the original style sheet, you need only load the BLUE style sheet, then print the chapter; load the RED style sheet, then print the chapter; and finally load the BLACK style sheet, and then print the chapter. In version 2.0, use Define Colors in the Paragraph menu and enable all colors not desired. There must be two colors active to print color separation. After this is finished, tag the text with the desired color in font option. Pull down the To Print menu and choose the Spot Color Overlay to ON. Ventura Publisher will then produce the desired effect by printing a different color for each page.

36. *I'm trying to print on film for color stripping using a Linotronic 300. I need to set some portions of my text to black on a black solid background so they would disappear. The actual text to be printed would be white on a black background.*

Ventura Publisher will allow text stripping only as a function of printing white text on a white background. Funny, but Header, Footer, and Graphic Caption text will disappear when the background is set to black; box and Frame text will not. The following batch files cause the printout to reverse video at the printer. Hidden text must be set to white on white. Normal text will appear at the printer as white on black. Two batch files are needed, one to turn on reverse video, and one to turn the effect off.

Batch files required to reverse video at printer:

```
Rev-On.ps
Serverdict begin 0 exitserver <R>
Statusdict begin<R>
True set default mirror print<R>
True set default negative print<R>
End
```

Batch File Required to Return to Normal at Printer:

```
Rev-Off.ps
Serverdict begin 0 exitserver<R>
Statusdict begin<R>
False setdefaultmirrorprint<R>
False setdefaultnegativeprint<R>
End
```

Steps Necessary to Print Stripped File On Linotronic 300:

Print Ventura Publisher document to disk file (filename.c00).
Exit Ventura Publisher.
Copy correct batch file to printer ie:
COPY REV-ON.PS COM(n):(where n = number) or
COPY REV-ON.PS LPT,(n):
Copy Ventura Publisher Print to Disk file to printer.
Then copy REV-OFF.PS to turn the effect off.

Ventura Release 2.0 Enhancements and Bugs

There are three different software packages available for the version 2.0 release—Base, Professional Extension, and Network. Each package has different memory requirements, all of which are more rigid than the 1.1 version. This means the configuration of your computer for 1.1 will probably not work for 2.0. For example, if you had space with Ventura Publisher 1.1 to run a network in the background for printing, this may not be true with 2.0.

The memory requirements for Ventura Publisher products with CGA or EGA color monitors are as follows:

Version	Memory	Expanded Memory	Monitor
Base	580k	0K	CGA / EGA 2 colors
Prof. Extension	560k	512K	CGA / EGA 2 colors
Network	500k	500K	CGA / EGA 2 colors
Base	585k	0K	VGA / EGA 16 colors
Prof. Extension	565k	512K	VGA / EGA 16 colors
Network	515k	500K	VGA / EGA 16 colors

NOTE
All numbers are + or − 5K

To be safe, don't install Ventura Publisher 2.0 unless you have kept your old version, and back up your chapter files before you install 2.0. This is important because once a chapter file has been loaded into 2.0 and saved, the 1.0 and 1.1 versions can't load the 2.0 chapter files or style sheet.

Version 2.0 may attempt to outthink you, especially when saving files or using the "Save As" option. Ventura Publisher 2.0 will save an untitled chapter in the same directory as the first text file you imported. For example, suppose you load a WordPerfect text file from the WordPerfect directory and you select "Save." Ventura Publisher 2.0 automatically names the chapter the same name as the text file and places the chapter file and utility files in the WordPerfect directory. In earlier versions the item selector appeared allowing the choice of where files would be located. As a user of the earlier versions of Ventura Publisher, I've found it very hard to remember where my files are located using 2.0. So I avoid using Ctrl-S when first saving an untitled chapter.

The "Save As" feature has been changed in version 2.0 so that it makes duplicates of the text files for different chapters instead of using the same text file over again. This can use up a lot of disk space with files that you didn't know would be there. Think about getting a WHEREIS.COM program, or find a program that will tell you where you have files that have the same names in different directories.

Another problem with 2.0 is that it uses a different subscript and superscript algorithm. This causes files to translate incorrectly if they have a lot of subscripts or superscripts. For example, the code "<^>1/<v>2<D>" in 1.1 will produce a "½" with the one over the two. Version 2.0 may not give you the same layout. I would avoid importing into Ventura Publisher 2.0 files that have this sort of information imbedded.

When installing 2.0, Ventura Publisher asks if you would like to "install the example chapter files?" If you say "No," Ventura Publisher will not copy the example files to the TYPESET directory. You may not need them, but I do suggest you copy the CHARSET.CHP and CAPABILI.CHP to your C:\TYPESET directory. These chapters are needed to determine if your printer can print rotated text and other Ventura Publisher special text.

Desk File Edit View Chapter Frame Paragraph Graphic Options

Xerox Desktop Publishing Series:
Ventura Publisher Edition

Standard, EMS-(SYS=0 kb, APP=0 kb)
Non-Network

Version 2.0 - (08/23/88)
Serial XBD-011184

Ventura
Software, Inc.

Don Heiskell
Lee Jay Lorenzen
John Grant
John Meyer

© Copyright Ventura Software, Inc., 1986-1988

OK

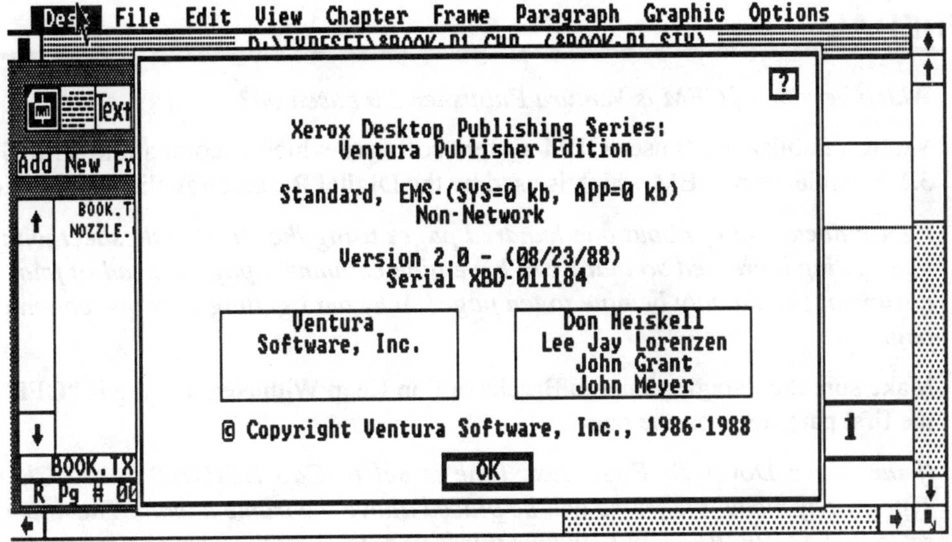

Topic Guide

GENERAL

1. *Which version of GEM is Ventura Publisher 2.0 based on?*

   Ventura Publisher 2.0 uses GEM system software which is compatible with GEM 3.1 (the release of GEM which is used by the Digital Research Artline application).

2. *I get a document of about one hundred pages using the Tabl2 style sheet with the tags setting increased so that I can have nine columns a page instead of four. The document should only be nine to ten pages. Why am I getting only one column per page?*

   Make sure the Paragraph menu Breaks option Keep With Next setting is "OFF" for the first paragraph on the page.

3. *If the Move Down To First Base Line is set to Cap HEIGHT in the Chapter Typography menu, the frame will be placed above the frame anchor. The anchor is set to RELATIVE, BELOW. Can I get this feature to place the frame below the frames anchor?*

   The feature Relative, Below Anchor Line in both 2.0 Base and Professional Extension works fine with "Move Down To 1st Baseline" by Cap HEIGHT. After inserting the frame anchor through Insert Special Item, you must select RE-ANCHOR FRAMES after naming the frame anchor.

Help Menus

4. *Can the help menus be optional or removed to give me more memory?*

   No.

OVERFLOW.MEM

5. *What is the file titled OVERFLOW.MEM which I found in my VENTURA directory?*

   This file is created in the Ventura subdirectory when working with large text files. Ventura Publisher reads in about six pages at a time and uses this file to swap out the text. This file is automatically deleted when no longer needed by Ventura Publisher. However, if any problem is encountered when working in the chapter, the file may be left in the Ventura subdirectory. The file is usually 0 bytes and can be deleted. If this file is present, you should also run CHKDSK, and you may find lost clusters.

Tag Attributes Lost at Page Break

6. *Why are tag attributes lost at a page break? For example, a Frame-Wide reverts to Column-Wide if the paragraph breaks across a page boundary. Also, In From Left spacing will be lost if the paragraph breaks across a page.*

These are bugs in 2.0. Because the problems occur in the underlying page, modifications may result in other problems.

Ruling Lines Shifting Upward

7. *My Xerox 4045 is shifting my ruling lines upward, making my document look different on paper than it looks on screen when printing in landscape mode.*

This is a bug in 2.0. If you upgraded to 2.0 you are in luck — you can replace the 2.0 driver with the old 1.1 driver. If you are just buying Ventura Publisher 2.0 for the first time, you can write to the software manufacturer to get a copy of the old 1.1 driver.

Decimal Tabs Not Aligning

8. *I am working on a document with decimal tabs and I have been unable to align the decimal points. For example, 489.357, jkl.sdf, wse.478 will all align properly, but 4c7.375 will not. In other words, if my string to the left of the decimal contains both alpha and numeric characters, it will not align with entries that have all alpha or all numeric characters to the left of the string. Is there a way that I can keep the decimal points aligned? For example:*

```
489.357
jkl.sdf
wse.478
 4c7.375
```

This is a software bug. In my experiments it was found that if a combination of alpha and numeric characters exist on the line and the alpha character is within three characters from the decimal point, the alignment was displaced.

HPDOWN.EXE Causing Page Ejects

9. *When HPDOWN.EXE is run to pre-download fonts, the printer ejects a page each time. Why?*

Check for a printer buffer. If one is installed then disable it. This should fix the problem.

CGM Conversion

10. *I'm using a conversion program called VPCGM.EXE to import Arts and Letters in the CGM file format. Version 1.1 loaded the file just fine, but the file is in reverse video when imported into 2.0. Why?*

CGM converter has been fixed in Ventura Publisher 2.0. You no longer require the VPCGM.EXE conversion program. Just bring the file directly into Ventura Publisher 2.0.

5¼" vs 3½" Disks

11. *I have 2.0 Base 5¼" and I just received Ventura Publisher Professional Extension on 3½" disk. Are these disks compatible? I can't seem to get Ventura Publisher Professional Extension installed.*

Ventura Publisher 2.0 Base and Professional Extension must be installed using the same size diskettes.

MEMORY

12. *Can you explain Professional Extension (PE), Network Base and Network Professional Extension memory architecture?*

As far as Expanded Memory (EMS) use, they are the same. EMS is first allocated for use by GEM.EMS if it exists. All the remaining EMS is allocated for use as an extended document area. You might think of this as a very fast disk paging area.

13. *I have Professional Extension with 572K bytes free using ASTEMM.SYS with 2.0Mb of EMS. Ventura Publisher loads with the EDCO dictionary. However, I looked at the diagnostic box and it says "Sys=1712,App=O" and "EMS in Use=0/0." Why is the system taking all of the EMS?*

The EDCO dictionary should take about 1.2 Mb of EMS, which will show up as system EMS. GEM.EMS will take an additional amount of memory; make sure that there is nothing else loaded into EMS (such as a disk cache or RAM disk). Professional Extension requires a minimum of 256K bytes of EMS available before it will even try to use it.

14. *While loading Professional Extension from Windows, the message "Not Enough Extended Memory" is appearing. Any explanations?*

    I would suggest that you either add some memory to your system or examine the .PIF file (using PIFEDIT) to determine whether the amount of memory which is indicated to be required can be lowered.

15. *Ventura Publisher 2.0 is supposedly written around LIM 3.2; however, no EMS driver below LIM 4.0 is supposed to be able to execute a file from expanded memory. This conflicts with Ventura Publisher's information.*

    Not just any executable code can be run in LIM 3.2 EMS. However, if sufficient care is taken with respect to what tasks the code performs while executing, it may run in LIM 3.2 EMS.

16. *Explain exactly how 2.0 Base is using expanded memory. Is there any way to make 2.0 Base use more expanded memory? How much conventional memory is actually saved when using EMS with 2.0 Base?*

    The only portion of 2.0 Base which uses expanded memory is GEM.EMS. This is a subset of the GEM system services which has been re-written by Ventura Software to be executable from EMS. Using GEM.EMS results in a saving of 31K bytes (31,744 bytes) of conventional memory. Note that GEM.EMS will result in the same savings when used with Professional Extension. There is no other way to make 2.0 Base use more expanded memory.

17. *I'm getting an "out of memory" message trying to load Ventura Publisher 2.0, yet I have plenty of RAM available, looking at CHKDSK. What's happening?*

    In this case the user's VP.BAT file showed /0=D: but there was no RAM disk configured. Taking the /0=D: out will fix the problem. Similarly, if a RAM disk is configured but the syntax is incorrect (for example, the colon is left off, as in /0=D), the same message will appear.

18. *If my driver is Intel compatible does it make it compatible with Ventura Publisher?*

    Yes, but with 286-class machines, limulators that place the 64K page frame into conventional memory do not truly emulate the LIM 3.2 or LIM 4.0 specification and will not allow Ventura Publisher to run.

COLOR

19. *When color separations are printed, each color prints as a solid black color. However, in 2.0 a color can be set to be a certain percentage of color (for example, 50%) to produce a tint. Why doesn't Ventura Publisher produce a 50% dot pattern when a color is set to 50% instead of solid black?*

   A 50% tint of a specific color is a different color, not a tint. It appears as a solid color on a separate page because it really is a separate color. Keep in mind that Ventura Publisher outputs color separations with every color on a separate page.

20. *Why are the colors in COLUMBIA.GEM turned off?*

   Because the color version looked bad when printed to a PostScript printer with Ventura Publisher 2.0. The colors appeared as dotted lines. However, the colors can all be set to black in the Define Colors dialog box.

NETWORK

21. *Does Ventura Publisher work on a network?*

   Yes. Ventura Publisher 2.0 Network is currently network compatible.

22. *Will Ventura Publisher recognize the NETPRINT.INF file in a subdirectory other than VENTURA?*

   No.

23. *My Network version of Ventura Publisher 2.0 will not load. I get a message that says it can't open a seat because someone is on it. I know there is no one on the network. What does it mean?*

   There is a file on the network that holds information such as who is on the network, on which seat, etc. This file must have a timeout factor. If you log out all the seats off the network for 5 to 10 minutes, the message should clear. If this does not happen, then you need to reinstall.

24. *My network version is getting a file handler error. Why?*

   Check to see if there is a typo in the VP.BAT file or a space that is not required.

25. *What does the error message, "Not Enough DOS File Handlers" mean when loading the Network version of Ventura Publisher?*

    If you have added additional workstations by copying the VPNET.BAT and/or VPPROF.BAT files, you must also update the "/I" parameter in the VPNET.BAT and VPPROF.BAT file(s) with the proper "<drive><subdir>." If this is not done properly, the error message will appear. The installation program will insert a statement "/I=<drive><subdir>" in the VPNET.BAT or VPPROF.BAT file. Make sure you are using the above method. This will prevent this message.

26. *I'm running a 3-Com Network emulation program named Starlan. Why is Ventura Publisher unable to load with it?*

    You must have Starlan 3.1 or higher. Check your version of the software.

27. *How do I get Ventura Publisher Network to load in 488K bytes running on a TOPS network?*

    You need a memory manager that will borrow your expanded memory to be used by conventional memory similar to Microsoft HIMEM.SYS.

28. *On the Network Base version, are the text files stored in expanded memory?*

    Yes. The Network Base version should be viewed as a Base product with Network features and EMS support.

29. *Can Ventura Publisher use a printer on a server other than the one that Ventura Publisher is installed on by using NETPRINT.INF?*

    No. This would require a friendly network environment and a loadable network module for that environment.

30. *If network users use the /O switch, will a local cache or RAM disk improve performance?*

    If a network user has EMS available, it is better used by Ventura Publisher as an extended document area, rather than as a local cache or overflow RAM disk with the /O switch. However, if the additional RAM must be used as extended memory instead of expanded, setting the /O switch will help if you work with documents which result in the overflow file being used. On non-network systems with extended memory only. Ventura Publisher prefers using the RAM as a disk cache to speed the Ventura Publisher overlay loading.

31. *What happens if two network users modify the same style sheet?*

The first person to save the style sheet will operate normally. When the second person saves the style sheet, analysis by Ventura Publisher of the style sheet file's date and time stamp will reveal that the file has been changed. At that point, an alert will be displayed which indicates that the style sheet has already been changed. You will be given the choice of abandoning the modifications, overwriting the existing file, or writing to a new style sheet file.

IPX.COM

32. *Where is the IPX.COM file located?*

IPX.COM is a file provided by Novell with the Netware software. It is located on the network server.

Novell Network

33. *What are the requirements for setting up the network to print Ventura Publisher over the Novell network?*

Printing over most any network involves asking the network to take over control of one of the printer ports. In most cases this will be Lpt1:. Usually this is handled by a batch file. The commands for Novell are as follows:

```
SPOOL (flags)
SPOOL S=name p=n L=n C=n B=(ascii) F=n
C=dr:\dir\filename T=n TI=n FF/NFF Disable/Enable show
```

The values for the Command Flags are as follows:

```
*=Ventura Publisher Needed
Command Flags Short Flag Data
* Server: S= Server_Name
* Printer P= Number 0 through 4 (LPT1 to COM2 of Server)
* Local= L= Number 1, 2, or 3 (LPT1 to LPT3 of local printer)
Copies C= Number 0 through 255
Forms F= Number (Identifies Form Alignment)
Create C= Dr:\directory\filename (Spool Filename)
Banner B= ASCII String (12 Characters)
"No Banner NB" Turns off Banner Output Sheet
Tabs T= Number (Spaces for ^I tabs)
No Tabs = NT Suppress Tab Spacing
* Timeout TI= Number of Seconds before File is Sent
No Form Feed: NFF= Suppress Form Feed at End of Job
```

Form Feed; FF= Send Form Feed at End of Job
Disable: D= Disable Spooling
Enable: E= ReEnable Spooling after Disable
Show: Show= Show Spool Settings on Screen

NOTE

The TI=120 (Seconds) should be sufficient time for Ventura
Publisher to format the document and go from initial access
of the port to placing data into the file. If this time is too short,
you will get blank pages ahead of or partial printouts of your
file.

34. *I'm running Ventura Publisher on a Novell network. When I try to access a file that
is currently being used by another user, I get an error message, "Output Device Not
Receiving Data." Why?*

When Ventura Publisher starts running on networks, one of the major headaches
will be two users trying to access the same style sheet or graphics file. The amount
of error trapping the network can do to prevent this is going to help prevent major
problems. This seems to be a problem with Ventura Publisher Network version.

SCREEN DRIVERS

35. *What are the names of the screen drivers?*

IBM color Card/Color Display (640x200): SD_CGA_5.CGA
IBM Enhanced Card/Color Display (640x200): SD_CGA_5.CGA
IBM Enhanced Card/Enhanced Display (640x350): SD_EGAH5.EGA
IBM Enhanced Card/Monochrome PC Display (640x350): SD_EGAM5.EGA
IBM Personal System/2 Model 50,60,80 VGA (640x480): SD_EGAU5.EGA
IBM Personal System/2 Model 30 MCGA (640x480): SD_MCGA5.EGA
IBM 3270 Pc 1 Monochrome PC Display (640x350): SD_32705.EGA
Hercules Card/Monochrome PC Display (720x348): SD_HERC5.EGA
Xerox 6065/AT&T 6300' (640x400): SD_X6655.EGA
MDS Genius Full Page Display (729 x 1000): SD_GENS5.EGA
Xerox Full Page Display (720x992): SD_XFUL5.EGA
Wyse Wy-700 Display (1280 x 800): SD_WY705.EGA

The following drivers should only be used with color printers:

IBM Enhanced Card 1 color Display 16 Colors 640x200: SDFEGALS.CGA
IBM Enhanced Card/Enhanced Display 16 Colors 640x350: SDFEGAH5.EGA
AT&T Display Enhancement Board (640 x 400) 16 colors: SD8XDEB5.EGA

PROFESSIONAL EXTENSION

36. *What are the conflicts between JRAM and Ventura Publisher Professional Extension?*

The biggest conflict occurs with JLaser and Professional Extension. Professional Extension goes out and grabs all available EMS; the JLaser driver is unable to allocate any when an attempt is made to print. This can be solved in one of two ways. You can use the /E switch to limit the amount of EMS Ventura Publisher uses, so that the JLaser will have 1Mb available to it, or you can upgrade the JRAM software to a version which supports pre-allocation (at boot time) of EMS for the JLaser. Another problem is that bugs existed in the original release of the JLaser driver in Base and old Professional Extension (i.e., before Network was released). The JLaser driver was fixed for the Network release. Take a look at the date on the driver file to determine which is which. Finally, problems also occur because many different versions of the JLaser software from Tall Tree Systems exist. You should contact Tall Tree Systems for the latest release of their software.

37. *Is it true that the size of a paragraph can be increased "ten times" with Professional Extension as the reference manual states? I've found this not to be true. The maximum size of a paragraph is still limited to 8,000 characters.*

The intention was probably to state that, with Professional Extension and expanded memory, Ventura Publisher will accept documents that can be ten times larger than the Base product can support.

Tables

38. *How do I clear the text out of a table but still leave the boxes?*

Make the text white.

39. *In the Professional Extension, if I delete a chapter, will the table file be deleted with it?*

Yes, if you use the DOS File Ops option in the File menu and type the name of the chapter file and an asterisk extension on the File Spec: line. For example, putting MYCHAP.* on the File Spec: line will delete not only the chapter file but all other files with that name and any extension. In other words, in this example the table file will be deleted.

40. *Can a table file be used with another chapter file like a frame?*

No, this file seems to be a special file that can only be used by the chapter where it was created. This file is much like the VGR and CIF files.

41. *How can I get two tables to act independently? I have two tables, one above the other. I would like for the bottom table to break to the next page. When I set Breaks to After for this table, both tables break to the next page as if they were anchored together.*

Insert a paragraph symbol between the two tables. Now if you set Break Across to NO for the bottom table, it will break to the next page, while the top table remains on the previous page.

42. *I'm using Professional Extension and I have 825K bytes of EMS memory, but when I attempt to save a table, Ventura Publisher tells me it doesn't have enough memory. Why won't it save my table?*

Look in the Ventura Publisher Desk menu Publishers Info option and Ventura Publisher will present an APP and SYS status line. If the APP shows zero, Ventura Publisher Professional Extension is saying there is no EMS memory available. This will cause your table not to save. If your APP shows zero, the SYS should show the balance. The only solution is to create and save smaller tables.

43. *Why did the text move from one cell in which it was placed into the next cell in the next column of my table when the chapter was loaded?*

Make sure a comma character (,) is not the only or first entry in a cell. A comma is used by the Table file as a delimiter to separate the entries in two cells. If it is necessary to have a comma as the only entry in a cell, place it in quotation marks "," to create a character string. Then set the font for the quotation marks (") to white in order to make them invisible.

Spreadsheet Columns

44. *I'm getting only eight columns to import into Ventura Publisher 2.0 Professional Extension when I bring in a much larger Lotus spreadsheet. Why?*

Set the margins in Lotus 1-2-3. Set the top, bottom, and left margins to zero, and the right to 240.

Variable Text

45. *Can you tell me how to create variable text insertions?*

Make sure text is displayed on the screen. For this example you can use the following text:

University

University welcomes all new students to the fall semester. We hope your stay at University will be a happy and productive one.

We are now ready to insert variable definitions. A good rule is to always put the variable definition at the beginning of the document. This way it is easy to locate when editing the document later. Now do the following steps to enter the variable definition for the text you just typed:

a. Activate Text Editing mode.

b. Click your left mouse button and plant your text cursor at the beginning of the title to the left of the U in University.

c. Pull down the Edit menu and select Ins Special Item or press Ctrl-C. The special items list will appear.

d. Select Variable Def from the special items list or press F8.

e. Ventura Publisher 2.0 Professional Extension will display the Insert / Edit Variable Definition dialog box.

f. Type the variable name, "State" and press the Down Arrow key to move to the Substitute Text line. Type "of Texas." The phrase, "of Texas" will be inserted after the word "University."

g. Select OK.

h. A degree symbol will appear at the position of the text cursor. Variable Def should be displayed in the Current Selection box.

At this point you're ready to enter the cross references. You must place a cross reference mark in front or behind each word where variable text is to be inserted.

   a. Click your cursor after the first appearance of the word "University."

   b. Pull down the Edit menu and select Ins Special Item or press Ctrl-C. The special items list will appear.

   c. Click on the Cross Reference option from the special items list or press F6. The Insert / Edit Reference dialog box will display.

   d. At The Name: line type in "State."

   e. Select V* on your Refer To option. "V*" tells Ventura Publisher that you want variable text to be inserted at this cross reference.

   f. Select OK. The degree symbol appears at the cursor and the word "Reference" appears in the Current Selection box.

   Repeat to insert multiple references.

To generate or update and automatically insert into the document your variable text, use the Renumber feature in the Multi-Chapter dialog box. This will require making this chapter a publication and renumbering the chapter as a publication.

Diagnostic

46. *Can I get an explanation of the Ventura Publisher 2.0 Professional Extension diagnostics pertaining to expanded memory?*

When initially entering the Publisher Info. dialog, the "SYS=" value indicates how much EMS has been used prior to the loading of Ventura Publisher, including EMS used by GEM.EMS. The "App=" value indicates how much EMS is available for use as an extended document storage area. This is actually used by Ventura Publisher Professional Extension to store the text and other document-related information. When you click on Ventura Publisher to enable the diagnostics, you have access to the EMS Memory in Use: line, which describes how much of the extended document area is actually being used by the current document (as well as the total amount of EMS available for use as the extended document storage area). Some of the extended document area memory is already in use even when you initially load Ventura Publisher. This is normal and indicates areas which are either pre-allocated or are constant overhead regardless of document.

1.1 VS 2.0

47. *I was editing a chapter in Ventura Publisher 2.0 which was created in Ventura Publisher 1.1 Patch 2. When I tried to save the chapter, I received the message, "This Chapter Is Used For Browsing Only No Changes Can Be Saved." The chapter is not a "Read Only" file, and I am not on a network. Why would I get this message?*

In a non-network environment, several situations could cause this message to appear:

    a. If you are using a floppy drive as the working drive, you could get this message if the disk fills before saving the chapter.

    b. Make sure you are within the DOS number-of-files-per-directory limits. They are as follows:

Single-sided 160/180Kb diskette	64 entries
Double-sided 320/360Kb diskette	112 entries
Double-sided HD 720Kb diskette	112 entries
Double-sided 1.44Mb diskette	224 entries
High-capacity 1.2Mb diskette	224 entries

If these DOS limits are reached or exceeded, even if there is space available on the disk, the browse message may appear when a Save is attempted.

48. *I've created a file with AutoCAD and it printed fine on my PostScript printer in Ventura Publisher 1.1. In 2.0 the lines that printed solid in 1.1, now print as shades of gray. Why?*

Check in the Ventura Publisher Paragraph menu Define Color option. If your Screen Display setting is set to Color, Ventura Publisher will print in shades of gray.

49. *On my HP LaserJet II, when printing a graphic larger than half the page, Ventura Publisher 2.0 bolds the output. Why?*

I noticed this problem in 1.1 Patch 2, and it was not fixed in version 2.0. Using the HP-150 dpi driver is the only solution I found for this problem.

50. *After installing Ventura Publisher 2.0 for the first time, it's taking the program a long time to load a chapter that took only a few seconds to load in 1.1. Why?*

Delete the entire 1.1 Ventura directory and reinstall 2.0. This will help in most occurrences.

51. *The screen does not seem to refresh as often in 2.0 and often leaves a trail on the screen. Why is this?*

    Many new features have been added with version 2.0 and, as with version 1.0 and 1.1, the screen may not always be completely refreshed. Use the Esc key to force the refresh whenever you are in doubt.

DOCUMENTATION ERRORS

52. *I was trying to import a dingbat character through my word processor by typing "<130>." In 2.0 the character I got is not the same as in the 2.0 Reference Guide. Why?*

    There is a documentation error in the Appendix E Character Sets and Codes. Dingbat characters from decimal 130 to 174 should be moved up by one. In other words, a dingbat character in the 2.0 Reference Guide has a decimal value of 130 but it should be 129. Dingbat characters from decimal 176 to 222 should be moved up by two. For example, a dingbat character in the 2.0 Reference Guide has a decimal value of 176 but it should be 174.

53. *I was trying to download my HP LaserJet fonts like it states in the 2.0 Reference Guide, but the program is not downloading the fonts. I looked at the HPLJPLUS.CNF file and it looked OK. What's wrong?*

    There is a documentation error in the 2.0 Reference Guide, Appendix K, Adding Fonts. The HPLJPLUS.CNF should contain the following:

    ```
    DOWNPATH(C:\FONTS)
    permfont(1    TMSN3010.SFL)
    permfont(2    TMSN3012.SFL)
    permfont(3    TMSB3010.SFP)
    permfont(4    TMSB3012.SFP)
    permfont(5    TMSB3014.SFP)
    ```

    The word "PERMFONT" should be in lower case. Capital letters will not work.

54. *On page K-18 in the Reference Guide it states, "For example, the first sans serif typeface not on the list should be assigned number 49, and the first serif number 99." Is this correct?*

    No, this is not correct. It should be the exact opposite. Instead of the number being one less than the first number, it should be one greater than the last number. For example, the serif fonts should be 40 to 49 and sans serif fonts should be 61 to 99.

MONITORS AND DISPLAY CARDS

55. *Which installation option installs the Orchid VGA card to use the 800 x 600 screen resolution?*

    Press the Page Down key when prompted for the graphics card by VPPREP, then select I, "TSENG Labs' VGA." The Orchid VGA card emulates the TSENG Labs' VGA card 800 x 600 screen resolution.

56. *How do I install Xerox Panorama monitor with Ventura Publisher 2.0?*

    Perform the following steps to install the Xerox Panorama monitor:

    a. Select 2 color VGA as the Display type.

    b. Then run VPDRV2_0 from the disk that came with the Xerox Panorama monitor. Answer the questions relating to installation.

    NOTE

    If using the Panorama with a Zenith 386 and EMS, modify the AUTOEXEC.BAT file by adding this line to the file: XRXSETUP C. The "C" is the memory block you are specifying (over the default E). The XRXSETUP file can be found on the Panorama disk that came with the monitor.

57. *I just installed 2.0 and now my Taxan monitor is giving me ghosts from my pull-down menu. Why?*

    A driver is available from Taxan for Ventura Publisher 2.0. You are probably using the 1.1 driver.

58. *I have a Wyse 700 and I'm using 2.0. In 1.1 I could see a full page. In 2.0 I see about 75% of the page in normal view. Is this the way the driver was written or is there something I can do to correct this?*

    In version 1.1 Ventura Publisher used the EGA fonts with the Wyse drive. In 2.0 Ventura Publisher uses the VGA fonts. It is the size of the fonts (in pixels) which determines how much of the page is viewable. If you were to use the EGA fonts with 2.0, the full page would again be displayed.

59. *The Vega VGA and Paradise VGA display drivers do not work. Why?*

    Quite a number of VGA problems can be related to the use of incorrect cabling.

PRINTS BLANK PAGES

60. *CGM files from Arts and Letters will load into Ventura Publisher but are not visible on the screen and print only blank pages. Why?*

There seems to be a color mapping inconsistency between Ventura Publisher and Arts and Letters. Ventura Publisher imports these files incorrectly. You can use the following procedure:

Change the color in Arts and Letters to a light shade. Save files to CGM format. Importing the file into Ventura Publisher now should clear the problem.

PRINTERS

61. *What are the settings for the Toshiba 24-pin printer?*

The settings for the Toshiba 24-pin printer are as follows:

FONT	:COURIER
PITCH	:10
QUIET MODE	:OFF
EMULTN	:TOSH/QUME
BIDIREC PRNT	:ON
LINES PER IN	:6
PAGE LENGTH	:66
CR FUNC	:CR ONLY
AUTO CR	:OFF
AUTO CH WRAP	:OFF
AUTO LF WRAP	:OFF
3 PASS GRAPH	:OFF
HEX DUMP	:OFF
INT'L CHR	:NORM
ASF BIN	:FIRST
RAM ALOC	:DLL
BUFFER SIZE	:4k
INTERFACE	:PARALLEL
PROTOCOL	:XON/XOF
BAUD RATE	:9600
PARITY	:EVEN
STOP BITS	:1
DATA BITS	:8
COUNTRY	:USA
AUTO LOAD ADJ	:6

```
SHT FEED ADJ          :9
ESC                   :OVR SCORE
IBM MODE              :PRO
ASF MODE              :OFF
ASF ADJ               :9
 HS                   :7
CORR.                 :7
HQ                    :7
HS COND               :7
CORR. COND            :7
GRP                   :6
HS COPY               :7
CORR. COPY            :7
HQ COPY               :7
HS CD COPY            :6
CORR. CD COPY         :7
GRP COPY              :6
HS COPY 2             :6
CORR. COPY 2          :7
HQ COPY 2             :6
HS CD COPY 2          :6
CO. CD COPY 2         :7
GRP COPY 2            :7
```

62. *How do I use the AST TurboLaser printer with 2.0?*

The AST TurboLaser printer is not supported by 2.0 since the vendor discontinued manufacturing this printer. For new 2.0 users there currently is no fix for this problem. If you have upgraded from Ventura Publisher 1.1 to 2.0, there is a way to use the 1.1 drivers with 2.0. Do the following:

a. Install 2.0

b. Copy VP.BAT file to another directory for protection.

c. Do a partial install using 1.1

d. Answer NO when Ventura Publisher asks if you are installing for the first time.

e. Answer installation questions about screen and mouse devices. When adding, you will have a choice to select AST TurboLaser.

Do not choose any other printer at this time.

After Ventura Publisher installs the printer, recopy the original VP.BAT that was developed by 2.0 back to its original directory.

63. *I'm attempting to use an HP Deskjet with Ventura Publisher 2.0. Is there a printer driver for this printer?*

There are two products out in the form of software packages. LaserGo Corporation makes a package named GoScript that allows a user to output to an HP DeskJet. The Software translates the printer code which is, at this time, a very slow process; but it does work. For additional information contact LaserGo at (619) 530-0099. Atech Software (629 S. Rancho Santa Fe Road; San Marcos, CA 92069) has a driver called Powerpak Ventura Publisher Edition, that works with Ventura Publisher 2.0 and 1.1 Patch 1. with the following limitations:

   a. Only Atech-provided typefaces are available.

   b. Does not support text hidden under solid graphics, ruling lines hidden under opaque graphics, or rotated text.

INTERNAL SYSTEM ERRORS

64. *I was attempting to load Professional Extension through Windows 386 Version 2.1 on a PS/2 Model 80 and I get an Internal System Error #13. Why?*

If you are using the IBM large screen monitor 8514A, Windows maps memory to the same address. You must use a different EMS driver to run Ventura Publisher.

65. *I have just upgraded to Professional Extension from Ventura Publisher Base and now I'm getting an Internal System Error #13 when loading Professional Extension. Why?*

This is a symptom of not having enough memory. Check for network cards and any resident memory programs. Perform a CHKDSK to insure you have at least 570K bytes free. You can get away with 560K bytes but only if EMS memory is available.

66. *Is there a good explanation that can be given to me regarding Internal System Errors?*

Internal System Error alerts are Ventura Publisher's attempt at being a good host and should be viewed in a positive light. Sometimes internal errors occur which do not cause an immediate crash to DOS or lockup, but do cause some slight corruption of data. This corruption may range from something minor to something which may be devastating if work is continued. Displaying the error alert gives you an opportunity to save all of the preceding work and to exit Ventura Publisher and reset the system to clear the error condition. It also lets you know that something strange has just occurred.

67. *I tried to print a job on a Compaq 286 20 MHZ machine and I received an Internal System Error #19. Can you tell me why?*

Reinstall Ventura Publisher at a slower clock speed. For best results always install Ventura Publisher at a slower clock speed, then switch to a faster speed for normal operation. Compaq machines are equipped with a Mode Command switch which controls the internal clock speed of the machine. This has been known to cause problems with Ventura Publisher printing.

CHAPTER 22

Error Messages and
Miscellaneous Problems

This chapter deals with problems that don't fit in any other chapter—for example, if Ventura Publisher just stops working. Usually, if Ventura Publisher stops working, it is due to lack of memory or disk space, which will result in losing data. If you have never lost data, thank your lucky stars and continue to read, because someday, when you least expect it, it could happen to you. Ventura Publisher may stop and give you an "Internal System Error" message. This chapter will not cure all internal system errors, but it will help you out of most and even avoid some. I hope this is helpful to you and good publishing.

Topic Guide

Topic Guide (Cont.)

Topic	Questions	Page
Frame too Complex	28	222
Printer Not Receiving Power	29 - 31	222
Printer Not Ready	32 - 33	222
Printer Not Receiving Data	34	223
Wish to Stop or Continue Printing	35	224
Fatal Error - GEMVDI	36	224
File Not Found	37	224
Atan Error	38	224
GEMVDI Screen Driver Could Not be Loaded	39	224
Language Error	40	225
Width Table Messages	41 - 42	225
Internal System Error	43	226
Internal System Error 21	44	226

GENERAL

1. *Does Ventura Publisher perform an automatic conversion to typographic characters?*

   No, Ventura Publisher can create documents with real typographic attributes, including em (—) dashes and typographic quotes (""). Since your keyboard doesn't contain these characters, Ventura Publisher lets you enter them using the Alt key. However, these characters can also be entered directly from your word processor by enclosing the decimal equivalent for the character inside the appropriate brackets. For instance, a left typographic quote can be inserted while using a word processor by typing <169>. These codes can be entered easily if your word processor supports keyboard macros. You can also use the search and replace function in your word processor.

2. *How many files of a particular extension will Ventura Publisher show in the scroll menus? For example, how many .STY, .CHP, or other files?*

   This is a limitation of the GEM environment. I found that Ventura Publisher can list 102 files. At 103 and beyond, Ventura Publisher will not show all the files.

3. *Can you get Ventura Publisher to redirect the backup files to a floppy disk?*

   No.

4. *How can I define or create a custom screen as referred to in the image settings help box? It's not mentioned in the manual.*

This requires a high degree of PostScript programming proficiency and is beyond the scope of the reference manual and this book. Users who are interested should read the "PostScript Language Reference Manual" by Adobe Systems (commonly called "the red book").

5. *Can you give me some examples of 1.1 keyboard shortcuts?*

Ctrl-Q shows all graphics associated with a frame.
Ctrl-E shows the screen in enlarged view.
Ctrl-2 activates the addition button on the side bar.

6. *Can you tell me how to use the DXFTOGEM.EXE file on Disk #11?*

Put Ventura Publisher #11 disk in drive A, then type "A:DXFTOGEM filename.DXF"; this should start the conversion.

7. *Can I put a trademark in a frame?*

Yes, you can do anything to text in a frame that you can do on the underlying frame. This is done by planting the text cursor in the position you want the trademark to appear. Hold down the Alt key and press 196 from the number pad. A hyphen will appear. Stay in Text mode and hold the mouse button and streak over the hyphen so that it appears in reverse video. Click on Set Font in the Paragraph menu and change the font to Symbol. This will make your TM.

LOCKUPS

Saved a Chapter on Floppy Drive

8. *I saved a chapter on the floppy drive and the system locked up. Why?*

When using the floppy drives, DOS gives you a DOS message across the screen, "PLEASE INSERT DISK INTO DRIVE AND PRESS RETURN," destroying the Ventura Publisher screen. If you are using a NEC Multisync color monitor, this message will not display. The system seems to have locked up; however, it is waiting for the Enter key to be pressed so it may not be locked at all.

100-page Book

9. *I have a 100-page book in several Ventura Publisher chapters. The longest is 16 pages with a 30K byte word processing file, but everything I do locks up the system. Why?*

   You do not have enough free memory for your chapters. Split the chapters in half, thereby creating smaller chapter files.

Text Mode

10. *I'm getting lockups while typing directly into Ventura Publisher in the Text mode. Is ANSI.SYS necessary in the CONFIG.SYS file?*

    The DOS command DEVICE=ANSI.SYS may be necessary in your CONFIG.SYS if you're experiencing lockups while typing in the Text mode in Ventura Publisher.

Lots of Graphics

11. *Ventura Publisher is locking up when I attempt to move a lot of graphics. Why?*

    This has been a known shortcoming in the programming of Ventura Publisher. They have been trying to improve this feature for a long time. The Patch 2 for Ventura Publisher version 1.1 went a long way in improving this problem.

ERROR MESSAGES

Frame is too Complex

12. *I'm getting an error message, "This frame is too complex to completely format. Try splitting it into two frames or reducing the number of columns, tabs, leaders, and lines of text." What should I do to correct this?*

    If too many tab characters are used, you may encounter this error message. Tabs should be used sparingly, because they consume internal memory. If you cannot create the document with fewer tabs or increase the space between your lines, then draw one or more frames on the page and flow the text into the first frame and then into the second frame. Select each frame individually and make it a repeating frame. These frames will automatically repeat on each page until the entire text file has been placed in the document. Some text must still flow into the underlying page in order to force Ventura Publisher to automatically create new pages.

Couldn't Find Overlay File

13. *What should I do for this error message: "Couldn't find overlay file. [Ok]?"*

One or more files in the Ventura directory has been modified or deleted. Reinstall Ventura Publisher.

VP.RSC File Couldn't be Found

14. *What should I do for this error message, "Fatal Error! The VP.RSC file couldn't be found or would not fit in memory. [Abort] Fatal Error! The GEM VDI screen driver couldn't be loaded. [Abort]?"*

The VP.RSC or screen driver file in the Ventura subdirectory has been modified or deleted. Reinstall Ventura Publisher.

Color Graphics Card Required

15. *I can't load Ventura Publisher after installation. When VP.EXE was executed, I received an error message, "Xerox Ventura Publisher: Color Graphics Card Required." Why?*

When you installed Ventura Publisher, you installed for a color graphics card. Ventura Publisher sees the Hercules graphics card and presents this message. Reinstall Ventura Publisher and select the Hercules card.

To Continue, Insert Your GEM Desktop Disk

16. *What does the error message, "To continue, insert your GEM DESKTOP disk into drive A:, and click on OK, or press the Enter key. To Return to DOS, click on cancel" mean?*

This is a message you receive from the GEM environment. It can be generated by two situations. The first is your VP.BAT file has been altered or the mouse statement, or "M," is changed to a "D." In this case, you will receive this message when you quit Ventura Publisher. The second case is having the DRVRMRGR statement in your VP.BAT file with no parameters. In this case, the message will appear at the beginning of executing Ventura Publisher.

Style Sheet Not in the Proper Format

17. *Ventura Publisher is giving me an error message that says the style sheet it is trying to load is not in the proper format. It then returns to the DOS prompt. Why?*

Go to the Ventura directory and delete the INF files. This is done by entering the following at the C: prompt:

```
cd\Ventura [Press Enter]
del *.inf [Press Enter]
```

This will return Ventura Publisher to its default setting and will allow Ventura Publisher to seek the default style sheet, not some style sheet that the INF files may be referencing. The INF files hold the name of the last style sheet loaded into Ventura Publisher. When Ventura Publisher starts to execute, it reads the INF files and attempts to load that style sheet.

18. *I recently installed 1.1 Patch 2 and I get a message that tells me that the style sheet I'm trying to use is a pre-beta format. What's wrong?*

This problem is not limited to 1.1 Patch 2, but also 1.1 Patch 1. The error message indicates a corrupted style sheet. You should recreate the style sheet by going to the File menu and selecting Save As New Style.

Abandon Changes to This Chapter

19. *What should I do for this error message: "Abandon changes to this chapter and revert to the previously saved version [OK|Cancel]?"*

You have selected the Abandon option in the File menu. Select OK to remove all changes made in this chapter and open the previously saved chapter.

Are You Sure You Wish to Delete All Files

20. *What should I do for this error message: "Are you sure you wish to delete all files that match: filename [Delete|Cancel]?"*

This message appears during DOS File Operations as a reminder that you are about to erase a file or files. Select Cancel if you do not want to continue with the delete operation.

Divide Overflow

21. *I received a "Divide Overflow" message when saving a chapter and the system locked up. What happened?*

After you rebooted your system and returned to Ventura Publisher, your chapter had Frame Too Complex on several pages. This indicates that your text is too large and complex for that frame. Adding another frame to distribute the text will correct the Divide Overflow problem.

22. *I try to print and get a lockup with "Divide overflow" error message. Why?*

Your CONFIG.SYS found FILES=99. Change this to FILES=20 and reboot. The problem will not occur again.

Insufficient Memory

23. *I have a 640K bytes machine and received an insufficient memory message when I tried to load a 10K bytes ASCII text file. Why?*

Normally a 640K bytes machine should be able to load a text file up to 150K bytes with version 1.0 or up to 500K bytes with version 1.1. Check the AUTOEXEC.BAT and make sure there are no memory-resident programs executed such as Sidekick, Super-key, Turbo-Lightning, Norton Utilities, etc. Background programs reduce the memory available to load files and programs. Ventura Publisher strongly suggests that all background utilities be deactivated before loading Ventura Publisher.

Check the number of buffers in the CONFIG.SYS file and make sure the number is not too large (over 25). Make sure your file is really an ASCII text file and not a word processing file. Perform a DOS CHKDSK to find out how much memory you have. You need 570K bytes for versions 1.0 and 1.1 and 575K bytes for version 2.0.

24. *I used Bitstream Fontware to add several fonts. Now when I load Ventura Publisher I get a message saying, "Insufficient Memory to load all of the requested fonts, some fonts may not display or print correctly." Why?*

This message is referring to screen fonts. It means Ventura Publisher has encountered a screen font file that is greater than 35K, which is Ventura Publisher's limit on screen font file size. Either rename the fonts extension or regenerate your fonts with a smaller character set to try and stay within the 35K bytes limit.

All Repeating Frames are Already in Use

25. *What should I do for this error message: "All 6 of your repeating frames are already in use [OK]?"*

Ventura Publisher allows up to six repeating frames per chapter. To fix this problem, you must make one of the existing six repeating frames a normal frame.

Remove Text From Selected Frame

26. *What should I do for this error message: "Do you wish to remove the text from the selected frame or cancel the request?[Remove Text |Cancel]?"*

When you type text directly into a frame, this text is stored in the chapter's caption file, along with all other captions, Box Text, and text typed into other frames. Later if you try to load a picture or text file to this frame, this message appears warning you that the text in this frame will be permanently lost.

Wish to Re-anchor Frames

27. *What should I do for this error message: "Do you wish to re-anchor just this page's frames, or all pages' frames, or cancel the request? [This Page\All Pages \Cancel]."*

If you select This Page, Ventura Publisher looks through all the text on this page for anchor entries and then moves frames throughout the document to these anchor points. If you select All Pages, this process is carried out across the whole document.

Frame too Complex

28. *I got an error message, "Frame too Complex." What can I do?*

In 1.0 this caused a disaster. In 1.1 and 2.0 everything that can be read into the frame will be. At the point of the error message, you can create additional frames on the page and use the Repeating Frame option in the Frame menu to complete the file transfer without losing data.

Printer Not Receiving Power

29. *I am trying to drive a Texas Instruments OmniLaser through a Western Telematics printer sharing device and I get a message, "Printer not receiving power." Why?*

The Western Telematics device allows you to tie several processors to one printer. However, it is a serial to parallel converter (serial ports from the processor to one parallel port on the printer) which may not pass DTR coming back to Ventura Publisher from the printer.

30. *When I try to print a document to an Apple Laserwriter, I get a message, "Device not receiving power." What is wrong?*

Typically this message indicates that there has been no indication received by Ventura Publisher that the printer is on and ready. Check the following:

  a The printer is turned on.

  b. You have the proper cables and they are secured as described in your printer's user manual.

  c. Try copying the file DRT.TXT using the DOS COPY command to the printer. This file is located on the Utilities Disk # 11.

31. *I am trying to print to a Texas Instruments OmniLaser (PostScript) through a switch box device, and I get a message, "printer not receiving power." Why?*

The switch boxes that allow multiple computers to share one printer are serial to parallel converters. Serial ports from the processor to one parallel port on the printer. The switch may not be passing DTR back to Ventura Publisher from the printer.

Printer Not Ready

32. *When I try to print, I get this error message, "Printer Not Ready etc," Why?*

This means your parallel or serial printer port is not providing the correct status of Ready to Ventura Publisher. Print &Book-pl.Chp Page 1 to a disk file and see if the problem is present at DOS level. At the DOS level type COPY FILENAME.C00 LPT(n:)/b or COM(n:)/b.

Add a DOS MODE statement to set the printer port inside the VP.BAT file and insure the statement ends with a "P" to set the port for maximum timeout value. Put the following statement in the VP.BAT file:

    MODE COM(n:) 96,n,8,1,p <cr> (for the serial port)
    MODE LPT(n:),p <cr> (for the parallel port).

33. *I can't print to my PostScript printer using Ventura Publisher AST Desktop Publishing setup at 10 mhz. When a DOS print to filename was done directly to LPT2, it printed to my AST printer as PostScript. Then DOS gave me the message after it printed, "Not Ready Error Writing Drive X " (Where X = drive letter). Why?*

Slowing the computer down to 8 mhz with a hotkey combination will make it work just fine. Use VP at fast speed but, before printing, slow down by using the hotkeys first.

Printer Not Receiving Data

34. *I have a QMS PS JET+ running in serial on my PC AT clone. I'm receiving an error message from Ventura Publisher, "printer not receiving data." Why?*

The solution to this problem is to have your printer print correctly with the printer set for DTR protocol. Execute a batch file containing the following DOS commands:

    MODE COM(n:)96,N,8,1,P.
    MODE LPT1:=COM1:

This file will allow you to print to the parallel port LPT1. Now Ventura Publisher is basically ignoring the serial port status that was originally confusing the driver.

Wish to Stop or Continue Printing

35. *What should I do for this error message: "Do you wish to stop or continue printing? (Stop! Continue)?"*

    This message appears when you press the Esc key while printing. Select Stop to abort the printing operation or select Continue to go ahead with printing.

Fatal Error - GEMVDI

36. *I received an error message, "FATAL ERROR - GEMVDI could not be loaded after printing from Ventura." What caused this?*

    You used the DOS ATTRIB command to change the attributes in several of your files to read-only status. Changing the file attributes back fixed the problem. This message may also occur when printing a very large chapter in version 1.0. When printing is completed, certain areas of memory may not be properly released and Ventura Publisher will display this message. To fix this problem in version 1.0, you must exit Ventura Publisher to clear the memory.

File Not Found

37. *When I try to print a file using Interpress, I get an XPRINT error message, "File not found." Why?*

    You probably did not copy the print file from the TYPESET or other directory into the root directory, or you gave the wrong filename and extension instead of XPRINT.IP.

Atan Error

38. *I'm receiving the error "ATAN ERROR" when printing to a Linotronic. There was an end of file character in the .C00 file which had to be removed before printing. Why?*

    This problem was caused by rescaling the page to the point where a Rounded Corner rectangle had a resulting 0" dimension in either horizontal or vertical direction. The workaround would be to delete this frame.

GEMVDI Screen Driver Could Not be Loaded

39. *Whenever I print to file for my PostScript printer, I get a message that the "GEMVDI Screen Driver could not be loaded." I've got 593K available when I load Ventura Publisher and my document is only two pages, so I don't think this could be a memory problem. What's happening?*

Ventura Publisher is looking for a file with a .SYS extension when it tries to reload the screen driver. If you did not delete the contents of the 1.01 Ventura directory prior to installing 1.1, there may be drivers left in the subdirectory from 1.01 with the .SYS extension. Ventura Publisher may mistakenly try to load one of these as a screen driver and, in failing to do so, display the GEMVDI message.

Language Error

40. *My 4045 printer won't print with Ventura Publisher and says "Language Error" on the configuration sheet. Why?*

The "Language Error" message on the Configuration sheet indicates a hardware problem on the printer itself. The configuration sheet does not reflect anything about the attached PC or software. If you get this message, I suggest you call your printer maintenance service. You may have a bad configuration cartridge.

Width Table Messages

41. *When I tried to load Ventura Publisher, I got a message on the screen that said, "The New Width Table file couldn't be loaded. You may wish to try reloading this width file after doing a New. For now, we are using the current file instead." My only option was to indicate OK, and when I did, the program aborted to DOS. What is happening?*

You do not have enough memory available to load Ventura Publisher. Check for background utilities loaded that you may have forgotten. Clear the utilities from memory and reboot your system.

42. *I was trying to create a width table for each typeface accessible on my Laserwriter Plus in version 1.0. I'm trying to load the width table for a typeface and I'm getting a message that, "the width table was not in the correct Ventura Publisher format." I have successfully created other width tables before and I'm doing everything the same. Is there a problem with certain fonts?*

Your font table may not have adequate fonts. In version 1.0 Ventura Publisher requires at least one of the standard Laserwriter fonts in the width table (those which appear above the comment line that says the following fonts are available only on the Laserwriter Plus). If it does not find one, it rejects the width table. You can insert just one font and one point size from the standard Laserwriter fonts and the width table will load (Ventura Publisher recommends Helvetica 10 pt). In version 1.1 the width table provided with Ventura Publisher already contains most available Adobe fonts, including Avant Garde. This will solve your problem.

INTERNAL SYSTEM ERROR

43. *I got an internal system error and now my system is locked up and will not release me no matter how long I click on "SORRY." What is wrong?*

When Ventura Publisher does not release something, it means you have run out of disk space. Ventura Publisher requires a minimum of 2 to 4Mb of disk space when processing and printing in portrait mode and 4 to 6Mb in landscape mode. This can be confirmed by running the CHKDSK DOS command on the disk drive that has Ventura Publisher installed. The bytes available on disk and total memory is the most important information. The memory free should be no lower then 570,000. Most internal system errors will be caused by not having enough memory or enough disk space.

Internal System Error 21

44. *My table with a lot of vertical graphic lines will not print completely on my HP LaserJet Plus, even though the printer has 4.5Mb memory. Only part of the page prints while the printer gives Internal System Error 21.*

Error 21 means too much data (rules, raster graphics, or dense text) has been sent to the printer. A large amount of printer memory and/or formatting power is apparently used up when the vertical graphic lines are present. Removing the vertical graphic lines enabled the page to print. Meanwhile here's a workaround:

Create Zero-Width Graphic Boxes that look the same as vertical graphic lines. This method uses printer memory more efficiently than vertical graphic lines. Incidentally, this trick makes it easy to draw perfectly horizontal or vertical lines, since the sides of a graphic box have no slant to them.

Index

Other Books of Interest to Desktop Publishers

Illustrated Ventura 2.0

GEORGE SHELDON

All the skills, techniques, and tips needed to master this top-selling desktop publishing program can be found in this comprehensive tutorial reference. Fully illustrated throughout, working examples demonstrate the enhanced user interface and technical publishing features designed to make desktop publishing more functional and easier to use. Step-by-step learning begins with a blank file that you develop into an impressive professional-quality document. New and experienced users will find the reference value of this book indispensable.

1-55622-104-5 • **$21.95**
softbound • 336 pages • 7 1/2 x 9 1/4

Handbook of Desktop Publishing
A Guide for Business and Professional People

JOHN C. SANS, JR.

This excellent information source examines the hardware and software capabilities, limitations, and purposes of desktop publishing. Sound advice, financial implications, and investment tips on acquiring, operating, and maintaining an inhouse publishing system are detailed. This handbook introduces Macintosh and IBM terms, principles, tools and techniques. Checklists and cost justification formulas help estimate your current and future needs while determining whether desktop publishing is for you.

0-915381-95-8 • **$19.95**
softbound • 192 pages • 7 1/2 x 9 1/4

Achieving Graphic Impact with Ventura 2.0

DEBORAH W. DICKSON   Illustrated by KEN PANNELL

Now you can learn to create and import graphic elements that add impact and professional appeal to your Ventura documents. Step-by-step instructions demonstrate ten popular Ventura-compatible graphic programs while detailing their capabilities and limitations. Guidelines on graphic design, page layout, and input/output devices are featured. Get the most out of Ventura 2.0 by learning more about prototyping, production strategies, scanning, and printing. This book is perfect for Ventura users who want to examine the variety of supplemental software packages available and who need tips on selecting Ventura-compatible graphics software.

1-55622-120-7 • **$21.95**
softbound • 352 pages • 7 1/2 x 9 1/4

Desktop Publisher's Dictionary

LARRY S. BONURA

Discover the language of desktop publishing with this comprehensive, one-stop reference to the terms used in this exploding industry. More than 4,000 terms, words, and abbreviations, from typography to binding and finishing, are clearly defined and frequently clarified by illustrations. Related terms and concepts are identified for easy cross-reference. Perfect for office, home, or school, this is an indispensable tool for today's contemporary professional.

1-55622-106-1 • **$21.95**
hardbound • 456 pages • 6 x 9

Business Professional

MegaTraits
12 Traits of Successful People
DR. DORIS LEE MCCOY

Dr. McCoy traveled extensively to interview over 1,000 "successful" people. Interviews with such people as Charlton Heston, Malcolm Forbes, and Ronald Reagan led Dr. McCoy to discover 12 traits of success. She sought consistencies and success patterns from which you can benefit. Are there specific points to help all of us become more successful? The answer is a resounding YES! There are traits consistently found in the lives of successful people. Discover how you too can develop and utilize these unique attributes. *MegaTraits* illustrates how you can make these successful qualities a part of your life.

1-55622-056-1 • **$17.95**
hardbound • 304 pages • 6 x 9

The Business Side of Writing
RUSSELL A. STULTZ

If you regard writing as a business rather than an art, this book can provide the reference information you need for a successful career in writing or publications management. These guidelines help organize and refine your approach to project planning, cost estimating, project research, financial control, development, and production. Mr. Stultz addresses the tools, techniques, methodologies, and processes to plan, manage, and automate publications development and production with emphasis on the bottom line.

1-55622-157-6 • **$15.95**
hardbound • 224 pages • 6 x 9

Innovation, Inc.
Unlocking Creativity in the Workplace
GROSSMAN, RODGERS, and MOORE

Unlock your hidden potential to reach a new plane of creative thinking. Seek new avenues of problem solving by elevating your ability to conceive ideas. Techniques and exercises in this book expand your creativity. The authors take you on a journey designed to spark confidence by reorganizing your thinking processes and patterns. Learn to use innovative thinking to inspire fresh ideas and formulate imaginative concepts.

1-55622-054-5 • **$14.95**
softbound • 256 pages • 6 x 9

Steps to Strategic Management
A Guide for Entrepreneurs
DR. RICK MOLZ

This book will help the entrepreneur uncover opportunities for a more successful business. A fictitious person, business, and product illustrate how this system works. Nine key steps to strategic management are developed and followed by real-world business applications. This system is used worldwide by sophisticated organizations of all types and sizes. The case example approach and readable style make this strategic method easy to understand and apply.

1-55622-050-2 • **$13.95**
softbound • 184 pages • 6 x 9

Illustrated

AutoSketch 2.0

PAUL SCHLIEVE and TOM BERGHAUSER

The authors of the popular *Illustrated AutoCAD* bring you detailed information on this entry-level, full-functioned, precision drawing tool. This complete AutoSketch introduction gets you up and running in about one hour. Hands-on activities step through the easy-to-use pull-down menus and dialog boxes that control sophisticated graphics manipulation functions. Details on how to import AutoSketch drawings to AutoCAD for additional refinements are included.

1-55622-113-4 • **$21.95**
softbound • 304 pages

Lotus 1-2-3 Release 3

Here is a complete, in-depth reference-tutorial for the long-awaited Release 3 from Lotus Development Corporation. Learn how to create spreadsheets that are three-dimensional. Specific, practical examples show you how to organize worksheets, consolidate templates, and create formulas within a worksheet using Lotus' new capabilities.

1-55622-160-6 • **$21.95**
softbound • 320 pages

Microsoft Windows 2.0

ROBERT E. WHITSITT II and LANA K. BRYAN

This comprehensive reference/tutorial now includes the latest updates of version 2.0. Learn to work with several applications simultaneously and shift among them easily and quickly. Complete and clear descriptions of the Program Information File (PIF) Editor, Print Spooler, and Clipboard features are included. Depend on this valuable guide to master the fundamentals as well as the subtle details of this popular, new operating system.

1-55622-069-3 • **$19.95**
softbound • 304 pages

Microsoft Word 5.0

JOHN MUELLER and WALLY WANG

Everything you need to know to use Microsoft Word 5.0 is included in this comprehensive guide. Working examples use, modify, and create Word stylesheets and provide working models that are easily adapted to your personal needs. Top-quality documents are easily achieved by following the step-by-step approach of this book. Ready access to commands and functions make this an in-depth reference tool.

1-55622-021-9 • **$21.95**
softbound • 384 pgs

Illustrated

MS/PC-DOS 4.0
Sixth Edition

RUSSELL A. STULTZ

This complete, timesaving reference contains all the significant updates to the world's most popular operating system. The novice-to-expert DOS user is led keystroke-by-keystroke through a sequence of exercises designed to provide hands-on experience. Use the new text-based DOSSHELL to initiate powerful DOS utilities. Each command is detailed in brief, easy-to-understand modules which make this book an indispensable reference.

1-55622-111-8 • **$21.95**
softbound • 272 pages

Novell NetWare 2.15

TIMOTHY K. McDONALD

Step-by-step techniques clearly demonstrate the fundamentals of this networking operating system from installation to operation. Master NetWare's user commands to effectively store, protect, and share company data and resources among personal computers. Learn to adapt essential software programs to NetWare's LAN for custom applications. Tips on a variety of security and printer options are included. A complete guide for effective communications between centralized personal computers. Reviewed for accuracy by Novell Corporation.

1-55622-065-0 • **$21.95**
softbound • 256 pgs

WordPerfect 5.0

JORDAN GOLD

Taste the latest, most significant capabilities of this top-selling word processing package. Create and save standard formats for document elements. Learn to size, rotate, crop, and position imported graphics. Preview pages that use a variety of fonts, sizes, column layouts, and graphics. New menu structure and mnemonic command selection is completely outlined. Hands-on exercises demonstrate the full macro language needed to create complex macros.

1-55622-063-4 • **$19.95**
softbound • 416 pages

WordStar Professional
Release 5

RUSSELL A. and DIANNE STULTZ

Master a host of new WordStar features including advanced page preview, footnotes/endnotes, windowing, TelMerge, ListMerge, and many more. Practical hands-on activities demonstrate the new user interface and the pull-down menus used to initiate the latest functions. This step-by-step learning guide is also a complete reference to the all-new advanced document features now available in WordStar 5.0.

1-55622-074-X • **$21.95**
softbound • 304 pages

Other Books from Wordware Publishing, Inc.

Artificial Intelligence
Illustrated VP-Expert

Business-Professional Books
Business Emotions
The Business Side of Writing
Consulting Handbook for the High-Tech Professional
Hawks Do, Buzzards Don't
How to Develop Company Policies
How to Win Pageants
Innovation, Inc.
Investor Beware
MegaTraits
Occupying the Summit
Steps to Strategic Management

Computer Aided Drafting
Illustrated AutoCAD (Release 9)
Illustrated AutoCAD (Release 10)
Illustrated AutoLISP
Illustrated AutoSketch 2.0
Illustrated GenericCADD Level 3

Database Management
The DataFlex Developer's Handbook
Illustrated dBASE II (2nd Ed.)
Illustrated dBASE III Plus
Illustrated dBASE IV
Illustrated Paradox Volume I 3.0 (2nd Ed.)
Illustrated Paradox Volume II 3.0 (2nd Ed.)

Desktop Publishing
Achieving Graphic Impact with Ventura 2.0
Desktop Publisher's Dictionary
Illustrated PFS:First Publisher 2.0
Handbook of Desktop Publishing
Illustrated Interleaf
Illustrated PageMaker 3.0
Illustrated Ready, Set, Go! 4.5 (Macintosh)
Illustrated Ventura 2.0
Ventura Troubleshooting Guide

General Advanced Topics
Consulting Handbook for the High-Tech Professional
Illustrated Dac Easy Accounting 3.0
Illustrated Dac Easy Accounting 4.0
Illustrated Harvard Graphics
Illustrated Novell NetWare 2.15
Novell NetWare: Advanced Techniques and
Applications

Programming Languages
Illustrated C Programming (ANSI) (2nd Ed.)
Illustrated Clipper 5.0
The FOCUS Developer's Handbook
Illustrated FoxBASE+ 2.01
Illustrated QuickBASIC 4.0
Illustrated Turbo C
Illustrated Turbo Debugger 1.0
Illustrated Turbo Pascal 4.0
Illustrated Turbo Pascal 5.5

Spreadsheet/Integrated
Illustrated Enable/OA
Illustrated Framework III
Illustrated Lotus 1-2-3 2.01
Illustrated Lotus 1-2-3 Rel. 3.0
Illustrated Lotus 1-2-3 2.2
Illustrated Microsoft Excel 2.10 (IBM)
Illustrated Microsoft Excel 1.5 (Macintosh)
Illustrated Microsoft Works 1.05
Illustrated Multiplan 2.0
Illustrated Q & A 3.0 (2nd Ed.)
Illustrated Quattro
Illustrated SuperCalc 5

Systems and Operating Guides
Illustrated Microsoft Windows 2.0
Illustrated MS/PC DOS 3.3
Illustrated MS/PC DOS 4.0 (6th Ed.)
Illustrated OS/2

Word Processing
Illustrated DisplayWrite 4
Illustrated Microsoft Word 5.0
Illustrated Microsoft Word for the Mac
Illustrated WordPerfect 1.0 (Macintosh)
Illustrated WordPerfect 4.2
Illustrated WordPerfect 5.0
Illustrated WordStar 3.3
Illustrated WordStar Professional (Rel. 5)
The New WordStar Customizing Guide 4.0
WordPerfect: Advanced Applications Handbook

Regional
This Dog'll Hunt
100 Days in Texas: The Alamo Letters
Exploring the Alamo Legends
Texas Wit and Wisdom
Forget the Alamo
Rainy Days in Texas Workbook

Call Wordware Publishing, Inc. for names of the bookstores in your area
(214) 423-0090